Entrepreneurial Women

ENTREPRENEURIAL WOMEN

New Management and Leadership Models
Volume 1

Louise Kelly, Editor

 PRAEGER

AN IMPRINT OF ABC-CLIO, LLC
Santa Barbara, California • Denver, Colorado • Oxford, England

Library of Congress Cataloging-in-Publication Data

Kelly, Louise, 1964–
    Entrepreneurial women : new management and leadership models / Louise Kelly.
        volumes ; cm
    Includes index.
    ISBN 978-1-4408-0077-1 (hardback : alk. paper) — ISBN 978-1-4408-0078-8
(ebook)   1. Women-owned business enterprises.   2. New business enterprises.
3. Businesswomen.   4. Women executives.   I. Title.
    HD6072.5.K45   2014
    338.04082—dc23   2014002911

ISBN: 978-1-4408-0077-1
EISBN: 978-1-4408-0078-8

18 17 16 15 14   1 2 3 4 5

This book is also available on the World Wide Web as an eBook.
Visit www.abc-clio.com for details.

Praeger
An Imprint of ABC-CLIO, LLC

ABC-CLIO, LLC
130 Cremona Drive, P.O. Box 1911
Santa Barbara, California 93116-1911

This book is printed on acid-free paper ∞
Manufactured in the United States of America

Contents

Introduction

An Overview of the Successes and Challenges of Entrepreneurial Women

Louise Kelly

Throughout the world, women play the most important roles in many spheres, including household, family, business, government, and now, more and more being entrepreneurs. They form around half of the total world population and play a significant role in economic development. There is clearly an established positive relationship between GDP and women's participation in the work-force (Baguant 2012; Blank 2000; Jaumotte 2003).

A significant body of research has emerged over the past 20 years on the growth and development of women entrepreneurs, their contribution to the economy, and why supporting them is of significance, and there is an argument to determine whether as a group they are now perhaps moving toward having a disproportionate impact on economic development (Edwards 2012). It has been found that women entrepreneurs' access to finance in the developing world can be a key factor to economic development, and as a result, many social entrepreneurs are turning their attention to the issues of microloans and microfinance. One such entrepreneur is Joanna Wasmuth, whose not-for-profit organization is called Erase Poverty, because she feels strongly that women starting businesses through access to microloans could be game changers.

In fact, if we look back into history, it has been documented how women entrepreneurs have shaped the development of different societies. For example, there are some studies of how the business activities of Jewish women entrepreneurs in medieval England had a major impact on the society. One such study documents how the medieval English Jewry was important, and how, for most of its existence, it was prosperous owing to its particular social organization,

1

which included a prominence of Jewish women in starting their own enterprises (Brown and McCartney 2001).

But yet their management and leadership styles were rarely studied in detail (Syal and Goswami 2012). Entrepreneurial activity relating to women entrepreneurs has been of interest to many researchers, as women have become the main contributors to today's economy. In recent years, women have shown an inclination toward taking self-oriented jobs and professions and have been succeeding at this at ever greater rates. They seem to do well, in particular, with their family support, financial assistance, and industrial guidance. Unfortunately, on a global scale, especially in rural settings, unequal access to education restricts women from acquiring even functional levels of literacy that impede the entrepreneurial process (Sukumar and Venkatesh 2012).

Women's entrepreneurship has played a major role in the empowerment of women, especially in developing countries, although there is a clear argument whether women's entrepreneurship has furthered the empowerment of women in the developed world as well. The role of medium and small enterprises toward the empowerment of women has improved; for example, a case study of entrepreneurs in Uhuru Market in Makadara District of Nairobi showed an increase in women's participation in entrepreneurship and other signs of empowerment (Mwangi 2012).

The study used a sample of respondents from the Uhuru Market's women entrepreneurs who were involved in making sweaters, clothes, and bags. There was a clear demonstration of a relationship between the enabling of women's participation and their prominence in society with their entrepreneurial activity. It seems that women who started their own business in this market district in Nairobi had higher self-esteem and a greater span of influence in the society.

One example of the empowerment of women and their entrepreneurship occurred during the employment crisis in Cameroon in the 1990s, which was in itself generated by the economic crisis and in fact led to many social upheavals. One result of this was the reconfiguration of socioeconomic relations, particularly, the renegotiation of power, which ended up with women having greater social and economic power based on their self-employment by running small and medium businesses (Fosso 2012).

Women entrepreneurs have become an important part of national development in recent years in many countries. A study was conducted to investigate factors influencing the success of the women entrepreneurs of Northeast India, and it found that there was a direct link between the empowerment of women entrepreneurs and the development of civil society.

Many authors highlight the relative lack of women's participation in entrepreneurship in absolute terms. Whereas the numbers are increasing geometrically on a global basis, the representation of women entrepreneurs is nowhere near equal to the percentage of women in the population. Much of the literature suggests ways that women can overcome the challenges they face so that they can increase the numbers. Though some disagree with what they consider as an overemphasis on the mythology of entrepreneurship (Huston 2010).

Another study in Vietnam considered the link between women's social empowerment and entrepreneurship. This empirical study investigated whether such increased economic participation of women entrepreneurs indeed improves household wealth and health. The empirical study did confirm that this link is indeed positive and significant (Anh et al. 2011).

There has been some agreement that the employment of young people in aboriginal communities is particularly significant. To ensure the economic, social, and cultural vitality of urban aboriginal communities, there has to be an understanding of the employment patterns. One study of young women aboriginal entrepreneurs in Canada focused upon the role of social capital in transitions to self-employment (Todd 2012). What the authors describe as the complex transitions of young women into self-employment occur at the same time as educational careers and family responsibilities are developing. In Canada, there is significant support for entrepreneurs in general, and in particular, young aboriginal people seeking self-employment are eligible for a number of government-supported programs. The young aboriginal women in this study, whose businesses are predominantly in creative and cultural industries, show the importance of their social networks within aboriginal and non-aboriginal communities. The young aboriginal women demonstrate their commitment to giving something back to their communities through their businesses. We have seen that this is typically a characteristic motivation of women entrepreneurs.

Often we can see a relationship between economic development and the creation of tourism-related businesses provides job opportunities for rural women in the tourist destinations, such as that seen in Aurangabad district of Maharashtra, India, a major tourist destination (Qureshi and Ahmed 2012). Often the tourism industry and the socioeconomic development of tourist areas are closely related to the development of the microcredit, which largely fuels women's entrepreneurship.

Motivation

However, not much is known about what motivates and hinders women entrepreneurs in their approach to starting businesses. There have been some exploratory studies of the motivations of women, such as the one looking at

Malaysian entrepreneurs, and we know that women entrepreneurs are generally not motivated by wealth accumulation but rather by a desire to help the community or provide employment for the family (Alam, Senik, and Jani 2012). We can say that women entrepreneurs, for profit or not, are often motivated by more altruistic motives—not exclusively, but on the balance. There have also been some interesting studies of first business idea labs such as the one in Costa Rica (Inlab SA) (Mora and Elizondo 2012), which elucidates how these motives are at play with women entrepreneurs.

One of the powerful approaches to women empowerment and rural entrepreneurship is the formation of self-help groups. This strategy has fetched noticeable results not only in India and Bangladesh but world over. Women self-help fits with a leadership and management model that taps into the networked model of leadership that women often favor (Vanithamani and Menon 2012).

There have been some studies that investigate personal and external factors that might influence women's decisions to become entrepreneurs, such as one study in Kuwait (Naser, Nuseibeh, and Al-Hussaini 2012) that reinforces the idea that women have a more personal and altruistic set of goals that motivate their business success. However, providing self-employment that is flexible and giving them some dignity and power of decision making and autonomy also come into play.

Some examples of these altruistic motives are often evident in developing countries and at times seem to fit very nicely with the sustainability paradigm of the triple bottom line. An example is, water is a key resource for the tourism industry, especially in countries lacking in drinking water and water infrastructures, such as Morocco. In one of the three case studies in Del Mar Alonso-Almeida's article (2012), she analyzes women's degree of empowerment for making significant decisions regarding water through their entrepreneurial undertakings. One study on water and waste management in the Moroccan tourism industry looked at the case of three women entrepreneurs and found that these women were strongly connected to their communities and were motivated by goals of strengthening the community (del Mar Alonso-Almeida 2012).

A study of the motivation of women entrepreneurs in Singapore examined the motives that stimulate women into becoming business owners. The important characteristic of a typical woman entrepreneur in Singapore, the motivational (Lee 1996) constellation, was confirmed as being based on autonomy for the women and agency and connection to the community.

There is a distinct trend that suggests women are naturally attracted to the new and emerging field of sustainable entrepreneurship (Shepherd and

Patzelt 2010).Women seem to show better attitudes and tendencies that drive them to engage themselves in environmentally concerned jobs (Glodež, Hribar, and Dolinšek 2011). There seems to be a positive relationship between women entrepreneurs and environmental and social entrepreneurship (López, Ramírez, and Casado 2012).

Factors Affecting the Success of Women Entrepreneurs

There are some fundamental questions about which factors affect the success of women entrepreneurs, and at this point, we do not yet have conclusive answers. It is important to consider the relationship between the skills possessed by women entrepreneurs and their motivations, challenges, and performances. Some of the factors that have been considered are the level of education, previous occupational experience, and prior business expertise and management skills. One study undertaken shows that the lack of education and the lack of managerial skills of women business owners are two of the most important variables when it comes to understanding the motivations and the difficulties they have to face (Huarng, Mas-Tur, and Hui-Kuang Yu 2012). The suggestion is that training is sometimes more effective for male entrepreneurs than their female counterparts, and this may be due to the framework that male entrepreneurs have developed through education and previous training.

Of course, when we look at the success of women entrepreneurs, there is great heterogeneity among women entrepreneurs. One study in rural Greece looked at the mix of locals, daughters-in-law from other cultures, and urban newcomers. The authors of this study investigated the heterogeneity of women entrepreneurs who are in involved in entrepreneurship in rural areas and found that the women who were successful in their business approach exhibited strong bonds and connections with the local society and the local economy (Iakovidou, Koutsou, and Partalidou 2012).

Another issue of inquiry is the role of immigrants and ethnic minorities and how this affects their success. The incidence of ethnic women entrepreneurs has risen in modern multicultural societies as women from ethnic minority immigrant backgrounds seek greater economic and societal recognition. Many migrant-receiving countries seek to support this entrepreneurial energy by trying to attract migrants from countries with a strong entrepreneurial tradition (De Vries and Dana 2012). For example, the Canadian government has had a policy of trying to attract Taiwanese immigrants because the culture has a strong tradition of entrepreneurialism, and the Canadian government believes that bringing Taiwanese immigrants to Canada will increase the entrepreneurial transnational connections.

One of the most consistent findings in the entrepreneurial literature is the relationship between self-efficacy and entrepreneurial success shown by Bandura (1997) (Wilson, Kickul and Marlino 2007). One qualitative study examined the self-perceived success factors of women entrepreneurs who consistently generate over $25,000 annually online (Vertel 2012). The results of the study suggested five themes—authenticity, prestige, persistence, speed of implementation, and reinvention—which highlighted what they referred to as the shared behaviors of the participants in their achievement of success. The study confirms that self-efficacy plays a key role in the success of entrepreneurial ventures, and women in particular view that role in a unique way.

Coping with the Stress of Women's Entrepreneurship

Modern life is full of stress and women entrepreneurs have to find a way of dealing with that stress (Shobha and Gopal 2012). This often high level of stress of the women entrepreneurs requires coping mechanisms, which is in the case of women who are distinctive. We have heard the oft-cited phrase *fight or flight*, in a complementary fashion, women often exhibit a reaction to stress called *tend and befriend*. This is a stress response that can be very beneficial to women entrepreneurs as it taps into the networking mode that can be so helpful to women entrepreneurs—a phenomenon treated in depth in Chapter 5 of Volume 2 of this book written by Hanson and Mah.

In one study, women entrepreneurs in Khadi village industries are seen as playing an important role in the Indian economy and creating income and employment opportunities, and this is often a characteristic motivation of women entrepreneurs (Shailaja and Swamy 2012). These particular industries are typical of many industries women entrepreneurs get involved in many different developing country settings. That is to say, the women's businesses generate production at low capital cost, promote the use of local material, utilize local skills, and prevent the youth from leaving these rural regions.

So the actual unique motivation of the women entrepreneurs, which often tends toward more altruistic or community-oriented relationships, can actually help them cope with the stress of the entrepreneurial endeavor, as the "tend and befriend" stress-coping mechanism is built into the core business model of the organization.

There have been some intriguing global studies on the unique networking approaches of the women entrepreneurs such as the one in Mauritius (Gungaphul and Kassean 2012). Studies on gender and entrepreneurship often attempt to compare personal characteristics, business practices, and behavior of male and female entrepreneurs. One key element in women's entrepreneurship that has started to gain attention is their networking capability, and this is one element that also helps women cope with the stress of entrepreneurship coupled with the stress of their roles as caregivers to their children and the elderly.

Women use the networking for the purpose of skill acquisition and bonding—the latter helps them cope with the insignificant stress of running a business. What is interesting is that the networking seems to have a direct effect of increasing the confidence of women, which in turn increase their chance of entrepreneurial success. One study examined the moderating effect of self-confidence in business on the relationship between loan access, skill acquisition, bonding, business performance. This quantitative research (Razak, Isidore, and Mat 2011) demonstrated a clear positive relationship among these factors.

Of course, expertise in the different functional areas of business can also be a key determinant of business success. With small enterprises promoted by women entrepreneurs, there has been an emphasis on marketing as a driver of success. Marketing is the performance of business activities that directs the flow of goods and services from producer to consumer or user and it has been seen as a key success driver. One study of marketing management gives us some sense of how marketing is considered to be a very important function by businesses irrespective of whether it is small, medium, or large or run by men or women (Rajitha 2012). So, marketing has to be considered in any discussion of entrepreneurial women.

Training Women Entrepreneurs

Many would argue that entrepreneurship is at the core of economic development. In fact, women are increasingly at the forefront of an ever-increasing number of businesses. Starting a business can perhaps best described as a multidimensional task that is essentially a creative undertaking (Nayyar et al. 2007). The word *entrepreneur*, which comes from the French word meaning "to grab," is a key factor in the entrepreneurial process. Women's entrepreneurship is a more recently emerging phenomenon, and in the process, women have to face up some of the gaps in their own education and training, especially on a global scale.

Often the training of women entrepreneurs will come through informally in the entrepreneurial process. For example, in the local markets in the Philippines, it is common for a more experienced entrepreneur (often a male) to lend the women a float to make it through the day's transactions. In the course of these interactions, the more experienced entrepreneur passes on some insights and business practices to the less experienced entrepreneurs. In one case, this led to the trainees achieving greater levels of success; for example, a female entrepreneur graduated from a marketplace stall to a grocery store and then multiple grocery stores. I know this particular story of one of my graduate students, Bonifacio Munar, who joined the navy and who along with his siblings emigrated from Philippines to the United States to do a PhD—and his start in life was facilitated by his mother's entrepreneurial endeavors, which helped to lay the financial foundations for his and his siblings' later success in life, and they moved from a lower economic status in the Philippines to a middle-class life in the United States.

Successful new business ventures produce economic development and further growth, however, these outcomes do not just happen. Instead, these are the results of right environment, planning, effort, and innovation. However, this mix is exactly what can be achieved only by the entrepreneurs and their unique view on the world. These people provide a clear plan for business success, and women are getting the mentoring needed to do this type of planning (Jagtap, 2012).

Work–Life Balance

There are some discernible issues that intersect around gender and work–life balance. For example, a recent phenomenological study of women entrepreneurs in Pakistan (Rehman and Roomi 2012) found that one of the consequences of increased participation of women in the labor force is that it creates challenges for them to balance work and family obligations. The situation becomes more complicated in patriarchal societies, especially, as Rehman and Roomi point out, in countries such as Pakistan, due to women's stereotypical domestic roles and religious and family obligations. This can be particularly true in rural areas.

Characteristics of Successful Women Entrepreneurs

Some studies have delved into the factors impacting successful women entrepreneurs. Some factors that have been identified include self-efficacy, risk taking, negative stereotypes, and embracing and upholding societal culture and traditions. For example, one exploratory study of Iranian women found that these factors were related to entrepreneurial women's success (Javadian and Singh 2012).

Despite the impressive growth in the number of firms run by women entrepreneurs, most of these businesses continue to remain small, and women-owned firms have not grown as fast as those of male entrepreneurs. In fact, one of the taglines that are used when discussing entrepreneurial women and their businesses is "smaller and slower." There are many reasons that may help explain the slower rate of growth of women's businesses (Arasti, Panahi, and Zarei 2012). One reason is environmental factors that work against entrepreneurial women's success, such as more restricted access to credit or lower levels of educational attainment in developing countries, as evidenced in a study of women entrepreneurs in Iran (Arasti et al. 2012). There are many reasons that may help explain the growth or lack thereof.

This Iranian qualitative study by Arasti et al. confirms the common finding in entrepreneurship literature that ventures owned by women tend to be smaller than those owned by men. This difference can be due to individual, organizational, and environmental factors. Some of the elements that were identified by the study are the following: goals and aspirations, motives, female identity, and personal characteristics all of which seem to be relevant to the growth aspirations and growth trajectories of women entrepreneurs. Iran's women population is in fact stepping up to attain higher education and make greater contributions to the society, and this is working in a virtuous cycle with their entrepreneurial participation.

However, we know, when it comes to entrepreneurship, women worldwide deal with more challenges than their male counterparts. So one conclusion from this research stream on "smaller and slower" is that there needs to be greater attention to the factors affecting growth orientation of women's ventures as this can have a significant impact on the economic development and national income.

Another internal factor that may limit women entrepreneur's growth rate could be the motivation of these women for starting a business in the first place—it is usually not wealth creation but the more social or altruistic motives previously discussed. We can summarize that women entrepreneurs who initiate, organize, and operate a business enterprise have mostly confined themselves to petty businesses and tiny cottage industries. Women entrepreneurs engage in business due to the factors previously discussed (Tyagi and Nangia 2012).

The entrepreneurial attitude model is becoming more prevalent as a framework to explain and describe new business creation and their success among entrepreneurial women. The attitude research approach suggests that the entrepreneurial behavior is based on the potential entrepreneur's attitudes such as self-efficacy, and in the case of women, a commitment to developing the community (López, Ramírez, and Casado 2012). Education can affect attitude and is clearly a key way to improve the role of women in business creation. For example, it has been recently shown that early school experiences have a strong impact on entrepreneurial motivation among women (Díaz-Pérez and González-Morales 2011).

A recent study in Kenya showed that women tended to operate enterprises associated with traditional women's roles, such as hairstyling. The small and medium enterprises play an important role in the developing economy, such as creating jobs. However, those run by women face particular challenges such as lack of finance, discrimination, problems with the city council, multiple duties, poor access to justice, and lack of education, among others (Mwobobia 2012).

The Kenyan study established that many stakeholders from both public and private sectors are helping empower women entrepreneurs in Kenya. This includes initiatives such as the formation of women enterprise fund, establishment of women's university of science and technology, formal and informal financial support, and donor initiatives among others. The study recommends that women's entrepreneurship needs to be accepted and supported financially and legally and more capacity building should be made available, and it demonstrates that there is a clear link between social empowerment and women's greater economic participation.

In writing this book, many have been enthusiastic and others have been dismayed that we still have to talk about women entrepreneurs. One study focuses on the way in which women entrepreneurs legitimate their place in what they refer to as a *gendered* economy by reifying or cementing a divide between real work and not-real work (Bourne and Calás 2013). This ethnographic study followed the everyday lives of several women who own and operate small businesses in the United States. The study shows that women entrepreneurs become perceived as productive workers by recasting reproductive work as nonproductive or not-real work. So as we continue to pursue this topic of women's entrepreneurship, it is important to consider the implications of what we are considering creative and productive work, not to exclude the very real work of raising children and caring for the elderly—work that is usually taken on by the female population.

References

Alam, Syed Shah, Zizah Che Senik, and Fauzi Mohd Jani. 2012. "An Exploratory Study of Women Entrepreneurs in Malaysia: Motivation and Problems." *Journal of Management Research* 4 (4): 282–97.

Anh, Pham Thi Ngoc, Peter Knorringa, Thanh Dam Truong, and Veronica Bayangos. 2011. "Women Micro-Enterprise Entrepreneurs in Vietnam: Does More Active Economic Participation Increase Social Empowerment?" Paper presented at the conference on "Rethinking Development in an Age of Scarcity and Uncertainty: New Values, Voices and Alliances for Increased Resilience," September 19–22. University of York, England.

Arasti, Zahra, Shirin Majd Shariat Panahi, Behrouz Zarei, and Sima Oliaee Rezaee. 2012. "A Qualitative Study on Individual Factors Affecting Iranian Women Entrepreneurs' Growth Orientation." *International Business Research* 5: 81–90.

Baguant, Priya. 2012. "The Dilemma of Women Entrepreneurs: A Case of Mauritius—A Small Island Economy." *Proceedings of International Conference on Business Management* 8.

Bandura, Anthony. 1997. *Self-Efficacy: The Exercise of Control.* New York: Worth Publishers.

Blank, Rebecca M. 2000. "Distinguished Lecture on Economics in Government: Fighting Poverty: Lessons from Recent U.S. History." *Journal of Economic Perspectives* 14: 3–19.

Bourne, Kristina A., and Marta B. Calás. 2013. "Becoming 'Real' Entrepreneurs: Women and the Gendered Normalization of 'Work.'" *Gender, Work & Organization* 20 (4): 425–38. doi:10.111/j.1468–0432.2012.00591.x. Accessed February 28, 2013.

Brown, Reva Berman, and Sean McCartney. 2001. "The Business Activities of Jewish Women Entrepreneurs in Medieval England." *Management Decision* 39: 699–709.

Del Mar Alonso-Almeida, María. 2012. "Water and Waste Management in the Moroccan Tourism Industry: The Case of Three Women Entrepreneurs." *Women's Studies International Forum* 35 (5): 343–53, http://dx.doi.org/10.1016/j .wsif.2012.06.002. Available at: http://www.sciencedirect.com/science/article/pii /S0277539512000957.

Díaz-Pérez, F. M., and O. González-Morales. 2011. "Desire of a Managerial Position and Entrepreneurial Motivation: The Influence of Gender and School Type in the Canary Islands Young People." *iBusiness* 3: 184–93.

Edwards, Akosua Dardaine. 2012. "Women Entrepreneurs Access to Finance in the Developing World." RIBM Doctoral Symposium, March 14–15. Manchester.

Fosso, Al. 2012. "The Emergence of Women Entrepreneurs in the Informal Sector in the Wake of Economic Crisis in Cameroon (1990s)." *Revue Européenne Du Droit Social* 3 (16): 211–24.

Glodež, N., T. Hribar, and S. Dolinšek. 2011. "Young People's (and Women in Particular) Priorities and Choices Related to Science and Technology Education: Case of Slovenia." Proceedings of the Fourth International Conference of Education, Research and Innovation, November 14–16, Madrid.

Gopal, Vennila, and K. Shobha. 2012. "Success Status of Women Entrepreneurs in a Globalized Environment-A Micro Level Study." *International Journal of Innovative Research and Development* 1 (4): 66–77.

Gungaphul, Mridula, and Hemant Kassean. 2012. "An Insight into the Networking Approaches of Women Entrepreneurs in Mauritius." Paper presented at the European Business Research Conference Proceedings, Roma, Italy.

Huarng, Kun-Huang, Alicia Mas-Tur, and Tiffany Hui-Kuang Yu. 2012. "Factors Affecting the Success of Women Entrepreneurs." *International Enterprise Management Journal* 8: 487–97.

Huston, Cate. 2010. "Q&A. Should All Women Aspire to Be Entrepreneurs?" *Technology Innovation Management Review* (July): Available at: http://timreview.ca /article/457. Accessed February 5, 2013.

Iakovidou, Olga, Stavriani Koutsou, Maria Partalidou, and Maria Emmanouilidou. 2012. "Women Entrepreneurs in Rural Greece: Do They Come from the Same "Neck of the Woods"? Locals, Daughters-in-Law and Urban-Newcomers." *New Medit* 11.

Jagtap, Kishor Nivrutti. 2012. "Rural Women Entrepreneurs—Opportunities and Challenges." *Golden Research Thoughts* 1 (12): 7–13.

Jaumotte, Florence. 2003. "Female Labor Force Participation: Past Trends and Main Determinants in OECD Countries." Working paper. Organisation for Economic Co-operation and Development, Paris.

Javadian, Golshan, and Robert P. Singh. 2012. "Examining Successful Iranian Women Entrepreneurs: An Exploratory Study." *Gender in Management: An International Journal* 27: 148–64.

Lee, Jean. 1996. "The Motivation of Women Entrepreneurs in Singapore." *Women in Management Review* no. 11: 18–29.

López, Jorge, Alicia Ramírez, and Pilar Casado. 2012. "Modelling Entrepreneurial Attitudes in Women Entrepreneurs with Bayesian Networks." *Psychology* 3: 265–79.

Mora, Johnny Poveda, and José Ronald Leandro Elizondo. 2012. "An Associative Entrepreneurship Productive Plan. The Contribution of Women Entrepreneurs to Local Economic Development: A Costa Rican Case Study." *Tec Empresarial* 6: 9–15.

Mwangi, Jane W. "The Role of Medium and Small Enterprises towards the Empowerment of Women: A Case Study of Entrepreneurs in Uhuru Market in Makadara District of Nairobi Province." PhD diss., 2012.

Mwobobia, Fridah Muriungi. 2012. "The Challenges Facing Small-Scale Women Entrepreneurs: A Case of Kenya." *International Journal of Business Administration* 3 (2): 112.

Naser, Kamal, Rana Nuseibeh, and Ahmad Al-Hussaini. 2012. "Personal and External Factors Effect on Women Entrepreneurs: Evidence from Kuwait." *Public Authority for Applied Education and Training Kuwait* 17: 23.

Nayyar, Pooja, Avinash Sharma, Jatinder Kishtwaria, Aruna Rana, and Neena Vyas. 2007. "Causes and Constraints Faced by Women Entrepreneurs in Entrepreneurial Process." *Journal of Social Sciences* 14 (2): 99–102.

Qureshi, Dulari, and M. L. Ahmed. 2012. "Strengthening Women Entrepreneurs through Tourism Employment and Entrepreneurship of the Rural Women in Aurangabad." *Journal of Hospitality Application and Research* 7 (1): 54–56.

Rajitha, G. 2012. "Small Enterprises Promoted by Women Entrepreneurs: A Study of Marketing Management." *Academicia: An International Multidisciplinary Research Journal* 1 (12): 107–22.

Razak, Razli Che, Isidore Ekpe, and Norsiah Mat. 2011. "A Qualitative Analysis of Micro-Credit Group Liability and Women Entrepreneurship's Performance." *Directory of Open Access Journals* 1 (5): 33–39.

Rehman, Sumaira, and Muhammad Azam Roomi. 2012. "Gender and Work–Life Balance: A Phenomenological Study of Women Entrepreneurs in Pakistan." *Journal of Small Business and Enterprise Development* 19: 209–28.

Sadhana, K. P. 2011. "A Study on Women Entrepreneurs in Coimbatore District." *Akshaya International Journal of Management Studies* 1: 55–63.

Shailaja, G., and T. L. N. Swamy. 2012. "Women Entrepreneurs in Khadi and Village Industries (KVI) Sector: A Case Study of Ranga Reddy district." *EXCEL International Journal of Multidisciplinary Management Studies* 2 (8): 271–87.

Shepherd, D. A., and H. Patzelt. 2010. "The New Field of Sustainable Entrepreneurship: Studying Entrepreneurial Action Linking 'What Is to Be Sustained' with 'What Is to Be Developed.' *Entrepreneurship: Theory and Practice* 35: 137–63. doi:10.1111/j.1540–6520.2010.00426.x.

Sukumar, Snigda, and S. Venkatesh. 2012. "Problems of Rural Women Entrepreneurs: An Empirical Study in Periyapatna Taluk." *International Journal of Business Economics and Management Research* 3: 103–10.

Syal, Subina, and Menka Goswami. 2012. "Efficiency of Banks in Providing Financial Assistance to the Women Entrepreneurs: A Case Study." *International Journal of Business and Management Tomorrow* 2: 1–5.

Todd, Roy. 2012. "Young Urban Aboriginal Women Entrepreneurs: Social Capital, Complex Transitions and Community Support." *British Journal of Canadian Studies* 25: 1–19.

Tyagi, Parul, and Richa Nangia. 2012. "Emergence of Indian Women as Global Entrepreneurs: Opportunities and Challenges." *International Multidisciplinary e-Journal* 1: 82–91.

Vanithamani, M. R., and S. Sandhya Menon. 2012. "Enhancing Entrepreneurial Success of Self-Help Group (SHG) Women Entrepreneurs through Effective Training." *EXCEL International Journal of Multidisciplinary Management Studies* 2: 60–72.

Vertel, Ann. 2012. "Self-Efficacy and Entrepreneurship: A Generic Qualitative Study of the Self-Perceived Attitudes and Behaviors of Successful Online Women Entrepreneurs." PhD diss. Capella University, Minneapolis, MN.

De Vries, Huibert P., and Teresa E. Dana. 2012. "Experiences of Ethnic Minority Immigrant Women Entrepreneurs in Contrast to Male Counterparts." *International Journal of Entrepreneurship and Small Business* 15: 502–15.

Wilson, Fiona, Jill Kickul, and Deborah Marlino 2007. "Gender, Entrepreneurial Self-Efficacy, and Entrepreneurial Career Intentions: Implications for Entrepreneurship Education." *Entrepreneurship: Theory and Practice* 31(3): 387–406.

Chapter 1

Gender and Entrepreneurial Intentions

Rotem Shneor and Jan Inge Jenssen

While women's entrepreneurship is growing in importance and numbers, academic research of it remains relatively limited (Baker, Aldrich, and Liou 1997; Brush 1992, 2006). One of the main reasons for this situation is an assumption that there are no differences between men and women entrepreneurs (Brush 2006). Indeed, the growing interest in women's entrepreneurship in recent decades has produced interesting studies, mainly highlighting women's greater tendency to concentrate in service and retail sectors (Hisrich and Brush 1983; Neider 1987), to experience challenges in access to finance (Carter and Rosa 1998; Coleman 2000), and to achieve more moderate results in terms of business growth and long-term performance (Boden and Nucci 2000; Cliff 1998; Rosa et al. 1994).

However, when placed in the context of the theory of planned behavior (TPB) (Ajzen 1991), it must be acknowledged that most of these studies examined women and men at stages of active entrepreneurial engagements, and hence at the action stage of behavior. As a result, insights into the similarities and differences between them at the intention formation stage remain scarce. In this context, it is worth noting that earlier studies showed that the TPB was particularly valuable for understanding and predicting new venture formations, thanks to the criticality of forming intentions prior to actually starting a business (Iakovleva and Kolvereid 2009; Krueger and Carsrud 1993; Krueger, Reilly, and Carsrud 2000; Liñán and Chen 2009).

According to Hindle, Klyver, and Jennings (2009), since women entrepreneurs systematically represent lower proportions of the population, and since they are relatively disadvantaged in terms of human capital in most countries, a woman may require more human and social capital than a man does, in order to form the same level of entrepreneurial intentions (EIs). Therefore, there is a need to draw clear distinctions between women and men with respect to the process of forming EIs. In turn, understanding gender differences in EIs may lead to better understanding of lower entrepreneurial activity among women in comparison to men (Yordanova and Tarrazon 2010).

Therefore, this chapter will focus on the intention formation stage of the TPB, attempting to identify commonalities and differences between men and women with respect to various factors assumed to influence their intentions to establish an entrepreneurial venture and/or being self-employed. First, we present a literature review of the models of EIs, concluding with a special focus on gender in the studies of EIs. Second, we present a new study that seeks to reveal some of the differences in the structure of relationships between different variables influencing the formation of EIs. Third, a discussion confronting our findings with those of earlier studies is presented, while identifying potential contributions, as well as limitations. Finally, the chapter concludes with a summary of main findings and suggestion for some venues for future research.

Literature Review

Being one of the pioneers to stress the centrality of intentions to entrepreneurial behavior, Bird (1988) broadly defined intentionality as "a state of mind directing a person's attention (and therefore experience and action) toward a specific object (goal) or a path in order to achieve something (means)" and more specifically, EIs as "aimed at either creating a new venture or creating new value in existing ventures."

Models of Entrepreneurial Intentions

Scholars concerned with the decision leading up to new venture creation quickly picked up on this notion and began developing models of EIs, mostly based on Shapero and Sokol's (1982) theory of the entrepreneurial event, and Ajzen's (1991) TPB. While the former focused on EIs in particular, the latter aimed at explaining planned behavior in general. The entrepreneurial event approach argues that an individual's perceptions of desirability, feasibility, and propensity to act influence his or her EIs. And the TPB argues that an individual's attitudes, subjective norms, and perceived feasibility influence his or her intentions in general, while EIs can be one type of such intentions. Having said that, the two models are conceptually similar (Krueger 2009). Shapero and Sokol equated intent with the identification of a credible and viable opportunity, which is achieved by the extent to which an individual perceives the opportunity as desirable (paralleling attitudes and social norms in the TPB) and feasible (paralleling self-efficacy in the TPB).

In any case, both models received empirical support in a series of studies (Krueger and Carsrud 1993; Krueger, Reilly, and Carsrud 2000; Shook, Priem, and McGee 2003), and some have even suggested integrative models building on components from both models(Iakovleva and Kolvereid 2009; Krueger, Reilly, and Carsrud 2000).

According to Hindle, Klyver, and Jennings (2009), although the different models of EIs come in many variations, they have more similarities than differences, as they essentially represent states of mind while underestimating the social contextualization of these states of mind. In particular, these authors suggest an informed intent model in which existing models are strengthened by incorporating human and social capital variables. Both the human capital and the social capital are viewed here as critical sources of information individuals use when forming EIs. Two main facets of human capital are education and experience, as both strengthen the cognitive capabilities of individuals to recognize opportunities by combining pieces of information effectively and as such inform judgments concerning new venture creation. Social capital resources such as professional networks, family members and friends in business, and personally known entrepreneurs are all sources of information, advice, support, and legitimacy when considering new venture creation. In addition, Hindle, Klyver, and Jennings (2009) also argue that gender in particular plays a critical role in moderating the effects of human and social capital, suggesting that females require higher education, greater start-up experience, and greater social capital than men in order to exhibit the same levels of EIs.

Gender and Entrepreneurial Intentions

In order to identify the role of gender in the formation of EIs, we conducted a systematic search for empirical studies examining EIs and including gender or sex as control or independent variable, as well as a basis for splitting samples and comparisons. All in all, 51 articles covering analyses of 60 independent samples were deemed relevant for review. Interestingly enough, while academic interest in EIs in general has increased during the past 15 years, the inclusion of a gender dimension to related analyses has only emerged in the past 5 years.

Overall, our review found that 28 studies used it as an independent variable, 17 as a control variable, and 6 as a basis for splitting samples for comparative analyses. Hence, the majority of studies were not concerned with gender differences per se, but rather with the existence or absence of the effect of gender on EIs. In any case, findings are nonconsistent to say the least. Direct effect of gender on EIs was identified in 21 samples across studies, while an absence of such effect was identified in 35 samples. The remaining samples were split by gender and traced gender differences. Possible explanation for such inconsistencies may be an identified moderator role of gender, which was suggested in some studies (BarNir, Watson, and Hutchins 2011; Díaz-García and Jiménez-Moreno 2010), or its indirect effect via other mediating variables, as suggested in others (Iakovleva, Kolvereid, and Stephan 2011; Liñán, Urbano, and Guerrero 2011; Shook and Bratianu 2010; Wilson et al. 2009; Yordanova and Tarrazon 2010).

Inspired by Hindle, Klyver, and Jennings's (2009) informed intent approach to EIs, the inconsistencies in findings surrounding the effect of gender, and acknowledging the potential complexity of relationships among the variables in EI models, we present in the remainder of this chapter a new independent study that attempts to address these issues. Later, findings from this study will be confronted by revisiting the theory, as well as earlier studies at the intersection of EIs and gender/sex.

Methodology

Research Context

The study of EIs requires an examination of entrepreneurial phenomena before they occur, while also including nonentrepreneurial intending subjects. Therefore, samples of students have been popular, as they reveal vocational preferences of individuals at a time when they face important career decisions (Krueger, Reilly, and Carsrud 2000). Indeed, students represent a section of public that can be characterized by the "between things" type of displacement, often associated with higher likelihood of starting a new venture (Shapero and Sokol 1982). Accordingly, such samples explicitly include subjects with a rather broad spectrum of intentions and attitudes toward entrepreneurship (Krueger, Reilly, and Carsrud 2000); and although details of a business may not have yet fully matured in subjects' minds, global career intentions should have (Scherer et al. 1989).

Moreover, Norway has been consistently recognized in Global Entrepreneurship Monitor (GEM) reports as an innovation-driven economy. In

2010, Norway had the second highest level of latent entrepreneurship within innovation-driven economies (only surpassed by Iceland), in addition to having the third highest level of early-stage entrepreneurial activity after Iceland and Australia (Kelley, Bosma, and Amorós 2010). Such conditions indicate a favorable environment for entrepreneurial development out of need for improvement rather than out of necessity, and may serve as fertile ground for those contemplating entrepreneurial careers and self-employment.

Therefore, and in accordance with our discussion in the previous paragraph, we focus our analysis on university students from Norway.

Data Collection and Sample

The data for our research are the results of a survey conducted among students from the University of Agder (UiA) in Norway, encompassing all departments and degree programs. Data were collected only from students and did not include members of faculty and/or staff. The survey was conducted from September to October 2009. The questionnaire was firstly pretested with 20 students, all of whom exhibited adequate understanding of all items. The final version of the questionnaire was then distributed as a web-based form by e-mail to 7,942 students on the UiA mailing list. Following Dillman's (2006) recommendations for four follow-ups, reminders were sent weekly to those who did not complete the survey within a time frame of one month. At the end of the process, we received 1,728 valid questionnaires, representing a response rate of 22 percent.

Our final data set included 42 percent male and 58 percent female respondents. In terms of age distribution, 82 percent were 35 or younger, while 18 percent were 36 or older. In terms of degree type, 59 percent were bachelor students, 25 percent master students, and 16 percent engaged in other degree programs. Finally, in terms of faculty affiliations, 33 percent of respondents were from the faculty of economics and social sciences, 22 percent from the faculty of humanities and education, 22 percent from the faculty of science and engineering, 19 percent from the faculty of health and sports, and 4 percent from the faculty of arts.

Measures

Measures employed in this study were adopted from earlier studies, with occasional adaptations as specified later in this chapter. Multiple-item constructs were assessed based on a factor analysis. Since normality of item distribution was not supported in a Kolmogorov–Smirnov test, the extraction method selected was principal axis factoring. A four-factor solution emerged, with each item loading on only one factor. The rotated solution suggested three factors with eigenvalues greater than 1 (including: EIs—4.019, self-efficacy—3.011, and social norms—2.513), whereas the fourth eigenvalue was 0.987 (capturing risk perceptions). Since our data set was large enough, the scree plot was considered, and it suggested a four-factor solution. Cumulative variance explained by the extraction was 70.2 percent. Later, the reliability of each factor was further assessed using Cronbach's alpha. Finally, for allowing correlations between our constructs, their scores were saved as averages of all their related items.

Dependent Variable

Entrepreneurial intentions have been captured in various ways in the literature, using both single (Fernández, Liñán, and Santos 2009; Lee and Wong 2004) and multiple items (e.g., Kolvereid 1996; Liñán and Chen 2009), mostly stressing both aspects of start-up/firm establishment and self-employment. In our study, a construct capturing EIs was measured through a 7-point Likert-type scale with five items (Cronbach's alpha = 0.949), where 1 stands for "strongly disagree" and 7 for "strongly agree." Of these five items, three items were adopted from Liñán and Chen's (2009) instrument: "My professional goal is to become an entrepreneur," "I am determined to create a firm in the future," and "I have the firm intention to start a firm someday." One item resembled an item used by Kuckertz and Wagner (2010), and was formulated as: "I intend to start a firm within five years after graduation." The last item was inspired by Grilo and Thurik (2005), and was formulated as: "I prefer to be self-employed."

Independent Variables

Drawing on findings from earlier studies, we adopted a number of variables that were frequently used, deemed relevant for students' EIs, and exhibited relative inconsistencies in terms of their impact on EIs in the different studies. In this section, we present and define each variable, and relate them to findings in earlier research, while highlighting inconsistent and contradictory findings. Finally, we summarize in Table 1.1 the actual measurements used for each variable, and the sources they were taken from, inspired by, or resembled to when self-created.

Table 1.1 Independent variables, measurements, and sources

Variable	Measurement	Source(s)
Self-efficacy	Five items: "I am able to deal effectively with unexpected events." "I can solve problems with my own efforts." "I have ability to solve and remain calm when facing difficulties." "I am resourceful and can handle unexpected challenges." "I can think of solutions if faced by several problems." 1- Strongly disagree, 7- Strongly agree.	Own instrument Inspired by items under the "coping with unexpected challenges" factor in DeNoble, Jung, and Ehrlich (1999), and the "risk-taking" factor in Chen, Greene, and Crick (1998) and Kolvereid and Isaksen (2006)
Social norms	Three items: "My closest family members think I should start my own business." "My friends and classmates think I should start my own business." "People who are important to me think I should start my own business." 1- Strongly disagree, 7- Strongly agree	As used in Kolvereid (1996), Iakovleva and Kolvereid (2009), and Liñán and Chen (2009)
Entrepreneurial attitudes/ risk perception	Two items: "Starting a new business is very risky." "The possibility of a new business doing poorly is very high." 1- Strongly disagree, 7- Strongly agree	Own instrument Inspired by the versions of Fitzsimmons and Douglas (2011), Fernández, Liñán, and Santos (2009)
Exposure to role models	"I know successful business operators I can follow as role models." 1- Strongly disagree, 7- Strongly agree	Extended version of Liñán and Chen (2009)

(Continued)

Table 1.1 (Continued)

Variable	Measurement	Source(s)
Parental entrepreneurial experience	"Have any of your parents ever been self-employed?" 0 - No, 1 - Yes	As used in Carey, Flanagan, and Palmer (2010), Kolvereid (1996), Iakovleva and Kolvereid (2009), and Lans, Gulikers, and Batterink (2010)
Motivation to comply	"I care about what my closest family and friends think about self-employment." 1- Strongly disagree, 7- Strongly agree.	Reduced version of Iakovleva and Kolvereid (2009) and Mueller (2011)
Entrepreneurial experience	"Have you ever been self-employed?" 0 - No, 1 - Yes	As used in Carey, Flanagan, and Palmer (2010), Hamidi, Wennberg, and Berglund (2008), Kolvereid (1996), Lans, Gulikers, and Batterink (2010), and Liñán and Chen (2009)
Entrepreneurial status	"Are you currently self-employed?" 0 - No, 1 - Yes	As used in Haase, Lautenschläger, and Rena (2011)
Entrepreneurial education	"Have you ever had entrepreneurship education/training?" 0 - No, 1 - Yes	As used in Franco, Haase, and Lautenschläger (2010), Hamidi, Wennberg, and Berglund (2008), and Tornikoski and Kautonen (2009)
Economics/business major	"In which faculty are you studying?" 0 - Other, 1 - Faculty of economics and social sciences	As used in Franco, Haase, and Lautenschläger (2010), Haase, Lautenschläger, and Rena (2011), Kristiansen and Indarti (2004), and Lans, Gulikers, and Batterink (2010)
Year of study	"In which year are you studying?" Number of years	As used in Zellweger, Sieger, and Halter (2011)
Age	"What is your age?" Number of years	As used in Iakovleva and Kolvereid (2009), Liñán and Chen (2009), and others.

Overall, our study included 12 independent variables. These comprise the three core variables of the TPB—self-efficacy, social norms, and risk perceptions (as proxy of attitudes); six variables capturing human capital—indications of entrepreneurial education, taking an economics major, years of education, having entrepreneurial experience, current entrepreneurial status, and age; and three variables capturing social capital—indications of exposure to entrepreneurial role models, parental entrepreneurial experience, and motivation-to-comply with social demands. Sex was used to split samples between male and female students, allowing us to compare the two.

Self-efficacy. Self-efficacy is a cognitive estimate that captures a person's belief in his or her own abilities to perform on the various skill requirements necessary for pursuing a new venture opportunity (Chen, Greene, and Crick 1998; DeNoble, Jung, and Ehrlich 1999). Earlier studies have shown a consistent positive direct effect of self-efficacy on EIs (e.g., BarNir, Watson, and Hutchins 2011; Carr and Sequeira 2007;Fernández, Liñán, and Santos 2009; Leffel and Darling 2009; Pejvak et al. 2009).

Various authors have used different operationalizations for capturing self-efficacy. Some authors have used both single items (e.g., Fernández, Liñán, and Santos 2009) and others have used multiple items (e.g., Lans, Gulikers, and Batterink 2010; Sequeira, Mueller, and McGee 2007; Zhao, Hills, and Seibert 2005).

In this study, we used five items that focus on the extent to which respondents believe in their ability to cope with uncertainty, change, and risk (Cronbach's alpha = 0.877), all reflecting important aspects of entrepreneurial management. All items were reformulated based on the previously published items, for example, by loading on the "risk-taking" dimension in Chen, Greene, and Crick (1998) and Kolvereid and Isaksen (2006), and the "coping with unexpected challenges" dimension in DeNoble, Jung, and Ehrlich's (1999). Respondents indicated the extent to which they agreed with each statement on a 7-point Likert scale, where 1 stands for "strongly disagree" and 7 for "strongly agree."

Social norms. Social norms is an estimate that captures normative beliefs about what important people think about an individual's choice to pursue an entrepreneurial career and/or self-employment (Yordanova and Tarrazon 2010), and the social pressures that are associated with him or her (Carey, Flanagan, and Palmer 2010). An overwhelming majority of studies have indicated a direct positive effect of social norms on EIs (e.g., Iakovleva and Kolvereid 2009; Kautonen, Luoto, and Tornikoski 2010; Kolvereid and Isaksen 2006; Leffel and Darling 2009; Liñán and Chen 2009; Pejvak et al. 2009). A single study has identified negative effects (Shook and Bratianu 2010), which have been explained by postcommunist realities and heritage in the specific transition economy context of Romania.

In line with earlier studies, we adopted Kolvereid's (1996) three items for capturing social norms, while relating to whether close family, friends, and people important to the individual encourage him or her to establish his or her own business (Cronbach's alpha = 0.951). Here as well, respondents were required to indicate the extent to which they agree with each statement on a 7-point Likert scale, as used earlier.

Motivation-to-comply. Motivation-to-comply is an estimate that captures the extent to which individuals care about the opinion of others. While earlier studies have computed the values of this dimension into an overall estimation of social norms (Iakovleva and Kolvereid 2009; Kolvereid 1996), we chose to treat it separately for two reasons. First, we did so in an attempt to identify whether the positive effect on EIs originates from motivation-to-comply or social norms, or both. Second, we wished to remain open to possibilities that motivation-to-comply may interact with other variables in influencing EIs, as part of the effort to uncover a more complex nature of relationships between variables.

Therefore, we created a single item—"I care about what my closest family and friends think about self-employment." Respondents were required to indicate the extent to which they agree with this statement on a 7-point Likert scale, as used earlier.

Risk perception. Risk perception is an estimate that captures the extent to which individuals associate entrepreneurship and self-employment with risk, and his or her attitudes toward it. Here, in order to reduce the potential complexity of capturing entrepreneurial attitudes in general we decided to focus on the perception of risk as a narrower proxy for entrepreneurial attitudes. Such approach is in tune with McMullen and Shepherd's (2006) claim that entrepreneurial action is an outcome of more willingness to bear uncertainty, and that attitude to risk is a sufficient proxy for perceived desirability (Fitzsimmons and Douglas 2011).

Various scholars have addressed the role of risk in studies of EIs. Some have shown that risk propensity is positively associated with EIs (e.g., Grilo and Thurik 2005; Gurel, Altinay, and Daniele 2010), while others have shown that risk aversion is negatively associated with EIs (e.g., Fernández, Liñán, and Santos 2009; Yordanova 2011), and so is the concern with job security (Haase, Lautenschläger, and Rena 2011). An exception here is a study by Hamidi, Wennberg, and Berglund (2008), who have found no effect, which can be explained by the specific item that was used, only addressing the perceptions of financial risk.

Therefore, we created a risk perception construct based on two items (see Tables 1.2 and 1.3), capturing the extent to which respondents associate entrepreneurship with risk (Cronbach's alpha = 0.656). Here, again, respondents were requested to indicate the extent to which they agree with each statement on a 7-point Likert scale, as used earlier.

Exposure to role models. Exposure to role models is an estimate that captures the extent to which respondents have been exposed to entrepreneurs who can serve as role models for them. While addressed in many studies, the operationalization of this variable remains problematic for two main reasons. First, some studies often relate this only to exposure to entrepreneurs, without necessarily associating this exposure with positive impression, success, or role model associations (e.g., Carey, Flanagan, and Palmer 2010; Franco, Haase, and Lautenschläger 2010; Liñán, Santos, and Fernández 2011). Three notable exceptions here are Walter, Parboteeah, and Walter (2011), who looked at the performance of entrepreneurial role models; Mueller (2011), who looked at students' evaluation of the entrepreneurs they met during an entrepreneurship course; and Zellweger, Sieger, and Halter (2011), who looked into the extent to which respondents associate their parents' entrepreneurial experiences with positive feelings. Second, in some cases, parents' entrepreneurial experiences were used as a proxy for exposure to role models (e.g., Kickul et al. 2008). However, role models may not necessarily be parents, they may also be the members of an extended network of relatives and friends, as well as media-profiled entrepreneurs.

Earlier studies considering family background and parental experiences have shown mixed results. Some have found direct positive effect (e.g., Carr and Sequeira 2007; Crant 1996; Gupta et al. 2009; Gurel, Altinay, and Daniele 2010), while others have found no effect on EIs (e.g., Ahmed et al. 2010; Kolvereid and Isaksen 2006; Singh and DeNoble 2003; Tornikoski and Kautonen 2009). Moreover, there are studies that have found both results in different samples of the same study (e.g., Kuckertz and Wagner 2010; Plant and Ren 2010; Veciana, Aponte, and Urbano 2005).

Similarly, inconsistencies are also evident with respect to the influence of knowing entrepreneurs in more extended social networks; while some studies have found direct positive effects (e.g., BarNir, Watson, and Hutchins 2011; Liñán, Urbano, and Guerrero 2011; Mueller 2011), others have not (e.g., Carey, Flanagan, and Palmer 2010; Franco, Haase, and Lautenschläger 2010; Hamidi, Wennberg, and Berglund 2008). In addition, there are studies showing both results in different samples of the same study (Liñán and Chen 2009; Liñán, Urbano, and Guerrero 2011). These different findings may be explained by different measurements, different samples collected in different contexts, and limited acknowledgment of complex relationships with other variables in the different models studied.

Based on this analysis, we used two separate variables. For capturing exposure to role models, respondents were asked to indicate the extent to which they agree with the statement: "I know successful business operators I can follow as role models" on a 7-point Likert scale, as used earlier. And for capturing parental entrepreneurial experience, we used a value-neutral dichotomous variable (as used in: Carey, Flanagan, and Palmer 2010; Kolvereid 1996; Kolvereid and Isaksen 2006; Kuckertz and Wagner 2010; Lans, Gulikers, and Batterink 2010; Tornikoski and Kautonen 2009), where respondents were required to indicate whether one of their parents has ever been self-employed or not.

Entrepreneurial experience. Entrepreneurial experience is an indication of whether a respondent has prior experience in being self-employed. Entrepreneurial experience has mostly been measured via dichotomous items tapping into whether one has previously been self-employed or not (e.g., Kolvereid 1996), whether one has previously owned a business or not (e.g., Gupta et al. 2009), and whether one is a novice entrepreneur versus a serial one (e.g., Kolvereid and Isaksen 2006). In this study, we used the same dichotomous indicator mentioned first.

Here, an overwhelming majority of studies have found a positive direct effect of entrepreneurial experience on EIs (e.g., Ahmed et al. 2010; Fitzsimmons and Douglas 2011; Kolvereid and Moen 1997; Zhao, Hills, and Seibert 2005), while a minority have found no effect (e.g., Kautonen, Luoto, and Tornikoski 2010; Liñán, Urbano, and Guerrero 2011).

Entrepreneurial status. Entrepreneurial status is an indication of whether the respondent is self-employed at the time of taking the survey. We identified a single study that controlled for actual entrepreneurial status when taking the survey, naturally finding significant positive effects on EIs (Haase, Lautenschläger, and Rena 2011). We adopted the same dichotomous variable, so as to differentiate between the effects of entrepreneurial experience in general and those of active entrepreneurial engagements at the time data were collected.

Year of study. Year of study is an indication in which year of higher education the respondent is enrolled. Year of study has been captured in the research of EIs either by number of years (e.g., Zellweger, Sieger, and Halter 2011) or in a categorical classification of seniority (e.g., Turker and Selcuk 2009). Here, while most studies have identified no direct effect on EIs (e.g., Gurel, Altinay, and Daniele 2010; Shook and Bratianu 2010; Turker and Selcuk 2009), some have identified a positive effect (e.g., Ahmed et al. 2010; Brice Jr. and Nelson 2008). Since our concern is with EIs among students, we opted for including year of study in our survey, which was measured by years of enrollment in higher education.

Entrepreneurial education. Entrepreneurial education is an indication of whether a respondent has ever attended an entrepreneurship course or training. Entrepreneurship education has been captured in the research of EIs either by using it as a dichotomous indicator of participation in an entrepreneurship course or training (e.g., Johansen and Clausen 2011; Tornikoski and Kautonen 2009), that is, as an indicator of whether respondents graduated with an entrepreneurship major (e.g., Kolvereid and Moen 1997), or by evaluating specific components and modules of an entrepreneurship education program (e.g., Franco, Haase, and Lautenschläger 2010). In this study, we used the same dichotomous indicator mentioned first.

Earlier research shows mixed results also with respect to the impact of entrepreneurship education on EIs. While some find a positive effect of entrepreneurial education on EIs (e.g., Hamidi, Wennberg, and Berglund 2008; Johansen and Clausen 2011; Jones et al. 2008; Kolvereid and Moen 1997), others find no effect (e.g., Ahmed et al. 2010; Tornikoski and Kautonen 2009).

Economics major. Economics major is an indication of whether a respondent is a student in the faculty of economics or other faculties. Earlier studies that wished to compare business and economics students versus students in other fields came up with mixed results. Some studies show higher levels of EIs among business/economics students (e.g., Schwarz et al. 2009), others show lower levels of EIs among them (e.g., Kristiansen and Indarti 2004), while others show no relationship between economics major and EIs (e.g., Zellweger, Sieger, and Halter 2011). These inconsistencies, again, may be explained by different contexts of study, potential complex relationships with the different variables of the models, and the existence of possible parallel conflicting effects of business/economics education.

Age. Age is an indication of how old a respondent was at the time of taking the survey in years. Age has been captured in the research of EIs mostly by the number of years (e.g., Sequeira, Mueller, and McGee 2007; Tornikoski and Kautonen 2009), but in some studies, also through categories of age ranges (e.g., Kautonen, Luoto, and Tornikoski 2010; Lee and Wong 2004). Some researchers have opted for more than one indicator of age using both years and years squared (e.g., Grilo and Thurik 2005; Lee et al. 2011; Raijman 2001). In our study, we used a single indicator of age by number of years.

Earlier studies show inconsistent results with respect to the effect of age on EIs. Some show a positive direct effect (e.g., Sequeira, Mueller, and McGee 2007), others show a negative direct effect (e.g., Vinogradov and Gabelko 2010; Yordanova 2011), while others show no effect (e.g., Iakovleva, Kolvereid, and Stephan 2011; Lee and Wong 2004). This inconsistency may be explained by claims of a curvilinear relationship of age and entrepreneurial behavior, based on the positive effects of experience, wealth, and credibility, as well as the negative effect of growing opportunity costs and resistance to change (Schwarz et al. 2009; Vinogradov and Gabelko 2010).

Method—Path Analysis

Our study has an exploratory nature in the way that it wishes to reevaluate existing knowledge by revealing the complex relationships among multiple variables, and hence explain inconsistencies in the literature about the effects of each. In order to do so, one must first acknowledge the need to identify correlations that may be spuriously present. Path analysis is suitable for this purpose, as it allows identifying parsimonious models where one has at least an implicit causal ordering and most variables correlated (Asher 1983). Indeed, in our case, we had both a causal ordering in mind and variables that were significantly correlated (see Table 1.2).

Since a majority of our variables were operationalized by single items, structural equation modeling was deemed less relevant, and instead we opted for using multiple regressions, gradually refining the model, while pruning out all nonsignificant paths, as suggested by Asher (1983), and already applied earlier in a research of entrepreneurial intensions by Krueger (1993). Such analysis entails regressing each model variable on all prior variables to control for spurious correlations. Exceptions here are the age and parental entrepreneurial experience variables, for which there is no theoretical or logical ground to assume that they are influenced by any of the remaining variables in the model. Moreover, to reduce model complexity we included only direct effects on EIs and direct effects on factors affecting EIs directly.

The standardized regression beta coefficients comprise the path weights (Krueger 1993), rendering them comparable across samples. Accordingly, for sex-based comparison purposes, our sample was split into two, one including males only and the other females only. Figures 1.1 and 1.2 present all significant paths, as emerged from our multiple regressions for males and females, respectively (Tables 1.3a and 1.3b). Each regression was run a number of times, while gradually removing variables with nonsignificant F values in the linear case, and nonsignificant Wald values in the logistic case (e.g., regressions where entrepreneurial experience, entrepreneurial status, entrepreneurial education, and an economics major served as dependent variables). Final regression for each variable includes only those variables that had significant univariate F values in the linear case or Wald values in the logistic case.

Table 1.2 Correlation matrix

	Mean	SD	(1)	(2)	(3)	(4)	(5)	(6)	(7)	(8)	(9)	(10)	(11)	(12)
(1) 1 Entrepreneurial intentions	2.87	1.61	—											
(2) Self-efficacy	5.23	0.92	0.220***	—										
(3) Social norms	3.16	1.47	0.591***	0.211***	—									
(4) Risk perceptions	4.57	1.20	-0.070**	-0.048*	-0.40*	—								
(5) Motivation to comply	3.80	1.73	0.090***	0.000	0.149***	0.109***	—							
(6) Age	27.36	8.94	-0.098***	0.124***	-0.030	-0.13***	-0.045*	—						
(7) Economics major	0.33	0.47	0.123***	0.065**	0.087***	0.09**	-0.040*	-0.071**	—					
(8) Year of study	2.48	1.532	-0.046*	0.129***	-0.050*	-0.079	-0.034	0.202***	0.058**	—				
(9) Entrepreneurial education	0.20	0.40	0.209***	0.098***	0.162***	0.001	-0.004	0.031	0.145***	0.082***	—			
(10) Parental entrepreneurial experience	0.43	0.50	0.068**	0.036	0.070**	-0.048	0.039	-0.015	-0.009	-0.030	0.036	—		
(11) Entrepreneurial experience	0.13	0.34	0.253***	0.113***	0.179***	-0.126***	-0.022	0.230***	-0.013	0.049*	0.212***	0.078***	—	
(12) Entrepreneurial status	0.06	0.24	0.232***	0.055*	0.165***	-0.113***	-0.001	0.104***	-0.038	0.057**	0.146***	0.023	0.609***	—
(13) Exposure to role models	4.05	1.90	0.343***	0.262***	0.430***	-0.057***	0.104***	0.050*	0.132***	0.036	0.210***	0.128***	0.127***	0.055*

Note: N = 1,728.
*p < .05; **p < .01; ***p < .001.

Table 1.3a Regression results in path analysis—males

Dependent Variable	Independent Variables (F values, significance)/(Wald values, significance)	Overall F/χ^2	Regression Statistics R-Squared
(1) Entrepreneurial intentions	Self-efficacy (6.0, $p < .05$) Social norms (189.5, $p < .001$) Risk perceptions (0.2, n.s.) Motivation to comply (0.0, n.s.) Age (3.8, n.s.) Economics major (9.6, $p < .01$) Year of study (1.1, n.s.) Entrep. education (0.3, n.s.) Parent entrep. experience (1.2, n.s.) Entrep. experience (8.8, $p < .01$) Entrep. status (4.1, $p < .05$) Exposure to role models (8.4, $p < .001$)	$F = 39.62$ (sig. at .001)	$R^2 = 0.401$ Adjusted $R^2 = 0.391$
(2) Entrepreneurial intentions	Self-efficacy (4.9, $p < .05$) Social norms (209.0, $p < .001$) Economics major (9.4, $p < .01$) Entrep. experience (8.4, $p < .01$) Entrep. status (6.7, $p < .05$) Exposure to role models (9.8, $p < .001$)	$F = 77.80$ (sig. at .001)	$R^2 = 0.395$ Adjusted $R^2 = 0.390$
(3) Self-efficacy	Social norms (10.0, $p < .01$) Risk perceptions (0.3, n.s.) Motivation to comply (2.8, n.s.) Age (1.3, n.s.) Economics major (0.0, n.s.)	$F = 8.70$ (sig. at .001)	$R^2 = 0.119$ Adjusted $R^2 = 0.105$

DV (Model)	Predictors (coefficient, sig.)	F	R^2
	Year of study (8.0, $p < .01$) Entrep. education (0.0, n.s.) Parent entrep. experience (0.1, n.s.) Entrep. experience (0.5, n.s.) Entrep. status (0.5, n.s.) Exposure to role models (39.0, $p < .001$)	$F = 30.22$ (sig. at .001)	$R^2 = 0.112$ Adjusted $R^2 = 0.108$
(4) Self-efficacy	Social norms (8.9, $p < .01$) Year of study (9.8, $p < .01$) Exposure to role models (41.8, $p < .001$)	$F = 23.35$ (sig. at .001)	$R^2 = 0.265$ Adjusted $R^2 = 0.254$
(5) Social norms	Self-efficacy (10.0, $p < .01$) Risk perceptions (0.1, n.s.) Motivation to comply (14.0, $p < .001$) Age (2.2, n.s.) Economics Major (0.2, n.s.) Year of Study (18.8, $p < .001$) Entrep. education (1.8, n.s.) Parent entrep. experience (0.3, n.s.) Entrep. experience (2.0, n.s.) Entrep. status (15.2, $p < .001$) Exposure to role models (94.9, $p < .001$)	$F = 49.90$ (sig. at .001)	$R^2 = 0.258$ Adjusted $R^2 = 0.253$
(6) Social norms	Self-efficacy (10.1, $p < .01$) Motivation to comply (15.6, $p < .001$) Year of study (20.3, $p < .001$) Entrep. status (38.7, $p < .001$) Exposure to role models (112.5, $p < .001$)	$F = 23.31$ (sig. at .001)	$R^2 = 0.289$ Adjusted $R^2 = 0.278$
(7) Exposure to role models	Self-efficacy (40.0, $p < .001$) Social norms (94.9, $p < .001$)		

(Continued)

Table 1.3a (Continued)

Dependent Variable	Independent Variables (F values, significance)/(Wald values, significance)	Overall F/χ^2	*Regression Statistics* R-Squared
	Risk perceptions (4.4, $p < .05$) Motivation to comply (6.7, $p < .01$) Age (0.2, n.s.) Economics major (16.0, $p < .001$) Year of study (0.1, n.s.) Entrep. education (10.4, $p < .001$) Parent entrep. experience (12.7, $p < .001$) Entrep. experience (1.1, n.s.) Entrep. status (3.2, n.s.)		
(8) Exposure to role models	Self-efficacy (41.5, $p < .001$) Social norms (97.0, $p < .001$) Risk perceptions (4.4, $p < .05$) Motivation to comply (6.6, $p < .01$) Economics major (17.2, $p < .001$) Entrep. education (12.1, $p < .001$) Parent entrep. experience (13.4, $p < .001$)	$F = 40.84$ (sig. at .001)	$R^2 = 0.286$ Adjusted $R^2 = 0.279$
(9) Economics major	Self-efficacy (0.0, n.s.) Social norms (0.2, n.s.) Risk perceptions (0.4, n.s.) Motivation to comply (3.7, n.s.) Age (1.6, n.s.) Year of study (13.8, $p < .001$) Entrep. education (18.3, $p < .001$)	$\chi^2 = 74.44$ (sig at .001)	Cox and Snell $R^2 = 0.098$ Nagelkerke $R^2 = 0.136$

(10) Economics major	Parent entrep. experience (5.0, $p < .05$) Entrep. experience (0.0, n.s.) Entrep. status (1.2, n.s.) Exposure to role models (15.8, $p < .001$)	
	Year of study (12.6, $p < .001$) Entrep. education (17.4, $p < .001$) Parent entrep. experience (5.4, $p < .05$) Exposure to role models (18.2, $p < .001$)	$\chi^2 = 65.59$ (sig. at .001) Cox and Snell $R^2 = 0.087$ Nagelkerke $R^2 = 0.120$
(11) Entrepreneurial experience	Self-efficacy (0.6, n.s.) Social norms (1.9, n.s.) Risk perceptions (3.0, n.s.) Motivation to comply (0.9, n.s.) Age (29.4, $p < .001$) Economics major (0.0, n.s.) Year of study (1.6, n.s.) Entrep. education (17.8, $p < .001$) Parent entrep. experience (3.7, n.s.) Entrep. status (68.5, $p < .001$) Exposure to role models (1.3, n.s.)	$\chi^2 = 299.10$ (sig. at .001) Cox and Snell $R^2 = 0.339$ Nagelkerke $R^2 = 0.551$
(12) Entrepreneurial experience	Age (32.2, $p < .001$) Entrep. education (23.2, $p < .001$) Entrep. status (75.4, $p < .001$)	$\chi^2 = 277.97$ (sig. at .001) Cox and Snell $R^2 = 0.319$ Nagelkerke $R^2 = 0.519$
(13) Entrepreneurial status	Self-efficacy (1.3, n.s.) Social norms (13.4, $p < .001$) Risk perceptions (4.3, $p < .05$) Motivation to comply (0.2, n.s.)	$\chi^2 = 247.42$ (sig. at .001) Cox and Snell $R^2 = 0.290$ Nagelkerke $R^2 = 0.634$

(Continued)

Table 1.3a (Continued)

Dependent Variable	Independent Variables (F values, significance)/(Wald values, significance)	Regression Statistics	
		Overall F/χ^2	R-Squared
	Age (0.3, n.s.) Economics major (1.9, n.s.) Year of study (5.6, $p < .05$) Entrep. education (0.1, n.s.) Parent entrep. experience (0.4, n.s.) Entrep. experience (65.4, $p < .001$) Exposure to role models (3.4, n.s.)		
(14) Entrepreneurial status	Social norms (10.5, $p < .001$) Risk perceptions (3.8, n.s.) Year of study (3.0, n.s.) Entrep. experience (63.3, $p < .001$)	$\chi^2 = 235.89$ (sig. at .001)	Cox and Snell $R^2 = 0.278$ Nagelkerke $R^2 = 0.609$
(14') Entrepreneurial status	Social norms (8.1, $p < .01$) Entrep. experience (67.5, $p < .001$)	$\chi^2 = 229.11$ (sig. at .001)	Cox and Snell $R^2 = 0.272$ Nagelkerke $R^2 = 0.594$

Abbreviations: Entrep, entrepreneurial; sig, significant; n.s., not significant.

Table 1.3b Regression results in path analysis—females

Dependent variable	Independent variables (F values significance)/ (Wald values, significance)	Regression statistics	
		Overall F/χ^2	R-squared
(1) Entrepreneurial intentions	Self-efficacy (11.1, $p < .001$) Social norms (320.2, $p < .001$) Risk perceptions (5.9, $p < .05$) Motivation to comply (1.8, n.s.) Age (30.3, $p < .001$) Economics major (1.9, n.s.) Year of study (1.5, n.s.) Entrep. education (17.1, $p < .001$) Parent entrep. experience (0.0, n.s.) Entrep. experience (6.8, $p < .01$) Entrep. status (4.6, $p < 0.05$) Exposure to role models (2.8, n.s.)	$F = 54.76$ (sig. at .001)	$R^2 = 0.398$ Adjusted $R^2 = 0.391$
(2) Entrepreneurial intentions	Self-efficacy (12.5, $p < .001$) Social norms (424.6, $p < .001$) Risk perceptions (5.5, $p < .05$) Age (35.7, $p < .001$) Entrep. education (19.6, $p < .001$) Entrep. experience (6.9, $p < .01$) Entrep. status (3.8, n.s.)	$F = 92.39$ (sig. at .001)	$R^2 = 0.393$ Adjusted $R^2 = 0.389$
(2') Entrepreneurial intentions	Self-efficacy (12.2, $p < .001$) Social norms (425.0, $p < .001$) Risk perceptions (5.7, $p < .05$) Age (36.2, $p < .001$) Entrep. education (21.0, $p < .001$) Entrep. experience (19.2, $p < .001$)	$F = 92.39$ (sig. at .001)	$R^2 = 0.393$ Adjusted $R^2 = 0.389$

(Continued)

Table 1.3b (Continued)

Dependent variable	Independent variables(F values, significance)/ (Wald values, significance)	Regression statistics	
		Overall F/χ^2	R-squared
(3) Self-efficacy	Social norms (13.3, $p < .001$) Risk perceptions (0.3, n.s.) Motivation to comply (0.0, n.s.) Age (16.4, $p < .001$) Economics major (2.0, n.s.) Year of study (12.6, $p < .001$) Entrep. education (1.4, n.s.) Parent entrep. experience (0.3, n.s.) Entrep. experience (2.3, n.s.) Entrep. status (0.3, n.s.) Exposure to role models (16.5, $p < .001$)	$F = 10.92$ (sig. at .001)	$R^2 = 0.108$ Adjusted $R^2 = 0.098$
(4) Self-efficacy	Social norms (16.3, $p < .001$) Age (21.0, $p < .001$) Year of study (12.9, $p < .001$) Exposure to role models (21.1, $p < .001$)	$F = 28.19$ (sig. at .001)	$R^2 = 0.101$ Adjusted $R^2 = 0.098$
(5) Social norms	Self-efficacy (13.3, $p < .001$) Risk perceptions (0.0, n.s.) Motivation to comply (13.5, $p < .001$) Age (3.6, n.s.) Economics major (3.7, n.s.) Year of study (1.1, n.s.) Entrep. education (3.9, $p < .05$) Parent entrep. experience (1.1, n.s.)	$F = 25.95$ (sig. at .001)	$R^2 = 0.223$ Adjusted $R^2 = 0.215$

Model	Predictors	Statistic	
	Entrep. experience (2.7, n.s.)		
	Entrep. status (1.8, n.s.)		
	Exposure to role models (15.0, $p < .001$)		
(6) Social norms	Self-efficacy (12.6, $p < .001$)	$F = 65.76$	$R^2 = 0.208$
	Motivation to comply (26.0, $F < .001$)	(sig. at .001)	Adjusted $R^2 = 0.205$
	Entrep. education (7.6, $p < .01$)		
	Exposure to role models (164.0, $p < .001$)		
(7) Risk perceptions	Self-efficacy (0.5, n.s.)	$F = 6.75$	$R^2 = 0.070$
	Social norms (0.0, n.s.)	(sig. at .001)	Adjusted $R^2 = 0.059$
	Motivation to comply (17.8, $F < .001$)		
	Age (27.7, $p < .001$)		
	Economics major (5.6, $p < .05$)		
	Year of study (0.0, n.s.)		
	Entrep. education (1.5, n.s.)		
	Parent entrep. experience (0.3, n.s.)		
	Entrep. experience (0.6, n.s.)		
	Entrep. status (1.0, n.s.)		
	Exposure to role models (8.7, $p < .01$)		
(8) Risk perceptions	Motivation to comply (17.6, $F < .001$)	$F = 17.89$	$R^2 = 0.067$
	Age (32.1, $p < .001$)	(sig. at .001)	Adjusted $R^2 = 0.063$
	Economics major (6.2, $p < .05$)		
	Exposure to role models (10.3, $p < .001$)		
(9) Entrepreneurship education	Self-efficacy (0.8, n.s.)	$\chi^2 = 84.91$	Cox and Snell $R^2 = 0.081$
	Social norms (3.9, $p < .05$)	(sig. at .001)	Nagelkerke $R^2 = 0.136$
	Risk perceptions (1.5, n.s.)		
	Motivation to comply (2.5, n.s.)		

(Continued)

Table 1.3b (Continued)

Dependent variable	Independent variables (F values, significance)/ (Wald values, significance)	Regression statistics	
		Overall F/χ^2	R-squared
	Age (2.5, n.s.) Economics major (4.8, $p < .05$) Year of study (0.5, n.s.) Parent entrep. experience (0.1, n.s.) Entrep. experience (7.2, $p < .01$) Entrep. status (4.7, $p < .05$) Exposure to role models (20.0, $p < .001$)		
(10) Entrepreneurship education	Social norms (4.2, $p < .05$) Economics major (7.0, $p < .01$) Entrep. experience (6.4, $p < .05$) Entrep. status (5.0, $p < .05$) Exposure to role models (19.6, $p < .001$)	$\chi^2 = 77.23$ (sig. at .001)	Cox and Snell $R^2 = 0.074$ Nagelkerke $R^2 = 0.124$
(11) Entrepreneurial experience	Self-efficacy (2.3, n.s.) Social norms (2.0, n.s.) Risk perceptions (0.6, n.s.) Motivation to comply (0.6, n.s.) Age (40.9, $p < .001$) Economics major (0.1, n.s.) Year of study (0.0, n.s.) Entrep. education (8.4, $p < .01$) Parent entrep. experience (5.8, $p < .05$) Entrep. status (62.9, $p < .001$) Exposure to role models (1.3, n.s.)	$\chi^2 = 232.95$ (sig. at .001)	Cox and Snell $R^2 = 0.207$ Nagelkerke $R^2 = 0.449$

(12) Entrepreneurial experience	Age (48.1, $p < .001$) Entrep. education (13.2, $p < .001$) Parent entrep. experience (7.6, $p < .01$) Entrep. status (66.7, $p < .001$)	$\chi^2 = 222.88$ (sig. at .001)	Cox and Snell $R^2 = 0.199$ Nagelkerke $R^2 = 0.432$
(13) Entrepreneurial status	Self-efficacy (0.0, n.s.) Social norms (1.5, n.s.) Risk perceptions (1.1, n.s.) Motivation to comply (0.0, n.s.) Age (1.4, n.s.) Economics major (1.9, n.s.) Year of study (0.6, n.s.) Entrep. education (4.7, $p < .05$) Parent entrep. experience (0.1, n.s.) Entrep. experience (63.0, $p < .001$) Exposure to role models (2.8, n.s.)	$\chi^2 = 172.06$ (sig. at .001)	Cox and Snell $R^2 = 0.157$ Nagelkerke $R^2 = 0.572$
(14) Entrepreneurial status	Entrep. education (3.4, n.s.) Entrep. experience (66.4, $p < .001$)	$\chi^2 = 163.41$ (sig. at .001)	Cox and Snell $R^2 = 0.150$ Nagelkerke $R^2 = 0.545$
(14') Entrepreneurial status	Entrep. experience (71.4, $p < .001$)	$\chi^2 = 159.99$ (sig. at .001)	Cox and Snell $R^2 = 0.147$ Nagelkerke $R^2 = 0.535$

Abbreviations: Entrep, entrepreneurial; sig, significant; n.s, not significant.

Furthermore, in order to ensure that the indirect paths included are those where mediation effects are evident, we tested for mediation effects, as reported in Tables 1.4a and 1.4b. We followed Baron and Kenny's (1986) procedures in the cases where regressions involved continuous variables as both dependent and mediator, and adjusted the procedures in line with MacKinnon and Dwyer (1993), when the mediator was a dichotomous variable. In step 1, we regressed the dependent variable on the independent variable, showing that there is an effect that may be mediated. In step 2, we regressed the mediator on the independent variable, showing that the two are correlated. In step 3, we regressed the dependent variable on the mediator while controlling for the effects of the independent variable. The results of the last stage help us establish whether a mediation effect is in place, and whether it is partial or full mediation. In addition, Sobel test values were calculated and are also reported in Tables 1.4a and 1.4b. Figures 1.1 and 1.2 include only indirect paths where mediation effect was confirmed.

Findings and Discussion

Our findings support the view that when studying EIs, one must acknowledge a complex network of relationships between the various variables of intentionality models, while acknowledging the social and human contextualization of such mind-set formation processes. This presents a shift from the common practice of mostly using hierarchical regressions in similar analyses. More concretely, our study shows strong support for the moderating role of gender in the formation of EIs, and presents its role in moderating both direct and indirect effects on EIs.

In this section, results of the study are presented by factor, while being compared with that of previous relevant literature.

Effect of Self-Efficacy

A direct positive effect of self-efficacy is evident in both males and females. In this sense, our study supports similar findings in studies that used mixed-gender samples (BarNir, Watson, and Hutchins 2011; Carr and Sequeira 2007; Fernández, Liñán, and Santos 2009; Zellweger, Sieger, and Halter 2011). However, our study extends our understanding by highlighting that the magnitude of this effect is greater in females than in males. These findings support similar findings in a study of Bulgarian students (Yordanova and Tarrazon 2010), as well as among middle and high school pupils in the United States (Kickul et al. 2008). However, it only partially supports a study of Swedish students (Pejvak

Table 1.4a Testing mediation effects on EIs—males

Variable	Step 1 Coeff. (SE)	Step 2 Coeff. (SE)	Step 3 Coeff. (SE)	Sobel Test Z Value	Conclusion
IV: Social norms	0.703*** (0.037)	0.143*** (0.025)	0.678*** (0.037)	2.880***	SE partially mediates the effect of SN on EIs.
M: Self-efficacy			0.180*** (0.054)		
Model fit	Adjusted R^2 = 0.338	Adjusted R^2 = 0.044	Adjusted R^2 = 0.347		
IV: Exposure to role models	0.328*** (0.031)	0.154*** (0.018)	0.295*** (0.033)	3.089***	SE partially mediates the effect of ERM on EIs.
M: Self-efficacy			0.212*** (0.064)		
Model fit	Adjusted R^2 = 0.132	Adjusted R^2 = 0.090	Adjusted R^2 = 0.143		
25	−0.069† (0.040)	0.062** (0.023)	−0.094* (0.039)	2.478**	SE partially mediates the effect of YOS on EIs.
M: Self-efficacy			0.403*** (0.064)		
Model fit	Adjusted R^2 = 0.003	Adjusted R^2 = 0.009	Adjusted R^2 = 0.053		
IV: Self-efficacy	0.387*** (0.064)	0.307*** (0.053)	0.180*** (0.054)	5.523***	SN partially mediates the effect of SE on EIs.
M: Social norms			0.678*** (0.037)		
Model fit	Adjusted R^2 = 0.047	Adjusted R^2 = 0.043	Adjusted R^2 = 0.347		
IV: Motivation to comply	0.090* (0.037)	0.143*** (0.030)	−0.011 (0.030)	4.625***	SN fully mediates the effect of MTC on EIs.
M: Social norms			0.706*** (0.037)		
Model fit	Adjusted R^2 = 0.007	Adjusted R^2 = 0.029	Adjusted R^2 = 0.337		
IV: Exposure to role models	0.328*** (0.031)	0.314*** (0.025)	0.130*** (0.030)	9.820***	SN partially mediates the effect of ERM on EIs.
M: Social norms			0.630*** (0.040)		
Model fit	Adjusted R^2 = 0.132	Adjusted R^2 = 0.176	Adjusted R^2 = 0.355		

(Continued)

41

Table 1.4a (Continued)

Variable	Step 1 Coeff. (SE)	Step 2 Coeff. (SE)	Step 3 Coeff. (SE)	Sobel Test Z Value	Conclusion
IV: Year of study	−0.069† (0.040)	−0.106*** (0.033)	0.005 (0.033)	−3.167***	SN fully mediates the effect of YOS on EIs.
M: Social norms			0.704*** (0.037)		
Model fit	Adjusted R^2 = 0.003	Adjusted R^2 = 0.013	Adjusted R^2 = 0.337		
IV: Entrepreneurial status	1.495*** (0.208)	1.067*** (0.174)	0.784*** (0.177)	5.806***	SN partially mediates the effect of EST on EIs.
M: Social norms			0.667*** (0.037)		
Model fit	Adjusted R^2 = 0.066	Adjusted R^2 = 0.048	Adjusted R^2 = 0.355		
IV: Self-efficacy	0.387*** (0.064)	0.594*** (0.070)	0.212*** (0.064)	6.154***	ERM partially mediates the effect of SE on EIs.
M: Exposure to role models			0.295*** (0.033)		
Model fit	Adjusted R^2 = 0.047	Adjusted R^2 = 0.090	Adjusted R^2 = 0.143		
IV: Social norms	0.703*** (0.037)	0.565*** (0.045)	0.630*** (0.040)	4.096***	ERM partially mediates the effect of SN on EIs.
M: Exposure to role models			0.130*** (0.030)		
Model fit	Adjusted R^2 = 0.338	Adjusted R^2 = 0.176	Adjusted R^2 = 0.355		
IV: Risk perceptions	−0.120* (0.052)	−0.153** (0.058)	−0.071 (0.049)	−2.557**	ERM fully mediates the effect of RP on EIs.
M: Exposure to role models			0.323*** (0.031)		
Model fit	Adjusted R^2 = 0.006	Adjusted R^2 = 0.008	Adjusted R^2 = 0.133		
IV: Motivation to comply	0.090* (0.037)	0.145*** (0.040)	0.043 (0.035)	3.424***	ERM fully mediates the effect of MTC on EIs.
M: Exposure to role models			0.323*** (0.031)		
Model fit	Adjusted R^2 = 0.007	Adjusted R^2 = 0.016	Adjusted R^2 = 0.132		

IV: Economics major	0.527*** (0.130)	0.732*** (0.143)	0.297* (0.124)	4.539***	ERM partially mediates the effect of EM on EIs.
M: Exposure to role models			0.314*** (0.032)		
Model fit	Adjusted R^2 = 0.021	Adjusted R^2 = 0.034	Adjusted R^2 = 0.137		
IV: Entrepreneurship education	0.630*** (0.145)	0.957*** (0.159)	0.332* (0.140)	5.117***	ERM partially mediates the effect of EED on EIs.
M: Exposure to role models			0.311*** (0.032)		
Model fit	Adjusted R^2 = 0.024	Adjusted R^2 = 0.046	Adjusted R^2 = 0.137		
IV: Parental entrepreneurial experience	0.257* (0.126)	0.535*** (0.138)	0.084 (0.118)	3.622***	ERM fully mediates the effect of PEE on EIs.
M: Exposure to role models			0.325*** (0.032)		
Model fit	Adjusted R^2 = 0.004	Adjusted R^2 = 0.019	Adjusted R^2 = 0.131		
IV: Year of study	−0.069† (0.040)	0.213*** (0.051)	−0.097 (0.040)	3.031***	EM partially mediates the effect of YOS on EIs.
M: Economics major			0.577*** (0.131)		
Model fit	Adjusted R^2 = 0.003	Nagelkerke R^2 = 0.034	Adjusted R^2 = 0.027		
IV: Entrepreneurship education	0.630*** (0.145)	1.010*** (0.181)	0.529*** (0.148)	2.799**	EM partially mediates the effect of EED on EIs.
M: Economics major			0.427*** (0.132)		
Model fit	Adjusted R^2 = 0.024	Nagelkerke R^2 = 0.058	Adjusted R^2 = 0.037		

(Continued)

43

Table 1.4a (Continued)

Variable	Step 1 Coeff. (SE)	Step 2 Coeff. (SE)	Step 3 Coeff. (SE)	Sobel Test Z Value	Conclusion
IV: Parental entrepreneurial experience	0.257* (0.126)	−0.242 (0.162)			No mediation effect. Did not pass step 2. (Removed)
M: Economics major					
Model fit	Adjusted R^2 = 0.004	Nagelkerke R^2 = 0.004			
IV: Exposure to role models	0.328*** (0.031)	0.226*** (0.046)	0.314*** (0.032)	2.153*	EM partially mediates the effect of ERM on EIs.
M: Economics major			0.297* (0.124)		
Model fit	Adjusted R^2 = 0.132	Nagelkerke R^2 = 0.049	Adjusted R^2 = 0.137		
IV: Age	−0.003 (0.008)				No mediation effect. Did not pass step 1. (Removed)
M: Entrepreneurial experience					
Model fit	Adjusted R^2 = −0.001				
IV: Entrepreneurial education	0.630*** (0.145)	1.221*** (0.205)	0.394** (0.144)	4.555***	EEX partially mediates the effect of EED on EIs.
M: Entrepreneurial experience			1.110*** (0.157)		
Model fit	Adjusted R^2 = 0.024	Nagelkerke R^2 = 0.076	Adjusted R^2 = 0.137		

IV: Entrepreneurial status	1.495*** (0.208)	5.171*** (0.604)	0.780** (0.265)	3.828***	EEX partially mediates the effect of EST on EIs.
M: Entrepreneurial experience			0.843*** (0.197)		
Model fit	Adjusted R^2 = 0.066	Nagelkerke R^2 = 0.427	Adjusted R^2 = 0.089		
IV: Social norms	0.703*** (0.037)	0.694*** (0.120)	0.667*** (0.037)	3.517***	EST partially mediates the effect of SN on EIs.
M: Entrepreneurial status			0.784*** (0.177)		
Model fit	Adjusted R^2 = 0.338	Nagelkerke R^2 = 0.120	Adjusted R^2 = 0.355		
IV: Entrepreneurial experience	1.209*** (0.153)	5.171*** (0.604)	0.843*** (0.197)	2.783**	EST partially mediates the effect of EEX on EIs.
M: Entrepreneurial status			0.780*** (0.265)		
Model fit	Adjusted R^2 = 0.078	Nagelkerke R^2 = 0.574	Adjusted R^2 = 0.088		

Note:

Step 1: effect of independent variable on dependent variable; Step 2: effect of independent variable on mediator; Step 3: effect of mediator on dependent variable controlling for independent variable.

†Significant at .1 level; *significant at .05 level; **significant at .01 level; ***significant at .001 level. Abbreviations: EED, entrepreneurial education; EEX, entrepreneurial experience; EIs, entrepreneurial intentions; EM, economics major; ERM, exposure to role models; EST, entrepreneurial status; IV, independent variable; M, mediator; MTC, motivation to comply; PEE, parental entrepreneurial experience; RP, risk perception; SE, self-efficacy; SN, social norms; YOS, year of study.

45

Table 1.4b Testing mediation effects on EIs—females

Variable	Step 1 Coeff. (SE)	Step 2 Coeff. (SE)	Step 3 Coeff. (SE)	Sobel Test Z Value	Conclusion
IV: Social norms	0.567*** (0.025)	0.116*** (0.018)	0.551*** (0.025)	2.873**	SE partially mediates the effect of SN on EIs.
M: Self-efficacy			0.138*** (0.043)		
Model fit	Adjusted R^2 = 0.337	Adjusted R^2 = 0.037	Adjusted R^2 = 0.343		
IV: Age	−0.017*** (0.005)	0.016*** (0.003)	−0.023*** (0.005)	4.242***	SE partially mediates the effect of age on EIs.
M: Self-efficacy			0.362*** (0.051)		
Model fit	Adjusted R^2 = 0.011	Adjusted R^2 = 0.029	Adjusted R^2 = 0.058		
IV: Exposure to role models	0.238*** (0.023)	0.105*** (0.014)	0.216*** (0.023)	3.743***	SE partially mediates the effect of ERM on EIs.
M: Self-efficacy			0.216*** (0.050)		
Model fit	Adjusted R^2 = 0.095	Adjusted R^2 = 0.049	Adjusted R^2 = 0.111		
IV: Year of study	−0.038 (0.031)				No mediation effect. Did not pass step 1. (Removed)
M: Self-efficacy					
Model fit	Adjusted R^2 = 0.001				
IV: Self-efficacy	0.319*** (0.051)	0.329*** (0.052)	0.138*** (0.043)	6.081***	SN partially mediates the effect of SE on EIs.
M: Social norms			0.551*** (0.025)		
Model fit	Adjusted R^2 = 0.037	Adjusted R^2 = 0.037	Adjusted R^2 = 0.343		
IV: Motivation to comply	0.086*** (0.026)	0.119*** (0.027)	0.018 (0.022)	4.326***	SN fully mediates the effect of MTC on EIs.
M: Social norms			0.564*** (0.025)		
Model fit	Adjusted R^2 = 0.009	Adjusted R^2 = 0.018	Adjusted R^2 = 0.337		

IV: Entrepreneurial education	0.904*** (0.121)	0.644*** (0.126)	0.552*** (0.101)	4.976***	SN partially mediates the effect of EED on EIs.
M: Social norms			0.545*** (0.025)		
Model fit	Adjusted R^2 = 0.052	Adjusted R^2 = 0.025	Adjusted R^2 = 0.356		
IV: Exposure to role models	0.238*** (0.023)	0.335*** (0.022)	0.059** (0.022)	11.908***	SN partially mediates the effect of ERM on EIs.
M: Social norms			0.535*** (0.028)		
Model fit	Adjusted R^2 = 0.095	Adjusted R^2 = 0.180	Adjusted R^2 = 0.341		
IV: Motivation to comply	0.086*** (0.026)	0.088*** (0.021)	0.092*** (0.026)	1.689*	RP partially mediates the effect of MTC on EIs.
M: Risk perceptions			−0.072† (0.039)		
Model fit	Adjusted R^2 = 0.009	Adjusted R^2 = 0.016	Adjusted R^2 = 0.012		
IV: Age	−0.017*** (0.005)	−0.025*** (0.004)	−0.019*** (0.005)	2.058*	RP partially mediates the effect of age on EIs.
M: Risk perceptions			−0.085* (0.039)		
Model fit	Adjusted R^2 = 0.011	Adjusted R^2 = 0.038	Adjusted R^2 = 0.015		
IV: Economics major	0.334*** (0.099)	0.210** (0.080)	0.348** (0.099)	−1.422	No mediation effect. Non-sig, Sobel stat. (Removed)
M: Risk perceptions			−0.066† (0.039)		
Model fit	Adjusted R^2 = 0.010	Adjusted R^2 = 0.006	Adjusted R^2 = 0.012		
IV: Exposure to role models	0.238*** (0.023)	−0.057** (0.020)	0.237*** (0.023)		No mediation effect. Did not pass step 3. (Removed)
M: Risk perceptions			−0.020 (0.037)		
Model fit	Adjusted R^2 = 0.095	Adjusted R^2 = 0.007	Adjusted R^2 = 0.095		

(Continued)

Table 1.4b (Continued)

Variable	Step 1 Coeff. (SE)	Step 2 Coeff. (SE)	Step 3 Coeff. (SE)	Sobel Test Z Value	Conclusion
IV: Social norms	0.567*** (0.025)	0.294*** (0.059)	0.545*** (0.025)	3.682***	EED partially mediates the effect of SN on EIs.
M: Entrepreneurial education			0.552*** (0.101)		
Model fit	Adjusted R^2 = 0.337	Nagelkerke R^2 = 0.043	Adjusted R^2 = 0.356		
IV: Economics major	0.334*** (0.099)	0.497** (0.172)	0.271** (0.097)	2.682**	EED partially mediates the effect of EM on EIs.
M: Entrepreneurial education			0.873*** (0.121)		
Model fit	Adjusted R^2 = 0.010	Nagelkerke R^2 = 0.014	Adjusted R^2 = 0.058		
IV: Entrepreneurial experience	0.885*** (0.158)	1.245*** (0.233)	0.701*** (0.158)	4.159***	EED partially mediates the effect of EEX on EIs.
M: Entrepreneurial education			0.808*** (0.122)		
Model fit	Adjusted R^2 = 0.029	Nagelkerke R^2 = 0.042	Adjusted R^2 = 0.069		
IV: Entrepreneurial status	1.231*** (0.241)	1.574*** (0.337)	0.971*** (0.239)	3.842***	EED partially mediates the effect of EST on EIs.
M: Entrepreneurial education			0.824*** (0.122)		
Model fit	Adjusted R^2 = 0.024	Nagelkerke R^2 = 0.033	Adjusted R^2 = 0.066		

IV: Exposure to Role models	0.238^{***} (0.023)	0.290^{***} (0.048)	0.212^{***} (0.023)	4.187^{***}	EED partially mediates the effect of ERM on EIs.
M: Entrepreneurial education			0.691^{***} (0.119)		
Model fit	Adjusted R^2 = 0.095	Nagelkerke R^2 = 0.065	Adjusted R^2 = 0.124		
IV: Age	-0.017^{***} (0.005)	0.073^{***} (0.010)	-0.026^{***} (0.005)	4.969^{***}	EEX partially mediates the effect of age on EIs.
M: Entrepreneurial experience			1.099^{***} (0.162)		
Model fit	Adjusted R^2 = 0.011	Nagelkerke R^2 = 0.113	Adjusted R^2 = 0.054		
IV: Entrepreneurship education	0.904^{***} (0.121)	1.245^{***} (0.233)	0.808^{***} (0.122)	3.413^{***}	EEX partially mediates the effect of EED on EIs.
M: Entrepreneurial experience			0.701^{***} (0.158)		
Model fit	Adjusted R^2 = 0.052	Nagelkerke R^2 = 0.055	Adjusted R^2 = 0.069		
IV: Parental entrepreneurial experience	0.885^{***} (0.158)	0.543^{*} (0.219)	0.192^{*} (0.093)	2.253^{*}	EEX partially mediates the effect of PEE on EIs.
M: Entrepreneurial experience			0.859^{***} (0.159)		
Model fit	Adjusted R^2 = 0.029	Nagelkerke R^2 = 0.013	Adjusted R^2 = 0.032		

(Continued)

Table 1.4b (Continued)

Variable	Step 1 Coeff. (SE)	Step 2 Coeff. (SE)	Step 3 Coeff. (SE)	Sobel Test Z Value	Conclusion
IV: Entrepreneurial status	1.231*** (0.241)	5.209*** (0.617)	0.691* (0.291)	3.046**	EEX partially mediates the effect of EST on EIs.
M: Entrepreneurial experience			0.627*** (0.192)		
Model fit	Adjusted R^2 = 0.024	Nagelkerke R^2 = 0.320	Adjusted R^2 = 0.034		
IV: Entrepreneurial experience	0.885*** (0.158)	5.209*** (0.617)	0.627*** (0.192)	2.286*	EST partially mediates the effect of EEX on EIs.
M: Entrepreneurial status			0.691* (0.291)		
Model fit	Adjusted R^2 = 0.029	Nagelkerke R^2 = 0.535	Adjusted R^2 = 0.034		

Note:

Step 1: effect of independent variable on dependent variable; Step 2: effect of independent variable on mediator; Step 3: effect of mediator on dependent variable controlling for independent variable.

†Significant at .1 level; *significant at .05 level; **significant at .01 level; ***significant at .001 level. Abbreviations: EED, entrepreneurial education; EEX, entrepreneurial experience; EIs, entrepreneurial intentions; EM, economics major; ERM, exposure to role models; EST, entrepreneurial status; IV, independent variable; M, mediator; MTC, motivation to comply; PEE, parental entrepreneurial experience ; RP, risk perception; SE, self-efficacy; non-sig., non-significant; SN, social norms; stat, statistic; YOS, year of study.

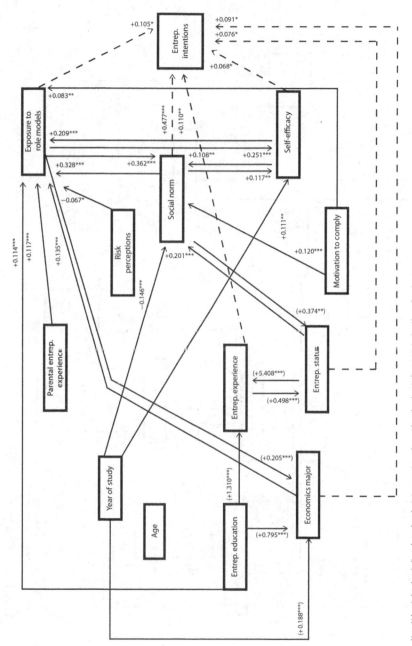

Note: Values in brackets indicate betas from logistic regression, values without brackets indicate standardized betas from linear regression.
*Significant at .05; **significant at .01; ***significant at .001.
Abbreviation: Entrep., entrepreneurial.

Figure 1.1 Path model: males

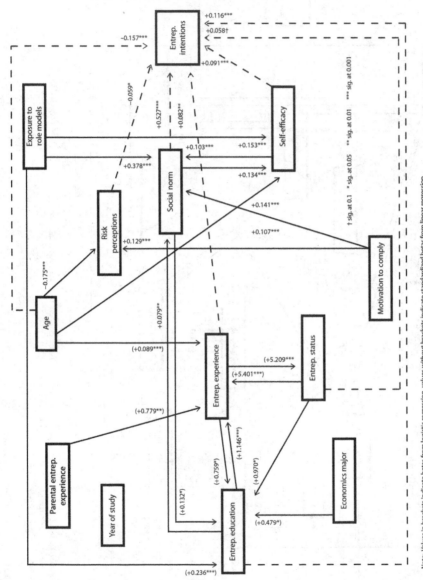

Figure 1.2 Path model: females

Note: Values in brackets indicate betas from logistic regression, values without brackets indicate standardized betas from linear regression.
†Significant at .1; *significant at .05; **significant at .01; ***significant at .001.
Abbreviation: Entrep., entrepreneurial.

et al. 2009), where such effects were evident in males but not in females. Since relative cultural and institutional differences between Sweden and Norway are low, possible reasons for this discrepancy may be associated with the different measurements that were used in both studies, as well as the relatively low Cronbach's alpha of 0.672 achieved for the measurement in the Swedish study.

In addition, our study shows that the effect of self-efficacy on EIs is mediated by a number of other factors. First, its effect is partially mediated by social norms in both males and females. Second, its effect is also partially mediated by exposure to role models in males, but not in females.

Effect of Social Norms

A direct positive effect of social norms is evident in both males and females. In this sense, our study supports similar findings in studies that used mixed-gender samples (Iakovleva and Kolvereid 2009; Kautonen, Luoto, and Tornikoski 2010; Kolvereid and Isaksen 2006; Liñán and Chen 2009). However, our study extends our understanding by showing that the magnitude of this effect is greater in females than in males. These findings support similar findings in Pejvak et al.'s (2009) study of Swedish university students. However, it only partially supports an earlier study of Bulgarian students (Yordanova and Tarrazon 2010), where such effects were evident among females but not in males. Since measurements are similar in these studies, possible reasons for such discrepancy may be associated with cultural differences between the more feminine Nordic societies and the more masculine Bulgarian one, if to use Hofstede's (2001) cultural dimensions framework. Here, harmony-inclined and inclusive feminine societies will be more concerned with social norms across sexes, while this will be more prominent among females rather than males in societies that are overall masculine, and hence more power- and achievement-inclined.

In addition, our study shows that the effect of social norms on EIs is mediated by a number of other factors. First, its effect is partially mediated by self-efficacy in both males and females. Second, its effect is partially mediated by entrepreneurial education in females, but not in males. And, third, its effect is partially mediated by entrepreneurial status and exposure to role models in males, but not in females.

Effect of Motivation-to-Comply

Our results indicate no direct effect of motivation-to-comply on EIs in either males or females. However, our mediation analyses show that while such effect exists, it is fully mediated by social norms in both males and females, as well as fully mediated by the exposure to role models in males only, and partially mediated by risk perceptions in females only. Hence, its use as an item of an overall measurement of social norms appears not to be as problematic as it was originally assumed.

Effect of Risk Perceptions

A direct negative effect of risk perceptions is evident in females, but not in males. This finding fits an earlier finding in a study among German university students (Walter, Parboteeah, and Walter 2011), exhibiting a significant effect of risk-taking propensity on self-employment intentions among males, but not significant for females. In this sense, the studies complement each other, where women's risk perceptions serve as an obstacle to risk-taking behavior, its undermining by males encourages them to take risks when pursuing entrepreneurial careers. However, our mediation analyses also show that while this effect also exists in males, it is fully mediated by exposure to role models.

Still, risk perceptions in this study were used as proxy for attitudes. Earlier studies examining the wider concept of attitudes provide contradictory findings from no direct effect in both males and females in the Bulgarian study (Yordanova and Tarrazon 2010), to positive direct effect in both males and females in the Swedish study (Pejvak et al. 2009). Differences between these two, as well as with our own findings, can all be explained by the different measurements used in each of these studies.

Effect of Exposure to Role Models

A direct positive effect of exposure to role models is evident in males, but not in females. These findings partially support findings from an earlier study among German students (Walter, Parboteeah, and Walter 2011), where a positive direct effect of the performance of role model on EIs was evident in both males and females. These differences may be explained both by differences in measurement and culture. In terms of measurement, the focus in the German study was on performance, and in our study it was on familiarity. Moreover, in terms of culture, differences between the feminine society of Norway and the masculine society of Germany, if to use Hofstede's (2001) framework, may also serve as potential explanation. Here, power- and achievement-focused masculine cultures will be more concerned with successful role models across sexes, while this will be more prominent among males rather than females in societies that are overall feminine.

In addition, our study shows that the effect of exposure to role models on EIs is mediated by a number of other factors. First, its effect is partially mediated by both self-efficacy and social norms in both males and females. Second, its effect is partially mediated by entrepreneurial education in females, but not in males. And, third, its effect is partially mediated by taking an economics major in males, but not in females.

Effect of Parental Entrepreneurial Experience

Our results indicate no direct effect of parental entrepreneurial experience on EIs in either males or females when all variables are included in the analysis. In this sense, our study supports a variety of earlier studies that found no effect while using mixed-gender samples (Carey, Flanagan, and Palmer 2010; Franco, Haase, and Lautenschläger 2010; Iakovleva, Kolvereid, and Stephan 2011; Kolvereid and Isaksen 2006; Tornikoski and Kautonen 2009). However, our mediation analyses show that while such effect exists, it is fully mediated by exposure to role models in males only, as well as partially mediated by entrepreneurial experience in females only.

This finding is partially supported in an earlier study among middle and high school students in the United States (Kickul et al. 2008), which also showed no direct effect in males, but identified a direct effect among females. A possible explanation for this discrepancy may be provided by differences in sample characteristics in terms of age. Here, the U.S. study relied on young teenagers who may be still more attached to and dependent on their parents, while our sample consisted of more mature and independent university students.

Effect of Entrepreneurial Experience

A direct positive effect of entrepreneurial experience is evident in both males and females. In this sense, this finding supports earlier findings in other mixed-gender samples (as shown in Ahmed et al. 2010; Fitzsimmons and Douglas 2011; Kolvereid 1996; Kolvereid and Isaksen 2006; Kolvereid and Moen 1997; Zhao, Hills, and Seibert 2005). However, our study extends this insight by showing that the magnitude of this effect is slightly greater among men.

Moreover, our study also shows that the effect of entrepreneurial experience on EIs is mediated by a number of other factors. First, its effect is partially mediated by entrepreneurial status in both males and females. And, second, its effect is also partially mediated by the effect of entrepreneurial education in females, but not in males.

Effect of Entrepreneurial Status

A direct positive effect of entrepreneurial status is evident in both males and females. Here, again, this finding supports earlier findings in other mixed-gender samples (Haase, Lautenschläger, and Rena 2011). However, our study extends this insight by showing that the magnitude of this effect is slightly greater among men.

Moreover, our study also shows that the effect of entrepreneurial status on EIs is mediated by a number of other factors. First, its effect is partially mediated by entrepreneurial experience in both males and females. And, second, its effect is partially mediated by the effect of social norms in males, but not in females.

Effect of Year of Study

Our results indicate no direct effect of year of study on EIs in either males or females when all variables are included in the analysis. Hence, it supports a variety of earlier studies that found no effect while using mixed-gender samples (Raijman 2001; Shook and Bratianu 2010; Turker and Selcuk 2009; Zellweger, Sieger, and Halter 2011). An exception here is a study done among Russians in Russia and Russian immigrants in Norway (Vinogradov and Gabelko 2010), which showed that a vaguely defined higher education indicator had a significant effect on EIs among males, but not females. A possible explanation for this discrepancy may be found in the different measurements used in the two studies, as well as in different sample characteristics. Here, while the Norwegian sample only included respondents with some level of higher education, the Russian sample included both those with and without higher education. Hence, an effect may be evident when considering differences between high and low education levels, but disappears when comparing different levels of higher education.

Moreover, our mediation analyses show that such effect exists only in males, but it is fully mediated by social norms, as well as partially mediated by self-efficacy and taking an economics major.

Effect of Entrepreneurial Education

A direct positive effect of entrepreneurial education is evident in females, but not in males.

However, our study also shows that when mediation analyses are consulted, such effect exists in both sexes, but is mediated differently. First, its effect is partially mediated by entrepreneurial experience in both males and females. Second, its effect is also partially mediated by the effect of both exposure to role models and taking an economics major in males, but not in females. And, third, its effect is partially mediated by the effects of social norms in females, but not in males.

In any case, the basic finding here contradicts that from an earlier study among German students (Walter, Parboteeah, and Walter 2011), which showed that participation in entrepreneurship programs had a significant effect in males, but not in females. This discrepancy may be explained by the fact that the German study did not include the factor of taking an economics major, which is critical in mediating the effect of entrepreneurial education in males, as well as the entrepreneurial experience factor, which is critical in mediating the effect of entrepreneurial education in both sexes.

Effect of Economics Major

A direct positive effect of taking an economics major is evident in males, but not in females.

However, our study also shows that when mediation analyses are consulted, such effect exists in both sexes, but is mediated differently. First, its effect is partially mediated by entrepreneurial education in females, but not in males. And, second, its effect is partially mediated by the effect of exposure to role models in males, but not in females.

In this sense, our findings here may suggest gender-based explanations for the inconsistent findings in mixed-gender samples, showing that taking an economics major can be associated with higher levels of EIs (e.g., Schwarz et al. 2009) in a male-majority sample of business students, or no effect on EIs (e.g., Zellweger, Sieger, and Halter 2011) in a female-majority sample of economics students.

Effect of Age

Our results indicate a direct negative effect of age on EIs in females but no effect in males. In this sense, it supports a number of earlier studies that found a similar effect while using mixed-gender samples (Grilo and Thurik 2005; Kautonen, Luoto, and Tornikoski 2010; Yordanova 2011). However, our study also shows that when mediation analyses are consulted, such effect exists in females only, and is partially mediated by self-efficacy, risk perceptions, and entrepreneurial experience.

Nevertheless, our findings do stand at odds with those in a study with gender-split samples of Russians in Russia and Russian immigrants in Norway

(Vinogradov and Gabelko 2010), where age had a significant negative effect on EIs among both males and females. A possible explanation for this discrepancy is the fact that the earlier study did not examine the effect of entrepreneurial experience in addition to age, and hence age may actually be representing experience rather than actual number of years alive.

Loop Effects

Interestingly, our findings suggest the existence of some loop effects among certain factors, reflecting both the complex nature of relationships among the various factors and the dynamic nature of the formation process of EIs.

Common to both males and females are the loop effects between self-efficacy and social norms, as well as the one between entrepreneurial experience and entrepreneurial status. The first loop effect may suggest that encouraging social environments may enhance one's beliefs in his or her abilities, and at the same time, those regarding themselves as competent enough to engage in entrepreneurship may seek social environments that are supportive of such activities. Moreover, the second loop effect may suggest that those currently engaged in entrepreneurship are gaining entrepreneurial experience through their activities, and at the same time, previous entrepreneurial experience, as well as the lessons learned from it, increases that likelihood of people remaining engaged in entrepreneurship.

In addition, unique to males are the loop effects of exposure to role models and economics major, self-efficacy, and social norms, as well as a loop effect between social norms and entrepreneurial status. In this sense, it is logical that exposure to entrepreneurial role models may influence field of study, as well as that the choice of economics may enhance students' exposure to such role models as part of their study program. Similarly, an exposure to charismatic role models may enhance individuals' self-efficacy, while at the same time exhibiting high self-efficacy will trigger a greater interest in exposure to exemplary role models. Furthermore, entrepreneurship encouraging social environments will enhance exposure to entrepreneurial role models, while at the same time, exposure to entrepreneurial role models may lead to self-selection of social environments appreciative of entrepreneurial behavior. Finally, an active engagement in entrepreneurship may influence the selection of social environments for support and network building, as well as engagement in supportive social environments may encourage individuals to actively pursue entrepreneurship.

Other loop effects unique to females are those between entrepreneurship education and entrepreneurial experience, as well as those between entrepreneurship education and social norms. Here, entrepreneurial education enhances opportunities to gain entrepreneurial experiences, while direct engagement in entrepreneurial experiences may enhance appreciation of associated complexity and lead to actively seeking guidance via related educational programs. Similarly, a supportive social environment may encourage its members to take up entrepreneurial education, while at the same time, taking entrepreneurial education exposes students to environments that are more interested in entrepreneurial activities.

Identifying Centers of Gravity

When incorporating insights about direct, indirect, and loop effects in which the various factors are involved, one can highlight a number of factors that appear more central to the model in the overall network of effects. Here, for both males and females, social norms and entrepreneurial experience seem to be key variables both directly affecting EIs and mediating multiple effects of other factors. Moreover, economics education in males and more specifically entrepreneurship education in females seem to do the same, and, hence, highlighting the criticality of education in encouraging the formation of EIs among students. Finally, unique to the case of males is the centrality of exposure to role models, which seems to be tightly linked to the effects of education, experience, and social norms, all of which provide opportunities of exposure to role models.

Acknowledging Limitations

Although presenting interesting findings, our study has limitations that should be acknowledged. First, while presenting a rich model incorporating multiple variables, our study does not account for all possible variables examined in earlier studies. For example, earlier studies have shown significant effects of personality dimensions (Singh and DeNoble 2003), career anchors (Lee and Wong 2004), innovativeness (Lee et al. 2011), general work experience (Carr and Sequeira 2007), and other influential factors, the incorporation of which, in future studies, may shed further light onto the complex network of relationships between variables influencing EIs.

Second, the generalizability of our findings is contextually constrained to students in Norway in 2009. Here, while students may represent an interesting public experiencing displacement and pressure to make critical employment decisions, they are also, at the same time, less experienced in judging the levels of commitment and risk that are associated with entrepreneurial activity, as well as the likelihood of its success. Moreover, Norway, representing an advanced innovation-driven economy with a generous welfare system and high levels of gender equality, may limit the generalizability of our findings to similar national contexts. Future studies in developing countries, more conservative cultures, and less generous national social systems may uncover different patterns. Finally, the timing of our study in late 2009 may represent responses that were influenced by the general notion of a global economic slowdown and recession. Study replications in times of more market optimism may further test the stability of our results.

Conclusions

The current study contributes to our understanding of EIs in the context of a complex network of relationships between variables, identifies the important moderating role of gender on these relationships, and highlights critical variables, which play influential roles in the network of relationships between variables in each group. In this sense, we support the earlier findings that different factors influence EIs in different ways across sexes (Kickul et al. 2008; Pejvak et al. 2009; Vinogradov and Gabelko 2010; Walter, Parboteeah, and Walter 2011; Yordanova and Tarrazon 2010). At the same time, our study extends these insights by highlighting the effects of additional variables, and the complex network of relationships among them via mediation and loop effects. Such analyses allow us to both pacify and challenge previous contradictory findings.

More specifically, our findings show that all factors included effect EIs differently in terms of prevalence, directionality, and magnitude between the sexes. Some of the main findings include the common influences, though to different magnitudes, of social norms, self-efficacy, entrepreneurial experience, and entrepreneurial status; the prevalence of direct effects of exposure to role models and an economics major in males only; and the prevalence of direct effects of entrepreneurship education, risk perceptions, and age in females only. Moreover, the study also identified the criticality of the variables that are uniquely influential in each sex group, based on their centrality in the overall network of effects. These include exposure to role models and economics education in males only, and entrepreneurship education in particular in females only.

In terms of policy implications, our findings exhibit the value of economics and entrepreneurial education in encouraging the formation of EIs among students. Accordingly, supporting such lines of study is one way policymakers can encourage EIs among young adults in their domains of influence. Furthermore, the identification of the critical effects of role models, entrepreneurial experience, and social norms all provide us with valuable insights when forming entrepreneurial education programs. Hence, it also encourages educators to incorporate modules exposing students to role models, real-time experiences, and simulations, as well as encourages public and social support for entrepreneurial venturing.

Finally, in terms of implications for research, future studies may further test the validity and generalizability of our findings across different contexts, such as similar and different public from developing nations, conservative cultures, less generous national social systems, and in periods characterized by greater market optimism. Furthermore, our models may be further expanded so as to incorporate other variables excluded from our analysis but identified in earlier research as influential on the formation of EIs, such as personality dimensions, career anchors, innovativeness, work experience, immigration status, and others.

References

Ahmed, Ishfaq, Muhammad Musarrat Nawaz, Zafar Ahmad, Muhammad Zeeshan Shaukat, Ahmad Usman, Rehman Wasim ul, and Naveed Ahmed. 2010. "Determinants of Students' Entrepreneurial Career Intentions: Evidence from Business Graduates." *European Journal of Social Sciences* 15 (2): 14–22.

Ajzen, Icek. 1991. "The Theory of Planned Behavior." *Organizational Behavior and Human Decision Process* 50 (2): 179–211.

Asher, Herbert B. 1983. *Causal Modeling. Quantitative Applications in the Social Sciences,* edited by Michael S. Lewis-Beck. 2nd ed. Newbury Park, CA: Sage Publications.

Baker, Ted, Howard E. Aldrich, and Nina Liou. 1997. "Invisible Entrepreneurs: The Neglect of Women Business Owners by Mass Media and Scholarly Journals in the USA." *Entrepreneurship & Regional Development* 9 (3) (January 1): 221–38.

BarNir, Anat, Warren E. Watson, and Holly M. Hutchins. 2011. "Mediation and Moderated Mediation in the Relationship among Role Models, Self-Efficacy, Entrepreneurial Career Intention, and Gender." *Journal of Applied Social Psychology* 41 (2): 270–97.

Baron, Reuben M., and David A. Kenny. 1986. "The Moderator–Mediator Variable Distinction in Social Psychological Research: Conceptual, Strategic, and Statistical Considerations." *Journal of Personality and Social Psychology* 51 (6): 1173–82.

Bird, Barbara. 1988. "Implementing Entrepreneurial Ideas: The Case for Intention." *Academy of Management Review* 13 (3): 442–53.

Boden, Richard J., and Alfred R. Nucci. 2000. "On the Survival Prospects of Men's and Women's New Business Ventures." *Journal of Business Venturing* 15 (4): 347–62.

Brice Jr., Jeff, and Millicent Nelson. 2008. "The Impact of Occupational Preferences on the Intent to Pursue an Entrepreneurial Career." *Academy of Entrepreneurship Journal* 14 (1/2): 13–36.

Brush, Candida G. 1992. "Research on Women Business Owners: Past Trends, a New Perspective and Future Directions." *Entrepreneurship: Theory and Practice* 16 (4) (Summer): 5–30.

Brush, Candida G. 2006. "Women Entrepreneurs: A Research Overview." Chap. 23. In *The Oxford Handbook of Entrepreneurship*, edited by Mark Casson, Bernard Yeung, Anuradha Basu, and Nigel Wadeson. 611–28. Oxford: Oxford University Press.

Carey, Thomas A., David J. Flanagan, and Timothy B. Palmer. 2010. "An Examination of University Student Entrepreneurial Intentions by Type of Venture." *Journal of Developmental Entrepreneurship* 15 (4): 503–17.

Carr, Jon C., and Jennifer M. Sequeira. 2007. "Prior Family Business Exposure as Intergenerational Influence and Entrepreneurial Intent: A Theory of Planned Behavior Approach." *Journal of Business Research* 60 (10): 1090–98.

Carter, Sara, and Peter Rosa. 1998. "The Financing of Male- and Female-OwnedBusiness." *Entrepreneurship & Regional Development* 19 (3): 225–41.

Chen, Chao C., Patricia Gene Greene, and Ann Crick. 1998. "Does Entrepreneurial Self-Efficacy Distinguish Entrepreneurs from Managers?" *Journal of Business Venturing* 13 (4): 295–316.

Cliff, Jennifer E. 1998. "Does One Size Fit All? Exploring the Relationship between Attitudes towards Growth, Gender, and Business Size." *Journal of Business Venturing* 13 (6): 523–42.

Coleman, Susan. 2000. "Access to Capital and Terms of Credit: A Comparison of Men- and Women-Owned Small Businesses." *Journal of Small Business Management* 38 (3): 37–52.

Crant, Michael J. 1996. "The Proactive Personality Scale as a Predictor of Entrepreneurial Intentions." *Journal of Small Business Management* 34 (3): 42–49.

DeNoble, Alex, Dong Jung, and Sanford B. Ehrlich. 1999. "Entrepreneurial Self-Efficacy: The Development of a Measure and Its Relationship to Entrepreneurial Action." In *Frontiers in Entrepreneurship Research*, edited by P. D. Reynolds, W. D. Bygrave, S. Manigart, C. M. Mason, G. D. Meyer, H. J. Sapienza, and K. G. Shaver. Wellesley, MA: Babson College.

Díaz-García, Maria Cristina, and Juan Jiménez-Moreno. 2010. "Entrepreneurial Intention: The Role of Gender." *International Entrepreneurship and Management Journal* 6 (3): 261–83.

Dillman, Don A. 2006. *Mail and Internet Surveys: The Tailored Design Method*. 2nd ed. New York: Wiley.

Fernández, José, Francisco Liñán, and Francisco J. Santos. 2009. "Cognitive Aspects of Potential Entrepreneurs in Southern and Northern Europe: An Analysis Using Gem-Data." *Revista de Economia Mundial*, no. 23, 151–78.

Fitzsimmons, Jason R., and Evan J. Douglas. 2011. "Interaction between Feasibility and Desirability in the Formation of Entrepreneurial Intentions." *Journal of Business Venturing* 26 (4): 431–40.

Franco, Mário, Heiko Haase, and Arndt Lautenschläger. 2010. "Students' Entrepreneurial Intentions: An Inter-Regional Comparison." *Education and Training* 52 (4): 260–75.

Grilo, Isabel, and Roy Thurik. 2005. "Latent and Actual Entrepreneurship in Europe and the US: Some Recent Developments." *International Entrepreneurship and Management Journal* 1 (4): 441–59.

Gupta, Vishal K., Daniel B. Turban, Arzu S. Wasti, and Arijit Sikdar. 2009. "The Role of Gender Stereotypes in Perceptions of Entrepreneurs and Intentions to Become an Entrepreneur." *Entrepreneurship: Theory and Practice* 33 (2): 397–417.

Gurel, Eda, Levent Altinay, and Roberto Daniele. 2010. "Tourism Students' Entrepreneurial Intentions." *Annals of Tourism Research* 37 (3): 646–69.

Haase, Heiko, Arndt Lautenschläger, and Ravinder Rena. 2011. "The Entrepreneurial Mind-Set of University Students: A Cross-Cultural Comparison between Namibia and Germany." *International Journal of Education Economics and Development* 2 (2): 113–29.

Hamidi, Daniel Yar, Karl Wennberg, and Henrik Berglund. 2008. "Creativity in Entrepreneurship Education." *Journal of Small Business and Enterprise Development* 15 (2): 304–20.

Hindle, Kevin, Kim Klyver, and Daniel F. Jennings. 2009. "An 'Informed' Intent Model: Incorporating Human Capital, Social Capital, and Gender Variables into the Theoretical Model of Entrepreneurship Intentions." In *Understanding the Entrepreneurial Mind: Opening the Black Box*, edited by Alan L. Carsrud and Malin Brännback. 35–50. New York: Springer.

Hisrich, Robert D., and Candida G. Brush. 1983. "The Woman Entrepreneur: Implications of Family, Educational, and Occupational Experience." In *Frontiers of Entrepreneurship Research*, edited by J. A. Hornaday, J. A. Timmons, and K. H. Vesper. 255–70. Boston: Babson College.

Hofstede, Gert. 2001. *Culture's Consequences: Comparing Values, Behaviors, Institutions, and Organizations across Nations*. 2nd ed. Thousand Oaks, CA: Sage Publications.

Iakovleva, Tatiana, and Lars Kolvereid. 2009. "An Integrated Model of Entrepreneurial Intentions." *International Journal of Business and Globalisation* 3 (1): 66–80.

Iakovleva, Tatiana, Lars Kolvereid, and Ute Stephan. 2011. "Entrepreneurial Intentions in Developing and Developed Countries." *Education and Training* 53 (5): 353–70.

Johansen, Vegard, and Tommy Høyvarde Clausen. 2011. "Promoting the Entrepreneurs of Tomorrow: Entrepreneurship Education and Start-Up Intentions among Schoolchildren." *International Journal of Entrepreneurship and Small Business* 13 (2): 208–19.

Jones, P., A. Jones, G. Packham, and C. Miller. 2008. "Student Attitudes towards Enterprise Education in Poland: A Positive Impact." *Education and Training* 50 (7): 597–614.

Kautonen, Teemu, Seppo Luoto, and Erno T. Tornikoski. 2010. "Influence of Work History on Entrepreneurial Intentions in 'Prime Age' and 'Third Age': A Preliminary Study." *International Small Business Journal* 28 (6): 583–601.

Kelley, Donna, Niels Bosma, and José Ernesto Amorós. 2010. "The Gobal Entrepreneurship Monitor 2010 Global Report." Babson College/Universidad del Desarrollo.

Kickul, Jill, Fiona Wilson, Deborah Marlino, and Saulo D. Barbosa. 2008. "Are Misalignments of Perceptions and Self-Efficacy Causing Gender Gaps in Entrepreneurial Intentions among Our Nation's Teens?" *Journal of Small Business and Enterprise Development* 15 (2): 321–35.

Kolvereid, Lars. 1996. "Prediction of Employment Status Choice Intentions." *Entrepreneurship: Theory and Practice* 21 (1) (Fall): 47–57.

Kolvereid, Lars, and Espen Isaksen. 2006. "New Business Start-Up and Subsequent Entry into Self-Employment." *Journal of Business Venturing* 21 (6): 866–85.

Kolvereid, Lars, and Oystein Moen. 1997. "Entrepreneurship among Business Graduates: Does a Major in Entrepreneurship Make a Difference?" *Journal of European Industrial Training* 21 (4/5): 154–60.

Kristiansen, Stein, and Nurul Indarti. 2004. "Entrepreneurial Intention among Indonesian and Norwegian Students." *Journal of Enterprising Culture* 12 (1): 55–78.

Krueger, Norris F. 1993. "The Impact of Prior Entrepreneurial Exposure on Perceptions of New Venture Feasibility and Desirability." *Entrepreneurship: Theory and Practice* 18 (1) (Fall): 5–21.

Krueger, Norris F. 2009. "Entrepreneurial Intentions Are Dead: Long Live Entrepreneurial Intentions." In *Understanding the Entrepreneurial Mind: Opening the Black Box*, edited by Alan L. Carsrud and Malin Brännback. 51–74. New York: Springer.

Krueger, Norris F., and Alan L. Carsrud. 1993. "Entrepreneurial Intentions: Applying the Theory of Planned Behaviour." *Entrepreneurship & Regional Development* 5 (4): 315–30.

Krueger, Norris F., Michael D. Reilly, and Alan L. Carsrud. 2000. "Competing Models of Entrepreneurial Intentions." *Journal of Business Venturing* 15 (5): 411–32.

Kuckertz, Andreas, and Marcus Wagner. 2010. "The Influence of Sustainability Orientation on Entrepreneurial Intentions—Investigating the Role of Business Experience." *Journal of Business Venturing* 25 (5): 524–39.

Lans, Thomas, Judith Gulikers, and Maarten Batterink. 2010. "Moving beyond Traditional Measures of Entrepreneurial Intentions in a Study among Life-Sciences Students in the Netherlands." *Research in Post-Compulsory Education* 15 (3): 259–74.

Lee, Lena, Poh Kam Wong, Maw Der Foo, and Aegean Leung. 2011. "Entrepreneurial Intentions: The Influence of Organizational and Individual Factors." *Journal of Business Venturing* 26 (1): 124–36.

Lee, Soo Hoon, and Poh Kam Wong. 2004. "An Exploratory Study of Technopreneurial Intentions: A Career Anchor Perspective." *Journal of Business Venturing* 19 (1): 7–28.

Leffel, A., and J. Darling. 2009. "Entrepreneurial versus Organizational Employment Preferences: A Comparative Study of European and American Respondents." *Journal of Entrepreneurship Education* 12: 79–92.

Liñán, Francisco, and Yi-Wen Chen. 2009. "Development and Cross-Cultural Application of a Specific Instrument to Measure Entrepreneurial Intentions." *Entrepreneurship: Theory and Practice* 33 (3): 593–617.

Liñán, Francisco, Francisco J. Santos, and José Fernández. 2011. "The Influence of Perceptions on Potential Entrepreneurs." *International Entrepreneurship and Management Journal*: 1–18.

Liñán, Francisco, David Urbano, and Maribel Guerrero. 2011. "Regional Variations in Entrepreneurial Cognitions: Start-Up Intentions of University Students in Spain." *Entrepreneurship and Regional Development* 23 (3/4): 187–215.

Mackinnon, David P., and James H. Dwyer. 1993. "Estimating Mediated Effects in Prevention Studies." *Evaluation Review* 17 (2): 144–58.

McMullen, Jeffery S., and Dean A. Shepherd. 2006. "Entrepreneurial Action and the Role of Uncertainty In the Theory of the Entrepreneur." *Academy of Management Review* 31 (1): 132–52.

Mueller, Susan. 2011. "Increasing Entrepreneurial Intention: Effective Entrepreneurship Course Characteristics." *International Journal of Entrepreneurship and Small Business* 13 (1): 55–74.

Neider, Linda. 1987. "A Preliminary Investigation of Female Entrepreneurs in Florida." *Journal of Small Business Management* 24 (4): 37–44.

Pejvak, Oghazi, Jung Marie-Louise, Peighambari Kaveh, and Tretten Phillip. 2009. "What Makes People Want to Become Self-Employed? Applying the Theory of Planned Behavior." *Advances in Management* 2 (11): 9–18.

Plant, Robert, and Jen Ren. 2010. "A Comparative Study of Motivation and Entrepreneurial Intentionality: Chinese and American Perspectives." *Journal of Developmental Entrepreneurship* 15 (2): 187–204.

Raijman, Rebeca. 2001. "Determinants of Entrepreneurial Intentions: Mexican Immigrants in Chicago." *Journal of Socio-Economics* 30 (5): 393–411.

Rosa, Peter, Daphne Hamilton, Sara Carter, and Helen Burns. 1994. "The Impact of Gender on Small Business Management: Preliminary Findings of a British Study." *International Small Business Journal* 12 (3) (April 1): 25–32.

Scherer, Robert F., Janet S. Adams, Susan S. Carley, and Frank A. Wiebe. 1989. "Role Model Performance Effects on Development of Entrepreneurial Career Preference." *Entrepreneurship: Theory and Practice* 13 (3) (Spring): 53–71.

Schwarz, Erich J., Malgorzata A. Wdowiak, Daniela A. Almer-Jarz, and Robert J. Breitenecker. 2009. "The Effects of Attitudes and Perceived Environment Conditions on Students' Entrepreneurial Intent: An Austrian Perspective." *Education and Training* 51 (4): 272–91.

Sequeira, Jennifer, Stephen L. Mueller, and Jeffrey E. McGee. 2007. "The Influence of Social Ties and Self-Efficacy in Forming Entrepreneurial Intentions and Motivating Nascent Behavior." *Journal of Developmental Entrepreneurship* 12 (3): 275–93.

Shapero, Albert, and Lisa Sokol. 1982. "The Social Dimensions of Entrepreneurship." In *Encyclopedia of Entrepreneurship,* edited by C. Kent, D. Sexton, and K. Vesper. 72–90. Englewood Cliffs, NJ: Prentice-Hall.

Shook, Christopher L., and Constantin Bratianu. 2010. "Entrepreneurial Intent in a Transitional Economy: An Application of the Theory of Planned Behavior to Romanian Students." *International Entrepreneurship and Management Journal* 6 (3): 231–47.

Shook, Christopher L., Richard L. Priem, and Jeffrey E. McGee. 2003. "Venture Creation and the Enterprising Individual: A Review and Synthesis." *Journal of Management* 29 (3) (June 1): 379–99.

Singh, Gangaram, and Alex DeNoble. 2003. "Views on Self-Employment and Personality: An Exploratory Study." *Journal of Developmental Entrepreneurship* 8 (3): 265–81.

Tornikoski, Erno T., and Teemu Kautonen. 2009. "Enterprise as Sunset Career? Entrepreneurial Intentions in the Ageing Population." *International Journal of Entrepreneurship and Small Business* 8 (2): 278–91.

Turker, Duygu, and Senem Sonmez Selcuk. 2009. "Which Factors Affect Entrepreneurial Intention of University Students?" *Journal of European Industrial Training* 33 (2): 142–59.

Veciana, José Ma, Marinés Aponte, and David Urbano. 2005. "University Students' Attitudes towards Entrepreneurship: A Two Countries Comparison." *International Entrepreneurship and Management Journal* 1 (2): 165–82.

Vinogradov, Evgueni, and Maria Gabelko. 2010. "Entrepreneurship among Russian Immigrants in Norway and Their Stay-at-Home Peers." *Journal of Developmental Entrepreneurship* 15 (4): 461–79.

Walter, Sascha G., Praveen K. Parboteeah, and Achim Walter. 2011. "University Departments and Self-Employment Intentions of Business Students: A Cross-Level Analysis." *Entrepreneurship: Theory and Practice.* doi:10.1111/j.1540-6520.2011.00460.x. Available at: http://onlinelibrary.wiley.com/doi/10.1111/j.1540-6520.2011.00460.x.

Wilson, Fiona, Jill Kickul, Deborah Marlino, Saulo D. Barbosa, and Mark D. Griffiths. 2009. "An Analysis of the Role of Gender and Self-Efficacy in Developing Female Entrepreneurial Interest and Behavior." *Journal of Developmental Entrepreneurship* 14 (2): 105–19.

Yordanova, Desislava I. 2011. "The Effects of Gender on Entrepreneurship in Bulgaria: An Empirical Study." *International Journal of Management* 28 (1): 289–305.

Yordanova, Desislava I., and Maria-Antonia Tarrazon. 2010. "Gender Differences in Entrepreneurial Intentions: Evidence from Bulgaria." *Journal of Developmental Entrepreneurship* 15 (3): 245–61.

Zellweger, Thomas, Philipp Sieger, and Frank Halter. 2011. "Should I Stay or Should I Go? Career Choice Intentions of Students with Family Business Background." *Journal of Business Venturing* 26 (5): 521–36.

Zhao, Hao, Gerald E. Hills, and Scott E. Seibert. 2005. "The Mediating Role of Self-Efficacy in the Development of Entrepreneurial Intentions." *Journal of Applied Psychology* 90 (6): 1265–72.

Chapter 2

Size and Growth Rate of Women-Owned Businesses in the United States[1]

Linda F. Edelman, Tatiana S. Manolova,
and Candida G. Brush

Women are the majority owners of an estimated 8 million businesses, or 28.2 percent of all businesses in the United States. These businesses create an economic impact of $3 trillion annually, which translates into the creation and/ or maintenance of more than 23 million jobs, or 16 percent of the total U.S. employment (CWBR, 2009). Further, majority women-owned (51%) businesses accounted for almost 30 percent of all businesses in the country as of 2009, but they generated only 4.2 percent of all revenues (CWBR, 2009). Analysis based on data from the U.S. Census Bureau shows female-owned businesses have lower survival rates, profits, employment, and sales, with sales roughly 80 percent lower than the average sales of male-owned firms (Fairlie and Robb 2009). Even though the number and importance of women-led ventures have grown substantially over the past two decades, they remain smaller than those of men-led ventures (Kelley, Brush, and Greene 2011). This performance disparity raises two important questions—namely, why are women-owned businesses smaller, and why do they grow more slowly than those led by men?

Surprisingly, there has been relatively little research that has examined women-led firms or analyzed firm performance by sex in the United States (Gatewood et al. 2003). Reasons offered for the systematic differences between women- and men-owned firms include human capital (Fairlie and Robb 2009), social capital (Renzulli, Aldrich, and Moody 2000), access to debt or equity financing (Robb and Wolken 2002; Brush et al. 2004), strategy (Chaganti and Parasuraman 1996; Gundry and Welsch 2001), industry sector (Robb and Wolken 2002; Anna et al. 2000), or personal motivations (Carter et al. 2003). However, given the variety of explanations for the growth differences of women- and men-led firms, empirical findings are not conclusive. For example, some research shows no differences in bank lending practices, approval rates, or terms between men- and women-owned businesses (Robb and Wolken 2002), while other research finds women are no different from men in terms of education (Fairlie and Robb 2009) and qualifications to grow ventures (Fischer, Reuber, and Dyke 1993). International studies also found no gender-based effects on the business potential to achieve significant growth (Westhead and Cowling 1995; Klofsten and Jones-Evans 2000). In sum, research explaining growth variations between men- and women-led firms is still sparse and largely inconsistent.

Research into the sociocognitive influences on entrepreneurial behavior in the early phase of new venture development has helped explain who pursues entrepreneurial opportunities, what the entrepreneurial process looks like, and what the outcomes of the entrepreneurial engagement turn out to be (Carsrud and Brännback 2011; Shane, Locke, and Collins 2003). Following this line of research, we explore nascent entrepreneurs' growth motivations, focusing on the gender differences in entrepreneurial motivations. More specifically, we adopt an expectancy theory perspective, following the *effort–performance–outcome* model (Gatewood 1993; Gatewood et al. 2002). We argue that nascent entrepreneurs will be motivated to expend effort toward the creation of a new venture if they believe the new business creation will lead to some desired outcomes (Gatewood et al. 2002). Further, we bring arguments from social learning theory to propose that the desired outcomes of a new venture creation differ by sex (Hackett and Betz 1981).

In this chapter, we first present a theoretical overview and develop our hypotheses. We then describe our methodology, and report the results from statistical tests. In conclusion, we discuss the theoretical, practitioner, and public policy implications of our study.

Theoretical Perspectives and Hypothesis Development

Expectancy Theory and Entrepreneurship

Expectancy theory, developed by Vroom (1964), is a dominant theoretical framework for explaining human motivation. The theory assumes that action will be taken when an individual believes that his or her efforts will lead to successful performance that will bring certain outcomes with direct positive value or will lead to other valued outcomes (Vroom 1964; Olson, Roese, and Zanna 1996). In other words, the perceived consequences of actions will rationally determine human behavior (Miller and Grush 1988).

Expectancy theory is also referred to as *VIE theory* because it is comprised of three relationships: *valence*, interpreted as the importance, attractiveness, desirability, or anticipated satisfaction with results; *instrumentality*, or the relationship between an outcome and another outcome; and *expectancy*, or the subjective probability that effort will lead to an outcome or performance (Vroom 1964; Mitchell 1974; Olson, Roese, and Zanna 1996).

Expectancy theory has been used in entrepreneurship research to explore the predictors of entrepreneurship as an occupational choice. Shaver, Gatewood, and Gartner (2001) found that entrepreneurs who believed in their skills and ability were motivated to exert necessary effort toward establishing a new venture. Douglas and Shepherd (2000) modeled the choice to pursue entrepreneurship as a utility function that reflected anticipated income, the amount of work effort anticipated to achieve this income, and the risk involved, as well as other factors such as the person's attitudes for independence and perceptions of the anticipated work environment, for example, the presence of funding or opportunities. Krueger, Reilly, and Carsrud (2000) compared the predictive power of two models of entrepreneurial intentions—Ajzen's (1987, 1991) theory of planned behavior (TPB) and Shapero's (1982) model of the entrepreneurial event. They found strong statistical support for both models, which led them to propose that intentions are the single best predictor of any planned behavior, including entrepreneurship, and that personal and situational variables typically have an indirect influence on entrepreneurship by influencing key attitudes and the general motivation to act (Krueger, Reilly, and Carsrud 2000, 412).

In this study, we follow Gatewood (1993) and Gatewood et al. (2002) and model new venture creation as an effort–performance–outcome process (see Figure 2.1). In this model, the effort expended to start a business (performance) leads to several desired outcomes. These outcomes include self-realization, roles or status, financial success, and autonomy. We present hypothesis 1 as follows,

> H1. *Entrepreneurial expectancy and entrepreneurial intensity will be positively and significantly associated with starting a business; and starting a business will be positively and significantly associated with desired outcomes (i.e., reasons or motivations to start a business).*

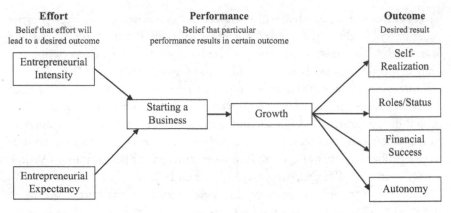

Effort	**Performance**	**Outcome**
Belief that effort will lead to a desired outcome	Belief that particular performance results in certain outcome	Desired result

Definitions
Effort
> *Entrepreneurial Intensity*. How focused or committed the entrepreneur is to his or her start-up endeavor.
> *Entrepreneurial Expectancy*. The belief that a particular action will result in a particular performance.

Performance
> *Starting a Business*. The perceived relationship between first-level outcomes (starting a business) and second-level outcomes (what the nascent entrepreneur desires to achieve from starting the business).
> *Growth*. Increasing the size of the business.

Outcomes
> *Self-Realization*. The pursuit of goals (typically beyond financial) that are of interest to the entrepreneur.
> *Roles/Status*. Role is the individual's desire to emulate the example of others. Status is an individual's position relative to others in a given social situation.
> *Financial Success*. Individual's intention to earn more money and achieve financial security.
> *Autonomy*. The desire for freedom, control, and flexibility in the use of one's time.

Figure 2.1   An expectancy framework including growth

Growth Expectancies

As a next step, we add the relationship between growth expectancies and desired outcomes from the entrepreneurial process. Growth is considered to be a measure of firm success (Davidsson 1991), and as such has received a great deal of attention in the entrepreneurship literature (Acs and Evans 1993; Delmar, Davidsson, and Gartner 2003). Based on Fishbein and Ajzen's (1975) and Ajzen's (1991) expectancy value model of attitude, Wiklund, Davidsson, and Delmar (2003) examined the relationships between expected consequences of growth and the overall attitude toward growth. They found that noneconomic concerns (particularly, the concern for employee well-being) may be more important than expected financial outcomes in determining the overall attitude toward growth. In a related study, Wiklund and Shepherd (2005) used Ajzen's (1987, 1991) TPB to examine the moderating effect of resources and opportunities on the relationship between growth aspirations and actual growth. They found that education, experience, and environmental dynamism magnify the effect that one's growth aspirations have on the realization of growth. These authors also reported that growth aspirations were significantly and positively associated with growth expectancies. Renko, Kroech, and Bullough (2011) examined the economic and noneconomic motivations of nascent entrepreneurs and found that valence, instrumentality, and expectancy were antecedents to the effort entrepreneurs put into the start-up process. They concluded that motivation distinguished those entrepreneurs who made progress from those who did not. Hypothesis 2 is formed as follows:

> H2. In the entrepreneurial expectancy framework, starting a business will be positively and significantly associated with growth expectations, and growth expectations will be positively and significantly associated with desired outcomes (i.e., reasons or motivations to start a business).

New Venture, Gender, and Growth

Social learning theory argues that as a result of factors such as peers, media, educational practices, or occupational systems affecting gender development, men and women grow up having different socialization experiences, which in turn influence their career preferences (Bandura 1977; Bussey and Bandura 1999; Hackett and Betz 1981). In the entrepreneurial context, performance accomplishments and vicarious learning are two major sources of differences (Hackett and Betz 1981). Performance accomplishments are those successful performances on a task that provide information increasing one's expectations of efficacy related to a specific task or behavior. For instance, boys might be more likely to gain experience in mechanical skills or sports, while girls might experience task accomplishment in home-related activities (Macoby and Jacklin 1974). Vicarious learning includes role models, sex role, and occupational stereotypes that can increase efficacy expectations by vicariously observing others succeed (Hackett and Betz 1981).

Early social learning experiences are related to career decisions, with males having a higher preference for entrepreneurship (Matthews and Moser 1996). In a national study of entrepreneurial tendencies among youth, Kourilsky and Walstad (1998) found that females were less interested in starting a business and less confident in their abilities. Chen, Greene, and Crick (1998) also reported that female students had lower self-efficacy than male students. Carter, Gartner, Shaver, and Elizabeth (2001) found that females scored lower than males on their confidence in starting a business, while Ljungren and Kolvereid (1996) concluded that during start-up, men were more likely to stress economic expectancies (risk and profitability) whereas women more often stressed personal expectancies (autonomy and challenge). Anna et al. (2000)

found that women in traditional businesses (e.g., services and retail) had stronger career expectations of security and balance between demands of work and home than women in nontraditional businesses (e.g., manufacturing). Finally, role models, self-assurance, and marriage were positively related to the supply of female entrepreneurs, while education and experience were negatively correlated with entrepreneurship (Shiller and Crewson 1997).

Other research found that women's intentions for launching and managing new businesses may differ from men's (Carter and Brush 2004), while a study of new venture strategies suggested that men and women entrepreneurs have different socialization experiences, which shape different expectancies, efforts, and beliefs explaining performance differences (Carter, Williams, and Reynolds 1997). Lee-Gosselin and Grise (1990) found that minimal prior business experience contributed to modest growth expectations for women, while Carter and Allen (1997) found that access to resources had stronger effects on growth than did intention or choice. Cliff (1998) found that personal considerations were more important than economic considerations for women in business expansion decisions, while Orser and Hogarth-Scott (2005) found that women weighted the opinions of their spouses more heavily as a key ingredient for growth than men did. Davis and Shaver (2012) investigated career motivations and growth of nascent firms and found that people's desires for growth vary by age *or* gender, and that *both* age and gender are key to understanding the antecedents of high growth intention.

Based on the expectancy theory argument, we suggest that women's and men's growth expectancy functions may differ substantively with respect to desired outcomes. Here is hypothesis 3:

H3. *In the entrepreneurial expectancy framework, desired outcomes (i.e., reasons or motivations to start a business) for starting and growing the new venture will differ between men and women.*

Figure 2.1 presents our hypothesized entrepreneurial expectancy framework including growth.

Methods

Sample

The data utilized for this investigation were drawn from the U.S. national Panel Study of Entrepreneurial Dynamics (PSED), a longitudinal study of nascent entrepreneurs, which was started in 1998. Nascent entrepreneurs were defined as individuals involved in attempting to start a new business on their own within the past 12 months (i.e., autonomous start-ups) before the study, as opposed to those doing so with sponsorship from existing firms. Motivated by a lack of understanding of who starts businesses, what process they undertake when starting a new business, and why some new businesses succeed, while others fail, the objective of the PSED was to gain an introspective understanding of how nascent entrepreneurs create new businesses and what activities and behaviors they engage in during the process of enterprise creation. As part of the national survey, a total of 64,622 individuals in the United States were contacted through random digit dialing by a marketing research firm. During these telephone interviews, two questions were used to identify those individuals who were in the process of starting a new venture: (1) "Are you alone or with others, now trying to start a business?"; and (2) "Are you alone, or with others, now trying to start a new venture for your employer?" Respondents who answered "yes" to either of these two questions were then asked two additional questions that determined whether they were actively involved in the start-up process and whether they would share in the ownership of the new venture. Positive answers to both of these questions qualified an individual as a nascent entrepreneur to be requested to participate in the PSED. Qualified individuals were offered a monetary inducement ($25) for their participation.

The PSED data were collected through a series of four waves of telephone interviews conducted at approximately one-year intervals by researchers at the University of Wisconsin between 1998 and 2003. In addition, a mail survey was also distributed after the first wave of phone interviews. To ensure that the entrepreneurs were "nascent," those cases in which the business had had a positive cash flow for more than three months were classified as "infant" businesses and were excluded from the sample. Given the complexity of the PSED, in 2004 a handbook was published as a guide for researchers using the PSED data set (Gartner et al. 2004). For researchers who are interested in examining the database, the first four iterations are available on the University of Michigan website (http://projects.isr.umich.edu/PSED) along with a codebook for deciphering the variables.

The sample of nascent-only entrepreneurs in the data from the phone surveys is 715. However, the sample was then reduced to $n = 469$, due to the reduced response rate in the mail survey. It is on this reduced sample that we present our descriptive statistics, reliability analysis, and correlation analysis. Since we were specifically interested in the differences between male and female nascent entrepreneurs, we then split the $n = 469$ sample by sex, which left us with two subsamples of $n = 231$ for men and $n = 238$ for women.

Measures

Both nominal and continuous measures were utilized in this study. We found strong support for the reliability and internal validity of our measures. The standardized factor loadings were all above 0.64 (the recommended minimum in the social sciences is usually 0.40 [Ford, McCallum, and Tait 1986]), and all alpha levels were above the 0.60 threshold (Nunnally 1970).

Independent Variables—Effort

Entrepreneurial intensity. Entrepreneurial intensity is a measure of how focused or committed the entrepreneur is to his or her start-up endeavor (Liao and Welsch 2004). To measure intensity, we used three 5-item Likert-type scale questions ("completely disagree" to "completely agree" with a defined neutral point) that reflect the level of dedication the nascent entrepreneur has toward the new venture: "I would rather own my own business than earn a higher salary employed by someone else,""There is no limit as to how long I would give a maximum effort to establish my business," and "My philosophy is to 'do whatever it takes' to establish my own business." The questions were confirmatory factors analyzed with factor scores of 0.64 or higher and a Cronbach's alpha of 0.65.

Entrepreneurial expectancy. Entrepreneurial expectancy is the belief that a particular action will be followed by a particular outcome (Gatewood 2004). To measure expectancy, we used four 5-item Likert-type scale questions ("completely disagree" to "completely agree" with a defined neutral point): "If I work hard, I can successfully start a business"; "My past experience will be very valuable in starting a business"; "Overall, my skills and abilities will help me to start a business"; and "I am confident that I can put in the effort needed to start a business." The four items were confirmatory factors analyzed with factor scores of 0.51 or higher and a Cronbach's alpha of 0.71.

Mediating Variables—Performance

Starting a business. Starting a business is the perceived relationship between first-level and second-level outcomes. First-level outcomes are ends in themselves (e.g., starting a business), while second-level outcomes are instrumental in achieving other results (e.g., reasons why entrepreneurs choose to start a business) (Gatewood 2004). Following Gatewood 2004, we measured this using a single item:—"If I start a business, it will help me to achieve other important goals in my life" ("completely disagree" to "completely agree" with a defined neutral point).

Growth. To measure growth, we followed Stewart and Roth (2001) and Stewart et al. (1998) (Human and Matthews 2004) and used a self-reported single-item dichotomous measure: "Which of the following two statements best describes your preference for the future size of this business?" (1) "I want the business to be as large as possible" (coded as 1), or (2) "I want a size I can manage myself or with a few key employees" (coded as 0).

Dependent Variables—Desired Outcomes

To measure the reasons why nascent entrepreneurs chose to start their own business (second-level outcomes), we factor analyzed a series of questions that address the reasons or motivations that nascent entrepreneurs have when starting a new venture (also referred to as *career reasons* [Carter et al. 2004]).[2] In our analysis, we found four naturally occurring factors, which roughly correspond to the second-level outcomes of the expectancy theory discussed in Gatewood (1993).

Self-realization. Self-realization is the pursuit of goals that are of interest to the entrepreneur. In our classification, this measure, albeit expanded, corresponds to Birley and Westhead's (1994) need for personal development. We measured self-realization using seven items: "To what extent is the following reason important to you in establishing this new business?" "To be innovative and in the forefront of technology," "To continue to grow and learn as a person," "To achieve something and get recognition," "To develop an idea for a product," "To fulfill a personal vision," "To lead and motivate others," and "To have the power to greatly influence an organization." Factor scores were at the 0.50 level or higher with a Cronbach's alpha of 0.82.

Role/status. Role is an individual's desire to emulate the example of others. Status is an individual's position relative to others in a given social situation. We follow Gatewood (1993), who posits in her framework for new venture development that status is a second-level outcome or reason for desiring to start a business. In our model, status corresponds to Shane, Kolveraid, and Westhead's (1991) typology for new firm formation, which presents four reasons why individuals desire to start their own firms. Our measure of status is a combination of what Shane et al. label as *recognition* (need to have status, approval, and recognition from those in the community) (Bonjean 1966) and *roles* (an individual's desire to follow family traditions or emulate the example of others) (Carter, Gartner, and Shaver 2004). We measured status using four items: "To what extent is the following reason important to you in establishing this new business?" "To achieve a higher position for myself in society," "To continue a family tradition," "To be respected by my friends," and "To follow the example of a person I admire." Factor scores for this measure are 0.60 or higher and the Cronbach's alpha is 0.69.

Financial success. Perhaps the most popular reason for starting a new business, financial success involves reasons that describe an individual's intention to earn more money and achieve financial security (Carter, Gartner, and Shaver 2004). In our study, we follow Birley and Westhead (1994) and Scheinberg and MacMillan (1988), who both label financial success as *perceived instrumentality of wealth.* To construct our measure, we used four items: "To what extent is the following reason important to you in establishing this new business?" "To give myself, my spouse, and children financial security"; "To build a business my children can inherit"; "To earn a larger personal income"; and "To have a chance to build great wealth or a very high income." Factor scores for this measure are 0.50 or higher with a Cronbach's alpha of 0.73.

Autonomy. Autonomy is an individual's desire for freedom, control, and flexibility in the use of his or her time (Schein 1978). We follow Birley and Westhead (1994), Scheinberg and MacMillan (1988), and Shane, Kolveraid, and Westhead (1991), who all discuss the importance of autonomy as a reason for nascent entrepreneurs to start a new business (Carter, Gartner, and Shaver 2004). Our measure has two items: "To what extent is the following reason important to you in establishing this new business?" "To have greater flexibility for my personal and family life" and "To have considerable freedom to adapt my own approach to work." Factor scores for this measure are 0.76 or higher and Cronbach's alpha is 0.61.

Table 2.1 presents descriptive statistics and zero-order correlations for the variables in our model. The operationalization of all of the measures can be found in the appendix.

Table 2.1 Means, standard deviations, and correlations for the variables in the model

	Mean	SD	1	2	3	4	5	6	7	8
Entrepreneurial intensity	3.86	2.32	1							
Expectancy	4.31	2.34	0.34**	1						
Starting a business	4.20	0.83	0.36**	0.39**	1					
Growth	1.90	0.39	0.11*	0.09*	0.07	1				
Self-realization	3.19	6.35	0.27**	0.26*	0.25**	0.17**	1			
Status/roles	2.10	3.51	0.28**	0.10*	0.14**	0.10*	0.55**	1		
Financial success	3.58	3.73	0.28**	0.22**	0.30**	0.23**	0.42**	0.37**	1	
Autonomy	4.16	1.70	0.20**	0.13**	0.26**	0.01	0.26**	0.23**	0.24**	1

Note:
$N = 469$; two-tailed tests.
*$p < .05$; **$p < .01$.

Analysis and Results

Measurement Model

To best capture the theoretical interdependencies between our constructs, we used structural equation modeling to test our hypotheses. This method allows for a fine-grained analysis of the hypothesized relationships within the context of the entire model; it is a particularly attractive choice when testing mediating variables in that all of the relevant paths are tested simultaneously and complications such as measurement error and feedback are directly incorporated into the model (Baron and Kenny 1986).

We followed the two-stage structural equation modeling procedure recommended by Anderson and Gerbing (1988). In the first stage, the measurement model was estimated using confirmatory factor analysis in order to test whether the constructs exhibited sufficient reliability and validity. The second stage identified the structural model(s) that best fit the data and tested the hypothesized relationships between the constructs. Due to our particular interest in the differences between men and women with respect to overall motivations and motivations toward growth, we ran structural equation models on both the full sample and on the split samples of men and women.

We checked the data for violations of the normality assumption, for missing data, and for outliers. We used mean substitution to eliminate missing data (Kline 1998). Mean substitution is a popular method of managing missing values in structural equation modeling. In addition, it is a conservative technique in that it makes the data less reactive. To compensate for the oversamples of women and minorities in the PSED data set, we weighted the data using the weighting scheme developed by Shaver (2004), before using the variance–covariance matrix as the input for the structural equation models.

Tables 2.2 and 2.3 present the fit statistics and path coefficients, respectively, for the measurement models.

Hypothesis Tests

To test our three hypotheses, we ran a series of structural equation models. In hypothesis 1, we hypothesized that the expectancy motivation theory will link effort and intensity expended toward the creation of the new venture (i.e., performance) and that performance will lead to desired outcomes (e.g., reasons or motivations to start a new venture). We found that the model fitted well with the data (see Table 2.2) and that with respect to the reasons for starting a new venture, the paths leading to the mediating variable—starting a new venture (i.e., performance)—from entrepreneurial intensity and expectancy, were both

Table 2.2 Structural equation model results: model statistics

Model	χ^2	df	χ^2/df	P_1	GFI	AGFI	NFI
Expectancy model—whole sample (H1)	0.76	1	0.76	0.38	1.00	0.99	0.99
Expectancy model with growth—whole sample* (H2)	7.54	4	1.89	0.11	0.99	0.96	0.99
Expectancy model with growth—men only* (H3)	3.95	4	0.99	0.41	0.99	0.96	0.99
Expectancy model with growth—women only* (H3)	5.44	5	1.09	0.36	0.99	0.96	0.99
Recommended value (Hair et al. 1995)			< 2.0	≥ 0.05	≥ 0.90	≥ 0.90	≥ 0.80

*Statistics presented are for the partially mediated models.
Abbreviations: GFI, goodness of fit; AGFI, adjusted goodness of fit; NFI, normed fit index; H1, Hypothesis 1; H2, Hypothesis 2; H3, Hypothesis 3.

Table 2.3 Structural equation model results: path estimates[a]

Path	Expectancy Model—Whole Sample (H1)	Expectancy Model with Growth—Whole Sample (H2)	Expectancy Model with Growth—Men Only (H3)	Expectancy Model with Growth—Women Only (H3)
Entrepreneurial intensity → starting a business	.110***	.093***	.089***	.097***
Expectancy → starting a business	.093***	.110***	.088***	.138***
Starting a business → growth	NA	.032	.032	.029
Starting a business → self-realization	.971**	1.054**	1.286*	4.390***
Starting a business → role/status	.224	.333*	.295	1.656*

(Continued)

Table 2.3 (Continued)

Path	Expectancy Model—Whole Sample (H1)	Expectancy Model with Growth—Whole Sample (H2)	Expectancy Model with Growth—Men Only (H3)	Expectancy Model with Growth—Women Only (H3)
Starting a business → financial success	.917***	.938***	.840***	2.602***
Starting a business → autonomy	.468***	.468***	.568***	.077***
Growth → self-realization	NA	2.121**	1.152	.640**
Growth → status/role	NA	.650	.237	.389*
Growth → financial success	NA	1.812***	1.328**	1.145***
Growth → autonomy	NA	−.074	−.083	.340**

Note:
Two-tailed tests.
*p < .05, **p < .01, ***p < .001.
ªPath estimates for the expectancy model with growth—whole sample; the expectancy model with growth—men only and the expectancy model with growth—women only are presented for the partially mediated model only.
Abbreviations: H1, Hypothesis 1; H2, Hypothesis 2; H3, Hypothesis 3; NA, not applicable.

significant (path estimate = 0.093; $p < .000$; path estimate = 0.110; $p < .000$, respectively). In addition, the paths leading from the mediating variable— starting a new venture—to the second-level outcomes or reasons to start a new venture were also all significant, save for the path leading to status, which was not significant (path estimate = 0.224; $p < 0.288$) (see Table 2.3). Therefore, we find strong support for the overall expectancy model as a way to understand entrepreneurial motivations to start a new venture.

In hypothesis 2, we added the mediating variable—growth—to the structural equation model. Specifically, we hypothesized that nascent entrepreneurs would associate the desired outcomes from the establishment of a new venture with growth expectancies. We tested this hypothesis on the entire (male and female) sample. We found that the fully mediated or hypothesized model did not fit well with the data, however, the partially mediated model, which allowed for a direct relationship from performance to growth, performance to desired outcomes, and growth to desired outcomes, did fit well with the data (see Table 2.4). In addition, in the partially mediated model, many of the specific paths were significant (see Table 2.3). Specifically, we found that like in the original expectancy model, the path between entrepreneurial intensity and the mediating variable—starting a new venture—and the path between expectancy and starting a new venture were significant (path coefficient = 0.093; $p < .000$; path coefficient = 0.110; $p < .000$, respectively). In addition, all of the paths

Table 2.4 Structural equation model results: nested model difference tests

Comparison	χ^2 Difference	Degree of Freedom Difference	Model Preference
Whole sample with growth as mediator			
Partial mediation vs. null	634.70**	24	Partial mediation
Hypothesized full mediation vs. partial mediation	2.58	0	Partial mediation[1]
Men-only sample with growth as mediator			
Partial mediation vs. null	275.22**	24	Partial mediation
Hypothesized full mediation vs. partial mediation	8.56*	2	Partial mediation
Women-only sample with growth as mediator			
Partial mediation vs. null	425.50**	23	Partial mediation
Hypothesized full mediation vs. partial mediation	7.07**	1	Partial mediation

Note:
A significant difference in χ^2 indicates that the more complex model provides a better fit with the data.
[1]Given the lack of degrees of freedom on which to calculate a χ^2, model preference was made based upon fit statistics.
*$p < .05$; **$p < .01$.

between starting a new business and desired outcomes were significant. However, when we examined the paths between starting a business and the mediating variable—growth—we found the path to be not significant (path estimate = 0.032; $p < .141$). This suggests that growth is not necessarily the reason why entrepreneurs start a new venture.

The paths between the mediating variable—starting a new venture—and desired outcomes were all significant when the mediating variable—growth—was introduced into the model (see Table 2.3). However, the paths between the mediating variable—growth—and the reasons to start a new venture were not all significant (see Table 2.3). Specifically, the paths between growth and status and growth and autonomy were not significant (path estimate = 0.650; $p < .101$; path estimate = −0.074; $p < .680$). This suggests that for the whole sample, the desire for status or autonomy is not a reason to grow a new venture. Therefore, while we do not find support for hypothesis 2 in its hypothesized fully mediated form, we do find support for a partially mediated model, which suggests that growth is not necessarily the sole generative mechanism through which the establishment of a new venture is expected to lead to desired outcomes.

In hypothesis 3, we posited that the reasons for the establishment and growth of a new business would vary by sex. To test this, we split the sample by sex and ran separate structural equation models on the men-only and women-only samples. Once again, we found that the hypothesized, fully mediated model did not fit as well with the data as did the partially mediated model (see Table 2.4). In the male-only sample, we found that entrepreneurial intensity and expectancy both led to starting a new venture (see Table 2.3), however, the path between starting a business and growth was not significant (path estimate 0.032; $p < .346$) (see Table 2.3). In addition, similar to the results for hypothesis 2, in the male-only model, we found that all the paths between starting a new venture and desired outcomes were significant, except the path between starting a new venture and roles/status, which was not significant (path estimate = 0.295; $p < .298$) (see Table 2.3). When we examined the relationship between growth and the desired outcomes however, we found very different results. Here, all of the paths between growth and the desired outcomes were not significant except the path between growth and financial success, which was significant (path estimate = 1.328; $p < .004$) (see Table 2.3). This suggests that while nascent entrepreneurs do not necessarily start their new venture for growth reasons, the predominant reason that men want to grow their new ventures is for financial success.

Interestingly, we found different results in the female-only sample. For women, we found significant results between entrepreneurial intensity and starting a new venture and between expectancy and starting a new venture (path estimate = 0.097; $p < .000$; path estimate = 0.138; $p < .000$, respectively), but similar to the men-only sample, there was no significant association between starting a new venture and growth (path estimate = 0.029; $p < .251$) (see Table 2.3). However, when we added growth to the model, we found different relationships between the mediating variables—starting a new venture and growth—and the desired outcomes. Specifically, we found that all paths between starting a new venture and desired outcomes and between growth and the desired outcomes were significant (see Table 2.3). This suggests that women aim at achieving a greater variety of goals through the establishment of a new venture (including status). Further, unlike men for whom financial success was the sole motivator of growth, women want to grow their business based on a need for self-realization, autonomy, and status, in addition to financial success. Therefore, while we do not find support for hypothesis 3 in its hypothesized fully mediated form, we do find support for a partially mediated model, which suggests that new venture creation and expected growth lead to different desired outcomes in men versus women.

Taken together, the results from our hypothesis testing suggest that nascent entrepreneurs expend effort toward the creation of a new venture, because they believe the establishment of a new venture would lead to some desired outcomes. Those desired outcomes, however, are not necessarily associated with the growth expectations of the new venture. Relative to men, women associate a greater number of desired outcomes with the establishment of a new venture and, in addition, they associate a variety of desired outcomes with the expected growth of the new venture (notably, while men associate growth solely with financial success, women associate growth with self-realization, status, and autonomy in addition to financial success). Our findings are discussed next.

Discussion

This study first provides statistical support for the expectancy theory's effort–performance–outcome framework. The expectancy model (hypothesis 1) showed both entrepreneurial intensity and entrepreneurial expectancy are significantly and positively associated with the expectation that the launch of the new venture would lead to desired outcomes. This expectation, in turn, was positively and significantly associated with three of the four desired outcomes we explored, self-realization, financial success, and autonomy. Our findings support previous literature that has demonstrated that entrepreneurs are motivated to start ventures to fulfill a need for personal development (Birley and Westhead 1994; Scheinberg and MacMillan 1988), to achieve financial success (Birley and Westhead 1994; Carter et al. 2003; Scheinberg and MacMillan 1988), and to have autonomy or independence (Birley and Westhead 1994; Scheinberg and MacMillan 1988).

At the same time, roles/status or having approval and recognition in start-ing a venture was not significant. Although previous research has shown that external validation (recognition and status) is an important reason for start-ing a venture, the previous research findings were drawn from international samples where perceptions of entrepreneurship as a career vary somewhat from those in the United States (Birley and Westhead 1994; Scheinberg and MacMillan 1988; Shane et al. 1991). Research by the Global Entrepreneurship Monitor project also reflects cultural differences showing that the U.S. index for perceived favorability of entrepreneurial conditions is higher than that of most countries (Kelley, Singer, and Herrington 2011). Therefore, the outcome of status/recognition may not be perceived as strongly desirable compared to the outcomes of other motivations for this U.S.-based nascent sample. Overall, our results confirm the explanatory power of expectancy theory in examining entrepreneurial start-up motivations.

A second major finding has to do with the inclusion of growth in our model (hypotheses 2 and 3). Our global model (whole sample) including growth is significant overall; however, specific paths in the model are not significant. For example, while nascent entrepreneurs associated the establishment of a new venture with all four specified desired outcomes (self-realization, sta-tus, financial success, and autonomy), there was no significant association between starting a new venture and growth in any of our specifications (the full sample, the men-only sample, or the women-only sample). This suggests that nascent entrepreneurs do not necessarily view achieving a business of a certain size as the generative mechanism that will translate the new business creation effort into certain desired outcomes. Similarly, Wiklund, Davidsson, and Delmar (2003) posit that while the supremacy of the economic motive is often taken for granted, people do start and operate their ventures for a variety of reasons other than growth or maximizing economic returns. This also supports findings from Renko, Kroech, and Bullough (2011), who found that those who were motivated by personal learning and personal growth spent more time on their ventures than those who had only finan-cial motivations. Orser and Hogarth-Scott (2005), in their study of Cana-dian businesses, also found that less than half of the sample intended to seek growth.

The lack of significant association between growth and autonomy, however, is thought-provoking. We speculate that autonomy (or independence) may reflect the desire to engage in, and maintain control over, independent actions. This flows from research that compares managers to entrepreneurs and the likelihood of self-employment (Shane, 2005). Indeed, starting a new venture is significantly and positively associated with the desire for autonomy. However, the link between expected new venture size and autonomy is negative, and fails to reach significance. We speculate that, on the one hand, a new venture that is "too small" may be perceived by the nascent entrepreneur as too precarious and vulnerable to guarantee self-sufficiency and autonomy. On the other hand, it may be that a business "as big as possible" is perceived as too large for an entrepreneur to effectively manage on his or her own, leading to a concern that control may be lost once a certain size threshold is reached. Taken together, these two conflicting tensions may lead to the ambivalent relationship between growth expectations and expected autonomy.

Lastly, we found significant differences between men and women in motivations for starting a new venture and growth. With respect to starting a new venture, men were motivated by self-realization, financial success, and autonomy, while women were motivated by all of the desired outcomes (self-realization, status, financial success, and autonomy). One interpretation for the difference in the significance in status between the two samples is that entrepreneurship is perceived as a "male" domain, for which positive value is perceived (Verheul, Uhlaner, and Thurik 2005). Given previously established relationships between entrepreneurial activity and perception, it may be that women being entrepreneurial (starting a venture) may be a desired outcome of greater perceived value, because it is a task more often associated with masculine behavior (Dickerson and Taylor 2000; Verheul, Uhlaner, and Thurik 2005). In addition, the desire to achieve status through the creation of a business venture among women may be induced by the gender-based horizontal and vertical market segregation, which influences the number and type of labor opportunities for women (Verheul, Uhlaner, and Thurik 2005). When there is disequilibrium between the aspirations of an individual and the perceived valuation of the labor market offerings, he or she is likely to be pushed into pursuing entrepreneurial opportunities (Lee and Venkataraman 2006).

In terms of the motivations for the growth of a new venture, men focused only on financial success, while women were motivated by a complex series of factors such as status/role and self-realization, in addition to financial success. This supports earlier research showing that men have higher salary expectations and that women perceive more barriers to achieving higher salary (Giles and Larmour 2000). In addition, research on women MBAs indicates that they desired more flexible careers, while male MBAs desired money (DeMartino and Barbato 2003). Another possible explanation is Cassar's (2005) finding that the women's sample is more heterogeneous, with some desiring higher growth and others desiring lower growth. In sum, our study offers empirical support to social learning theory's argument that different socialization and social learning experiences shape different approaches to venture creation and different business and growth expectancies among men and women nascent entrepreneurs (Brush 1992; Cliff 1998).

Implications and Conclusions

In this paper, we used the entrepreneurial expectancy theory of motivation to explain the differences between men and women with respect to their motivations in starting and growing a new business. Our findings reveal significant differences based on sex, supporting our contention that motivations for starting and growing a new venture are very different between men and women, and suggesting that a finer-grained analysis is appropriate when looking at start-up behaviors.

As with all empirical research, our study has a number of limitations. In particular, we are relying on survey data, and as a result, our model is not as rigorous as a test of the expectancy framework, including experimental control group, as a pure laboratory setting would provide. However, given that limitation, our entrepreneurial expectancy model draws on structural equation modeling techniques, which permit a holistic examination of all of the variables in the framework. This suggests that while imperfect, our method has attempted to capture all of the variances inherent in the framework, and hence is a better test of expectancy theory than other linear methods.

In addition to our method, our study was constrained by the data available in the PSED data set. For example, our study measured expectations for growth presented in a dichotomous variable. Another weakness is in our measure of starting a new business, which while continuous, is a single-item measure. As with all research using the PSED, our design presents the researcher with the trade-off between unparalleled access to data about a large number of nascent entrepreneurs and the data collection limitations.

Notwithstanding limitations, the inclusion of growth in our model provides an important extension to expectancy theory and to research on women's entrepreneurship. We find significant differences in the motivations to start a business between men and women, which are magnified when growth is considered. Our results support an expectancy lens toward entrepreneurial motivations and call for a finer-grained sex-based perspective. In starting and growing a new venture, an appreciation of the differences based on sex is essential for researchers to understand the cognitive basis for new venture creation.

APPENDIX

Independent Variables

Entrepreneurial Intensity (5-Point Likert Scale)

I would rather own my own business than earn a higher salary employed by someone else.

There is no limit as to how long I would give a maximum effort to establish my business.

My philosophy is to "do whatever it takes" to establish my own business.

Entrepreneurial Expectancy (5-Point Likert Scale)

If I work hard, I can successfully start a business.

My past experience will be very valuable in starting a business.

Overall, my skills and abilities will help me to start a business.

I am confident that I can put in the effort needed to start a business.

Mediating Variables

Performance (5-Point Likert Scale)

If I start a business, it will help me to achieve other important goals in my life.

Growth (Dichotomous Variable)

Which of the following two statements best describes your preference for the future size of this business?

    I want the business to be as large as possible.

    I want a size I can manage myself or with a few key employees.

Dependent Variables

Self-Realization (5-Point Likert Scale)

To what extent is the following reason important to you in establishing this new business?

    to be innovative and in the forefront of technology

    to continue to grow and learn as a person

    to achieve something and get recognition

    to develop an idea for a product

    to fulfill a personal vision

to lead and motivate others

to have the power to greatly influence an organization

Role/Status (5-Point Likert Scale)

To what extent is the following reason important to you in establishing this new business?

to achieve a higher position for myself in society

to continue a family tradition

to be respected by my friends

to follow the example of a person I admire

Financial Success (5-Point Likert Scale)

To what extent is the following reason important to you in establishing this new business?

to give myself, my spouse, and children financial security

to build a business my children can inherit

to earn a larger personal income

to have a chance to build great wealth or a very high income

Autonomy (5-Point Likert Scale)

To what extent is the following reason important to you in establishing this new business?

to have greater flexibility for my personal and family life

to have considerable freedom to adapt my own approach to work

Notes

1. A previous version of this paper was presented at the Academy of Management Conference, Atlanta, GA, 2006.

2. In contrast to the *Handbook of Entrepreneurial Dynamics*, in which the authors specified that their analysis should identify six factors, in this study, we chose to use naturally occurring factors. To do so, we conducted exploratory factor analysis from which we identified four factors, and then confirmatory factor analysis to check the internal validity of those factors.

References

Acs, Z., and D. Evans. (1993). "Entrepreneurship and Small Business Growth: A Case Study." In *Advances in the Study of Entrepreneurship, Innovation and Economic*

Growth: New Learning on Entrepreneurship, edited by G. Libecap. Vol. 6, 143–76. Greenwich, CT: JAI Press.

Ajzen, I. 1987. "Attitudes, Traits, and Actions: Dispositional Prediction of Behavior in Social Psychology." *Advances in Experimental Social Psychology* 20: 1–63.

Ajzen, I. 1991. "The Theory of Planned Behavior." *Organizational Behavior and Human Decision Processes* 50: 179–211.

Anderson, J. C., and D. W. Gerbing. 1988. "Structural Equation Modeling in Practice: A Review and Recommended Two-Step Approach." *Psychological Bulletin* 103: 411–23.

Anna, A., G. Chandler, E. Jansen, and N. Mero. 2000. "Women Business Owners in Traditional and Non-Traditional Industries." *Journal of Business Venturing* 15 (2): 279–303.

Bandura, Albert. 1977. "Self-Efficacy: Toward a Unifying Theory of Behavioral Change." *Psychological Review* 84 (2): 191.

Baron, R. M., and D. A. Kenny. 1986. "The Mediator–Moderator Variable Distinction in Social Psychological Research: Conceptual, Strategic, and Statistical Considerations." *Journal of Personality and Social Psychology* 51: 1173–82.

Birley, S., and P. Westhead. 1994. "A Taxonomy of Business Start-Up Reasons and Their Impact on Firm Growth and Size." *Journal of Business Venturing* 9: 7–31.

Bonjean, C. M. 1966. "Mass, Class, and the Industrial Community: A Comparative Analysis of Managers, Businessmen, and Workers." *American Journal of Sociology* 72 (2): 149–62.

Brush, C. G. 1992. "Research on Women Business Owners: Past Trends, a New Perspective and Future Directions." *Entrepreneurship: Theory and Practice* 16 (4): 5–30.

Brush, C. G., N. Carter, E. Gatewood, P. G. Greene, and M. Hart. 2004. *Clearing the Hurdles: Women Building High-Growth Businesses*. Englewood Cliffs, NJ: Prentice Hall Financial Times.

Brush, C. G., N. Carter, P. G. Greene, M. Hart, and E. Gatewood. 2002. "The Role of Social Capital and Gender in Linking Financial Suppliers and Entrepreneurial Firms: A Framework for Future Research." *Venture Capital Journal* 4 (4): 305–23.

Bussey, K., and A. Bandura. 1999. "Social Cognitive Theory of Gender Development and Differentiation." *Psychological Review* 106: 676–713.

Carsrud, A., and M. Brännback. 2011. "Entrepreneurial Motivations: What Do We Still Need to Know?" *Journal of Small Business Management* 49 (1): 9–26.

Carter, N. M., and Kathleen R. Allen. 1997. "Size Determinants of Women-Owned Businesses: Choice or Barriers to Resources?." *Entrepreneurship & Regional Development* 9 (3): 211–20.

Carter, N. M., and C. G. Brush. 2004. "Gender." In *Handbook of Entrepreneurial Dynamics: The Process of Business Creation*, edited by W. B. Gartner, K. G. Shaver, N. M. Carter, and P. D. Reynolds, 12–25. Thousand Oaks, CA: Sage.

Carter, N. M., W. Gartner, K. Shaver, and E. Gatewood. 2003. "The Career Reasons of Nascent Entrepreneurs." *Journal of Business Venturing* 18 (1): 13–39.

Carter, N. M., W. B. Gartner, Kelly G. Shaver, and Elizabeth J. Gatewood. 2003. "The Career Reasons of Nascent Entrepreneurs." *Journal of Business Venturing* 18 (1): 13–39.

Carter, N. M., M. Williams, and P. D. Reynolds. 1997. "Discontinuance among New Firms in Retail: The Influence of Initial Resources, Strategy, and Gender." *Journal of Business Venturing* 122: 125–45.

Cassar, G. 2005. "Entrepreneur Motivation, Growth Intentions and Preferences." Paper presented at the Babson–Kauffman Entrepreneurship Research Conference, June. Babson College, Wellesley, MA.

Center for Women's Business Research (CWBR). 2009. "The Economic Impact of Women-Owned Businesses in the United States." Available at: http://www.nwbc.gov/sites/default/files/economicimpactstu.pdf.

Chaganti, R., and S. Parasuraman. 1996. "A Study of the Impacts of Gender on Business Performance and Management Patterns in Small Businesses." *Entrepreneurship: Theory and Practice* 21 (1): 73–89.

Chen, C., P. Greene, and A. Crick. 1998. "Does Entrepreneurial Self-Efficacy Distinguish Entrepreneurs from Managers?" *Journal of Business Venturing* 13 (4): 295–316.

Cliff, J. E. 1998. "Does One Size Fit All? Exploring the Relationship between Attitudes towards Growth, Gender, and Business Size." *Journal of Business Venturing* 13 (6): 523–42.

Davidsson, P. 1991. "Continued Entrepreneurship: Ability, Need and Opportunity as Determinants of Small Firm Growth." *Journal of Business Venturing* 4: 211–26.

Davis, A., and K. Shaver. 2012. "Understanding Gendered Variations of Business Growth Intentions across the Life Course." *Entrepreneurship: Theory and Practice* 36 (3): 495–512.

Delmar, F., P. Davidsson, and W. Gartner. 2003. "Arriving at the High-Growth Firm." *Journal of Business Venturing* 18 (2): 189–216.

DeMartino, R., and R. Barbato. 2003. "Differences between Women and Men MBA Entrepreneurs: Exploring Family Flexibility and Wealth Creation as Career Motivators." *Journal of Business Venturing* 18: 815–32.

Dickerson, A., and A. Taylor. 2000. "Self-Limiting Behavior in Women: Self-Esteem and Self-Efficacy as Predictors." *Group and Organization Management* 25 (2): 191–210.

Douglas, E. I., and D. A. Shepherd. 2000. "Entrepreneurship as a Utility Maximizing Response." *Journal of Business Venturing* 15: 231–51.

Fairlie, R. W., and A. M. Robb. 2009. "Gender Differences in Business Performance: Evidence from the Characteristics of Business Owners survey." *Small Business Economics* 33: 375–95.

Fischer, E., R. Reuber, and L. Dyke. 1993. "A Theoretical Overview and Extension of Research on Sex, Gender, and Entrepreneurship." *Journal of Business Venturing* 10 (5): 371–91.

Fishbein, M., and I. Ajzen. 1975. *Belief, Attitude, Intention, and Behavior: An Introduction to Theory and Research*. Reading, MA: Addison-Wesley.

Ford, J. C., R. C. McCallum, and M. Tait. 1986. "The Application of Exploratory Factor Analysis in Applied Psychology: A Critical Review and Analysis." *Personnel Psychology* 39: 291–314.

Gartner, William B., ed. 2004. *Handbook of Entrepreneurial Dynamics: The Process of Business Creation*. Sage.

Gatewood, E. J. 1993. "The Expectancies in Public Sector Venture Assistance." *Entrepreneurship: Theory and Practice* (Winter): 91–95.

Gatewood, E. J. 2004. "Entrepreneurial Expectancies." In *Handbook of Entrepreneurial Dynamics: The Process of Business Creation*, edited by W. B. Gartner, K. G. Shaver, N. M. Carter, and P. D. Reynolds. 153–62. Thousand Oaks, CA: Sage.

Gatewood, E. J., N. Carter, C. Brush, P. Greene, and M. Hart. 2003. *Women Entrepreneurs, Their Ventures, and the Venture Capital Industry: An Annotated Bibliography*. Stockholm: Entrepreneurship and Small Business Research Institute.

Gatewood, E. J., K. J. Shaver, J. B. Powers, and W. B. Gartner. 2002. "Entrepreneurial Expectancy, Task Effort, and Performance." *Entrepreneurship: Theory and Practice* 27 (2): 187–206.

Giles, Melanie, and Sonya Larmour. 2000. "The Theory of Planned Behavior: A Conceptual Framework to View the Career Development of Women." *Journal of Applied Social Psychology* 30 (10): 2137–157.

Gundry, L., and H. Welsch. 2001. "The Ambitious Entrepreneur: High Growth Strategies of Women-Owned Enterprises." *Journal of Business Venturing* 12 (5): 453–70.

Hackett, G., and N. E. Betz. 1981. "A Self-Efficacy Approach to the Career Development of Women." *Journal of Applied Social Psychology* 30: 2137–57.

Human, S., and C. Matthews. 2004. "Future Expectations for the New Business." In *Handbook of Entrepreneurial Dynamics: The Process of Business Creation*, edited by W. B. Gartner, K. G. Shaver, N. M. Carter, and P. D. Reynolds. 386–400. Thousand Oaks, CA: Sage.

Kelley, D., C., Brush, and P. Greene. 2011. "Global Entrepreneurship Monitor 2012 Women's Report." Wellesley, MA: Babson College. Available at: http://www.babson.edu/Academics/centers/blank-center/global-research/gem/Documents/GEM%202012%20Womens%20Report.pdf.

Kelley, D., S. Singer, and M. Herrington. 2011. "Global Entrepreneurship Monitor 2011 Global Report." Wellesley, MA: Babson College. Available at: http://www.gemconsortium.org/docs/download/2409.

Kline, R. B. 1998. *Principles and Practices of Structural Equation Modeling*. New York: The Guildford Press.

Klofsten, M., and D. Jones-Evans. 2000. "Comparing Academic Entrepreneurship in Europe: The Case of Sweden and Ireland." *Small Business Economics* 14 (4): 299–309.

Kourilsky, M. L., and W. B. Walstad. 1998. "Entrepreneurship and Female Youth: Knowledge, Attitudes, Gender Differences, and Educational Practices." *Journal of Business Venturing* 13: 77–88.

Krueger, N. F., M. D. Reilly, and A. L. Carsrud. 2000. "Competing Models of Entrepreneurial Intentions." *Journal of Business Venturing* 15: 411–32.

Lee, J. H., and S. Venkataraman. 2006. "Aspirations, Market Offerings, and the Pursuit of Entrepreneurial Opportunities." *Journal of Business Venturing* 21 (1): 107–24.

Lee-Gosselin, H., and J. Grise. 1990. "Are Women Owner-Managers Challenging Our Definitions of Entrepreneurship? An In-Depth Survey." *Journal of Business Ethics* 9 (4/5): 432–33.

Liao, J., and H. Welsch. 2004. "Entrepreneurial Intensity." In *Handbook of Entrepreneurial Dynamics: The Process of Business Creation*, edited by W. B. Gartner, K. G. Shaver, N. M. Carter, and P. D. Reynolds, 186–95. Thousand Oaks, CA: Sage.

Ljungren, E., and L. Kolvereid. 1996. "New Business Formation: Does Gender Make a Difference?" *Women in Management Review* 11 (4): 3–11.

Macoby, E., and C. Jacklin. 1974. *The Psychology of Sex Differences*. Stanford, CA: Stanford Press.

Matthews, C., and S. Moser. 1996. "A Longitudinal Investigation of Family Background and Gender on Interest in Small Firm Ownership." *Journal of Small Business Management*, 34 (2): 29–43.

Miller, L. E., and J. E. Grush. 1988. Improving Predictions in Expectancy Theory Research: Effects of Personality, Expectancies, and Norms. *Academy of Management Journal* 31 (1): 107–22.

Mitchell, T. R. 1974. "Expectancy Models of Job Satisfaction, Occupational Preference, and Effort: A Theoretical, Methodological, and Empirical Appraisal." *Psychological Bulletin* 81 (12): 1053–77.

Nunnally, J. C., Jr. 1970. *Introduction to Psychological Measurement*. New York: McGraw Hill.

Olson, J. M., N. J. Roese, and M. P. Zanna. 1996. "Expectancies." In *Social Psychology: Handbook of Basic Principles*, edited by E. T. Higgins and A. W. Kuglanski. 211–38. New York: Guilford Press.

Renko, M., K. G. Kroech, and A. Bullough. 2011. "Expectancy Theory and Nascent Entrepreneurship." *Small Business Economics*. Available at: https://datapro.fiu.edu/campusedge/files/articles/kroeckk062712001992.pdf

Renzulli, L., H. Aldrich, and J. Moody. 2000. "Family Matters: Gender, Networks, and Entrepreneurial Outcomes." *Social Forces* 79 (2): 523–46.

Robb, A., and J. Wolken. 2002. "Firm, Owner, and Financing Characteristics: Differences between Female- and Male-Owned Small Businesses." Working paper presented at the University of North Carolina Boot camp on Women and Minority Entrepreneurship Research, August, 2002. Available at: http://www.federalreserve .gov/pubs/oss/oss3/ssbf98/FEDS_robbwolken.pdf.

Schein, E. H. 1978. *Career Dynamics: Matching Individual and Organizational Needs.* Reading, MA: Addison-Wesley.

Scheinberg, S., and I. MacMillan. 1988. "An 11 Country Study of Motivations to Start a Business." In *Frontiers of Entrepreneurship Research,* edited by B. A. Kirchoff, W. A Long, W. E. McMullan, K. H. Vesper, and W. E. Wetzel, Jr. 669–84. Wellesley, MA: Babson College.

Schiller, B., and P. Crewson. 1997. "Entrepreneurial Origins: A Longitudinal Inquiry." *Economic Inquiry* 35 (3): 523–31.

Shane, S. 2005. *A General Theory of Entrepreneurship: The Individual–Opportunity Nexus.* Cheltenham, UK: Edward F. Elgar.

Shane, S., L. Kolveraid, and P. Westhead. 1991. "An Exploratory Examination of the Reasons Leading to New Firm Formation across Country and Gender." *Journal of Business Venturing* 6: 431–46.

Shane, S., E. A. Locke, and C. J. Collins. 2003. "Entrepreneurial Motivation." *Human Resource Management Review* 13 (1): 257–79.

Shapero, A. 1982. "Social Dimensions of Entrepreneurship." In *The Encyclopedia of Entrepreneurship,* edited by C. Kent, D. Sexton, and K. Vesper. 72–90. Englewood Cliffs, IL: Prentice Hall.

Shaver, K. G. 2004. *Cleaning of ERC Data from ISR Web Site.* Available at http://www .wm.edu/psyc/kscleans04.sps.

Shaver, Kelly G., E. J. Gatewood, and W. B. Gartner. 2001. *Differing Expectations: Comparing Nascent Entrepreneurs to Non-Entrepreneurs.* Washington, DC: Academy of Management.

Stewart, W. H., and P. L. Roth. 2001. "Risk Propensity between Entrepreneurs and Managers: A Meta-Analytic Review." *Journal of Applied Psychology* 86 (1): 145–53.

Stewart, W. H., W. E. Watson, J. C. Carland, and J. W. Carland. 1998. "A Proclivity for Entrepreneurship: A Comparison of Entrepreneurs, Small Business Owners, and Corporate Managers." *Journal of Business Venturing* 14 (2): 189–214.

U.S. Small Business Administration (SBA) Office of Advocacy, and U.S. Census Bureau Office of Statistics. 2002. "Firm Data." Available at http://www.sba.gov/advo /research/data.html.

Verheul, I., L. Uhlaner, and R. Thurik. 2005. "Business Accomplishments, Gender, and Entrepreneurial Self-Image." *Journal of Business Venturing* 20: 483–528.

Vroom, V. H. 1964. *Work and Motivation*. New York: Wiley.

Westhead, P., and M. Cowling. 1995. "Employment Change in Independent Owner-Managed High-Technology Firms in Great Britain." *Small Business Economics* 20 (4): 62–71.

Wiklund, J., P. Davidsson, and F. Delmar. 2003. "What Do They Think and Feel about Growth? An Expectancy-Value Approach to Small Business Managers' Attitudes toward Growth." *Entrepreneurship: Theory and Practice* 27 (3): 247–70.

Wiklund, J., and D. Shepherd, D. 2003. "Aspiring for, and Achieving Growth: The Moderating Role of Resources and Opportunities." *Journal of Management Studies* 40 (8): 1919–41.

Wiklund, J., and D. Shepherd. 2005. "Entrepreneurial Orientation and Small Business Performance: A Configurational Approach." *Journal of Business Venturing* 20 (1): 71–91.

Chapter 3

Breaking the Glass Ceiling through Entrepreneurship

Jay M. Finkelman and Louise Kelly

This chapter considers the barriers that women face in traditional organizational environments. This chapter then analyzes their options and describe the increasingly prevalent practice of women moving from organizational management into entrepreneurial leadership roles. While this change is often done reluctantly, it is frequently done successfully.

Unfortunately, this progression, though often an effective solution to discrimination and harassment in the workplace, is not a good business model universally—in part because, the skill sets involved in organizational management do not always overlap with those that ensure entrepreneurial success (Bell, McLaughlin, and Jennifer 2002). However, the increasing success rate of entrepreneurial ventures in general and the slightly negative aspect that women's businesses tend to be "smaller and slower" in growth are two important factors that need to be considered regarding women's transition into specific types of entrepreneurial activity.

We can only speculate as to how much more successful women might have been, had discriminatory practices not precluded their presence in traditional organizational environments. It is probably a tribute to the versatility—perhaps the desperation—of women entrepreneurs that so many of them are able to manage this difficult transition (Weiler and Bernasek 2001, 85). But necessity is the mother of invention, and this has proven to be a surprisingly viable option for many women dissatisfied with their experiences in traditional organizations (Bible and Hill 2007, 69; Boyd 2000).

While some talented women have certainly been successful in traditional organizations, that is not the typical experience (Chernesky 2003). Many high-achieving women in traditional organizations report that they had success despite the obstacles and discrimination that they encountered (Brizendine 2008). Women executives vary dramatically in their tolerance for chauvinistic and otherwise inappropriate behavior in the workplace (Hoobler, Wayne, and Lemmon 2009). From our perspective, those who can "take it" and have learned to play the game are more likely to rise in the traditional organizational hierarchy (Fogliasso and Scales 2011).

Women who are less tolerant of the "game playing" that takes place in many corporate environments or offended by the need to change their demeanor in order to accommodate the "old boys" culture that still prevails in many organizations are more likely to leave (Estrin and Mickiewicz 2011). Some of these women leave demoralized and humiliated, while others leave motivated to be successful in their own right and on their own terms. The latter group of women are the most likely to seek entrepreneurial leadership roles (Carnes and Radojevich-Kelley 2011, 78). Sometimes anger can be an effective incentive to achieve!

Not all women executives are predisposed to an entrepreneurial lifestyle; however, some leave the workplace entirely (Hull 2012). Some make lateral moves in an effort to avoid the unpleasantness of their current situation. Sometimes this strategy works, but often it does not (Reinhold 2005, 47). Instead, it may create a short buffer until the realities of alternative positions become apparent (Stokes and Merrick 2013). Another strategy, in which some women engage, is to downsize the organization in which they work, in the hope of finding a more receptive environment within smaller organizations (McKeown 2011).

Gender Discrimination by Occupation

Some of the patterns of gender discrimination are quite situation-specific, although there usually is a common theme that relates to the perception of the status and place of women in the workplace (O'Neill and Boyle 2011). We will offer a number of examples that we have witnessed to illustrate the patterns across various professions. This will highlight some of the different ways in which overt and covert discrimination against women in the workforce becomes manifest (Bell, McLaughlin, and Jennifer 2002, 72).

Lawyers

In our experience, female attorneys are rarely perceived as not being on the same level as their male colleagues, with respect to legal prowess, either in the courtroom or in the law firm. But they are less likely to be the litigators, judges, and managing partners (Purie 2011). While there is little objective rationale for this, the pattern continues (Fuller and Batchelder 1953, 116). It may be self-correcting, to some degree, as an increasing percentage of women enter law schools (according to a survey by the National Association of Women and the Law of the nation's 200 largest law firms, women make up 47 percent of first- and second-year associates), and thus the legal profession.

It is true that there is a legitimate time lag before new female lawyers are typically permitted to try cases in larger law firms. And the delay before female lawyers are considered for judgeships is considerably longer. We suppose that the same might be said for managing partners of law firms, but other factors appear to be operating there as well, to the detriment of qualified women candidates (Pinto 2009, 11).

In the top echelons of power at certain large law firms, women are recognized for their legal skills and acumen, but not as readily for their management and leadership skills. "Those" responsibilities are best left to men, who, as often thought, are genetically equipped to do the job better! This thinking, though presented only in jest in this chapter, is not unheard of in the profession. One of the this chapter's authors has worked as an expert witness for talented women who have felt the need to change firms—and occasionally departed the profession—in response to this very transparent glass ceiling (Adams and Funk 2012).

In a pattern somewhat similar to the departure of women from large corporate positions, a number of these frustrated attorneys have elected to start their own successful practices, often attracting colleagues and clients to join them. This should not be construed as suggesting those women are incapable of "playing rough" and are engaging in self-serving politics. They can and they do—but seemingly less frequently than men—and with a smaller network of like-minded women to support this unfortunate behavior.

Other female attorneys, who have not yet advanced to the level of senior partnership and eligibility for managing committee membership, report that they are more likely to be used in a clerical capacity, or for functions typically performed by paralegals or legal secretaries. Sometimes the differences are subtle—and difficult to detect from the outside. But the participants sense the difference and it can be demoralizing and humiliating. Very few women confront this perception directly, in part because it is difficult to prove, and in part because it might be a career-ender for those with partnership ambitions (Zipfel and Kleiner 1998, 91).

In a somewhat reciprocal and strangely symbiotic pattern, from the male-dominated power end of the (dysfunctional) law firm senior management, there often appears to be a disconnection between what managing partners know about gender equity and appropriate conduct in the workplace and how they elect to behave as leaders themselves (Zipfel and Kleiner 1998, 89). While their behavior may often be perceived as "merely" chauvinistic, it occasionally rises to a more serious level of misconduct.

While this escalation of the behavior to the level of misconduct is certainly the exception, one of the authors of this chapter was engaged to do executive coaching for two managing partners of different law firms, in the aftermaths of internal sexual harassment investigations. Despite their obvious intelligence, the men were neither particularly receptive to coaching, nor insightful as to what had occurred that triggered the need for such an intervention. While the law firms were pleased with the outcomes, it seemed to be more cosmetic and superficial—intended to mitigate liability rather than effect real attitudinal change.

Police Officers

Women police officers are becoming more common—sometimes this is in response to court-ordered corrective action. "Pioneer" women officers often encountered hazing and harassment from their fellow police and management. They were often perceived as less-worthy colleagues and "dangerous" partners, because they were thought to not be able to hold their own in barroom brawls and similar altercations.

It is true that women, in general, have less upper body strength than men, although the distribution curves do overlap. But that is not the appropriate predictor of the effectiveness of police officers. Today, in most cities, police do not spend a lot of time in physical combat, such as breaking up barroom brawls (Burke and Mikkelsen 2005, 134)! In those rare events, smart police officers call for backup before wading into the melee.

The great equalizer in police work is the firearm. To the chagrin of many male police officers, female police officers are quite adept with weapons—and often outshoot the male police officers!

Anecdotally, women also appear more capable in de-escalating volatile situations, thus obviating the need for force to begin with. They are less likely to engage in macho competition with bad guys (and gals) and more likely to simply finesse the situation, thus contributing to everyone's safety.

Through these and related skills, more women are also advancing to senior management positions within police and sheriffs' departments. Nonetheless, women who are not prepared to deal with some level of testing and teasing probably need not apply. The law is one thing, but practice on the ground may deviate from the pristine ideal. We note this reality with sadness and reluctance.

Firefighters

Women as firefighters face different and more onerous challenges than they do as police officers. There are no equalizers in firefighting, such as firearms for police officers. Women typically need to be able to carry at least 130 pounds of equipment and/or people up a ladder to qualify as firefighters. Size and strength matters less for police officers than it does for firefighters. This may be counterintuitive at first, but it is supported in the literature.

Most men cannot meet the physical requirements for firefighters, but a far higher percentage of women are able to meet those requirements. What may be more ironic is that the need for physical strength and agility diminishes as firefighters escalate through the ranks. Yet, women who do qualify for the entry firefighter position are almost never eligible for promotion to higher ranks.

This discussion is not meant to excuse the unprofessional and boorish behavior that occasionally occurs when strong, qualified women elect to join departments that are almost exclusively staffed by men. While vigilant senior fire department management can do a great deal to ease the transition of women into these "minority" roles and protect them from harassment, they cannot be there all the time to supervise every interaction (Yap and Konrad 2009).

Despite the best of intentions and credible training, violations still occur and female firefighters may suffer taunting and abuse within their own engine companies. One of the authors of this chapter testified for a large municipality in defense of their fire department in which sexual vulgarities were apparently carved on the axe handle of a female firefighter, among other alleged abuses. The defense prevailed at trial but it was rather precarious.

Teachers and Administrators

Women in education and the teaching profession and health care have traditionally fared better than those in many other occupations, and that trend still continues (Weil and Mattis 2003). Michele Nealon-Woods, the national president of a major graduate school with campuses in three states, notes that this apparent success is often at the expense of equitable salary scales, which are notoriously deflated because of the abundance of women in the profession (Weinberger 2011). It is a vicious cycle for women. However, the good news is that educational systems tend to be more progressive than most other organizations, and women have generally fared well and been promoted to senior academic administrative positions (Ragins, Townsend, and Mattis 1998).

The Franchise Option

For most women, the entrepreneurial route, though tempting, is fraught with risk. Professional women are smart enough to perform due diligence before taking such a big step in their lives and their careers. Often, the results of this analysis are sufficient to give women pause before taking steps that might put their savings and earning potential at risk. There is an option that generally reduces the risk for those who can afford it and are willing to share the proceeds of their effort (Coyne, Issacs, and Schwartz 2010, 613). This option is the franchise alternative, which historically has had a much higher success rate than starting new businesses from scratch.

Franchises are not guarantees of success for either gender, but major brand-name franchises seem to enjoy greater returns and more certainty than their smaller and less well-known counterparts. The implication is that successful business women are more likely to have accumulated the capital necessary to secure the most desirable franchises in the better locations—and the staying power to sustain the initial negative cash flow that is inevitable in almost any franchise. Without these resources, slight miscalculations in growth rate or in expenses can prematurely bring down what might otherwise have developed into a successful enterprise. With these resources, women can further increase the odds of success in their favor.

The Entrepreneurial Challenge for Business Women

This issue is often unanticipated, as successful women make the decision to peruse entrepreneurial alternatives to their corporate careers (Ramona, Emanoil, and Andrada 2010). Too often they get used to the many comfortable entrapments associated with their organizational status (Bible and Hill 2007, 73). These expensive amenities, including executive assistants, luxurious offices, and maintained vehicles, are typically absent from most entrepreneurial arrangements, franchise, or otherwise.

For some women, this may simply be a bit of a shock, while for others it may trigger deep feelings of regret that they gave so much up because of political issues or perceived gender discrimination (Williams 2010). Making your own coffee is one thing, but not having calls screened, visitors escorted, travel arrangements made, expenses reimbursed, and copies run may be more than some former executives were prepared to handle. While it may sound petty when presented this way, it can have a cumulative psychological impact that is demoralizing and discouraging to new entrepreneurs who had not always intended to be entrepreneurs.

It is surprising how quickly people get used to—and then expect—high service and deferential behavior from their subordinates. Executives accustomed to staying at the Ritz-Carlton Hotels typically do not take kindly to a Motel 6, or even to a Holiday Inn, despite the complimentary breakfasts. Similarly, executive travelers who have gotten used to business class have a difficult transition flying behind the (coach) curtain!

In Chapter 8 of this volume, Bett Mickels highlights the specific challenges women face when moving from the corporate suite to the entrepreneurial chief. We have seen examples of certified public accountants who got frustrated in being overlooked for promotions and who ended up training the men who were promoted above them and used that anger and gave voice to their values and started their own accounting firms; examples of health care executives who decided that their jobs supervising 3,500 indirect reports were not compatible with raising two kids; and examples of managers of not-for-profit organizations who said, "I know a better way to do this, nobody is listening and so let me start my own agency." In all three examples, the women who chose the entrepreneurial route were very successful—but we also know that with the "smaller and slower" phenomenon, that is not always the case. Frustration can be a motivator, as can be a violation of values that happens with discrimination. As we encourage women to explore the entrepreneurial route, it is also our view that it is necessary to work tirelessly to eradicate the discrimination that often drives women to the entrepreneurial route.

References

Adams, Renée B., and Patricia Funk. 2012. "Beyond the Glass Ceiling: Does Gender Matter?" *Management Science* 58 (2): 219–35..

Bell, Myrtle P., Mary E. McLaughlin, and Sequeira M. Jennifer. 2002. "Discrimination, Harassment, and the Glass Ceiling: Women Executives as Change Agents." *Journal of Business Ethics* 37 (1): 65–76.

Bible, Dana, and Kathy L. Hill. 2007. "Discrimination: Women in Business." *Journal of Organizational Culture, Communications and Conflict* 11 (1): 65–76.

Boyd, Robert L. 2000. "Survivalist Entrepreneurship among Urban Blacks during the Great Depression: A Test of the Disadvantage Theory of Business Enterprise." *Social Science Quarterly* 81 (4): 972–84.

Brizendine, Louann. 2008. "One Reason Women Don't Make It to the C-Suite." *Harvard Business Review* 6: 36.

Burke, Ronald J., and Aslaug Mikkelsen. 2005. "Gender Issues in Policing: Do They Matter?" *Women in Management Review* 20 (1): 133–43.

Carnes, William. J., and Nina Radojevich-Kelley. 2011. "The Effects of the Glass Ceiling on Women in the Workforce: Where Are They and Where Are They Going?" *Review of Management Innovation & Creativity* 4: 70–79.

Chernesky, Roslyn H. 2003. "Examining the Glass Ceiling: Gender Influences on Promotion Decisions." *Administration in Social Work* 27 (2): 13–18.

Coyne, Christopher J., Justin P. Isaacs, and Jeremy T. Schwartz. 2010. "Entrepreneurship and the Taste for Discrimination." *Journal of Evolutionary Economics* 20 (4): 609–27. doi:http://dx.doi.org/10.1007/s00191-009-0164-6.

Estrin, Saul, and Tomasz Mickiewicz. 2011. "Institutions and Female Entrepreneurship." *Small Business Economics* 37 (4): 397–415. doi:http://dx.doi.org/10.1007/s11187-011-9373-0.

Fogliasso, Christine, and Janel Scales. 2011. "Women in Management: Observations and Trends." *Franklin Business & Law Journal* 3: 108–16.

Fuller, Frances M., and Mary B. Batchelder. 1953. "Opportunities for Women at the Administrative Level." *Harvard Business Review* 31 (1): 111–28.

Hoobler, Jenny M., Sandy J. Wayne, and Grace Lemmon. 2009. "Bosses' Perceptions of Family–Work Conflict and Women's Promotability: Glass Ceiling Effects." *Academy of Management Journal* 52 (5): 939–57.

Hull, Janet. 2012. "Women on Boards: Through the Glass Ceiling." *Market Leader* Quarter 1: 50–52.

McKeown, Eileen. 2011. "Top Suite in Corporate America still Eludes Women." *T + D* 65 (1): 18. Available at: http://search.proquest.com/docview/846785817?accountid=34120.

O'Neill, Colleen, and Stacey Boyle. 2011. "Leadership Challenges for Women at Work." *Chief Learning Officer* 10 (6): 76–78.

Pinto, Consuela A. 2009. "Eliminating Barriers to Women's Advancement: Focus on the Performance Evaluation Process." *Perspectives: A Magazine for and about Women Lawyers* 17 (4): 10–14.

Purie, Aroon. 2011. "What Glass Ceiling?" *Business Today* (October 2): 114–17.

Ragins, Belle Rose, Bickley Townsend, and Mary Mattis. 1998. "Gender Gap in the Executive Suite: CEOs and Female Executives Report on Breaking the Glass Ceiling." *The Academy of Management Executive* 12 (1): 28–42.

Ramona, Todericiu, Muscalu Emanoil, and Ghitulete Andrada. 2010. "Breaking the Glass Ceiling: Female Entrepreneurship." *Annals of the University of Oradea, Economic Science Series* 10: 1048–54.

Reinhold, Barbara. 2005. "Smashing Glass Ceilings: Why Women still Find It Tough to Advance to the Executive Suite." *Journal of Organizational Excellence* 24 (3): 43–55.

Stokes, Paul, and Lis Merrick. 2013. "Designing Mentoring Schemes for Organizations." *The Wiley-Blackwell Handbook of the Psychology of Coaching and Mentoring*: 195–216.

Weil, Peter A., and Mary C. Mattis. 2003. "To Shatter the Glass Ceiling in Healthcare Management: Who Supports Affirmative Action and Why?" *Health Services Management Research* 16 (4): 224–33.

Weiler, Stephan, and Alexandra Bernasek. 2001. "Dodging the Glass Ceiling? Networks and the New Wave of Women Entrepreneurs." *The Social Science Journal* 38 (1): 85–103.

Weinberger, Catherine. 2011. "In Search of the Glass Ceiling: Gender and Earnings Growth among U.S. College Graduates in the 1990s." *Industrial and Labor Relations Review* 64: 949–80.

Williams, Matt. 2010. "Do Women Still Face a Glass Ceiling?" *Campaign*: 17.

Yap, Margaret, and Alison M. Konrad. 2009. "Gender and Racial Differentials in Promotions: Is There a Sticky Floor, a Mid-Level Bottleneck, or a Glass Ceiling?" *Industrial Relations* 64 (4): 593–619.

Zipfel, Krista S., and Brian H. Kleiner. 1998. "Developments Concerning Gender Discrimination in the Workplace." *Equal Opportunities International* 17 (3–5): 89–91.

Chapter 4

Exploring a Feminine Leadership Model among Women Entrepreneurs

Jennifer Walinga and Virginia McKendry

Entrepreneurs are leaders—leaders of their own vision, their supporters, and their business. The chapter will explore the management and leadership models that women entrepreneurs are uniquely poised to enact, including networked leadership, community building, ethical and altruistic practices, sustainability, and work–life balance. Women entrepreneurs are unique in that they are both "in the ring" of business leadership and out of it. Women struggling for equality and acknowledgment within a corporate landscape tend to first fight to get into the ring. Women entrepreneurs, on the other hand, define the "ring" in which they conduct their leadership, and as such, have the freedom, power, and opportunity to operationalize a feminine approach to doing business. More than that, women entrepreneurs who deliberately design their organizational culture through a feminine leadership model contribute to the evolution of wider cultural assumptions that underpin the default masculine leadership model of "command and control" that has dominated the social discourse of entrepreneurship and leadership.

Later in this chapter, we present a cultural analysis of the challenges facing feminine leaders and a case for the unique role that feminine entrepreneurs hold in advancing the feminine model of leadership and interaction. We then present a vision for how the feminine leadership model could itself be better leveraged to facilitate a shift in cultural assumptions and beliefs. Leveraging this alternative and equally legitimate leadership model lays the groundwork for its own acceptance at the executive level. A shift in values toward more systematic, integrated, and collaborative ways of seeing social interactions and transactions coupled with institutionalizing measures for evaluating outcomes arising from those values must take place in order to truly allow for feminine models of leadership to take hold. As Minnich (1990) calls for in her seminal work *Transforming Knowledge*, we must not only "liberate our minds" but also "the systems we live within from concepts that rationalize inequality" before we can begin to truly implement a feminine leadership model.

It's a Man's World

Consider this illustration of the gendered context of leadership in which a professional woman seeks to practice feminine leadership values in a masculine organizational culture, in this case, a university. A new professor was tasked with leading and revising a program within her department. She set about arranging consultative meetings across the organization and across her department seeking insight, input, and historical knowledge to inform her revisions. As ideas and directions emerged from the discussions, she presented these ideas at departmental meetings for further feedback, only to be met with defensiveness, attack, and outcry. No matter how she explained or presented topics for discussion, they were perceived to be pronouncements of change and were met with resistance and argumentation rather than the extended thought, reflection, and discussion she sought. At one point, a colleague called her process "complicated." At the same time, she watched a fellow professor who without any consultation walked a program revision through a single meeting with minimal reaction, let alone resistance or argument. He was admired for "keeping it simple" and for his "direct" approach. Several months later, the department's advisory board reviewed the program revisions. The board passed our young female professor's revision smoothly and applauded her for its comprehensiveness. Her colleague's revision, on the other hand, met with concern, negative feedback, and requests for changes.

What stands out for us in this case is that a participatory leadership model that involves collaborative discussion, reflection, and iterative processes tends to take longer and be more complex (not necessarily more complicated) than a more autocratic model of leadership. Ultimately, however, a democratic model has greater potential to produce more integrated, enduring, and satisfactory outcomes. What also becomes clear is that the true leadership challenge for women lies not in establishing which model works best, but rather in overcoming a cultural inability to value a more democratic, inclusive, or participatory model at its outset. The academic setting offers a similar opportunity for women: the female professor is equally poised to advance what is understood culturally as a "feminine" approach to leadership and interaction. Because of her relative freedom to determine her own leadership style, the academic, like the entrepreneur, is "in the ring," possessing freedom, power, and opportunity with equanimity.

Leadership research shows that professional women tend to lead with a participatory style. A meta-analysis of leadership models demonstrated that women leaders are typically more democratic and participative in their approach than men, who lean toward autocratic, command, and control models of leadership or management (Eagly and Johnson 1990). Research on gender and leadership resulted in the construction of a feminine style of leadership. Therefore, the sex and gender identity of the leader emerges as irrelevant in the discussion of management style; in this chapter, we prefer to refer to feminine and masculine leadership models as *styles*, as they are known in the literature (Helgesen 1995, 2012). Helgesen (2012) states in the Human Resources iQ website, that talented and confident women leaders have seven characteristics in common:

1) they place a high value on relationships and judge the success of their organizations based on the quality of relationships within them;

2) they prefer direct communication;

3) they are comfortable with diversity, having been outsiders themselves and knowing what kind of value fresh eyes could bring;

4) they are unwilling (and unable) to compartmentalize their lives and so draw upon personal experience to bring private sphere information and insights to their jobs;

5) they are skeptical of hierarchies and surprisingly disdainful of the perks and privileges that distinguish hierarchical leaders and establish their place in the pecking order;

6) they preferred leading from the center rather than the top and structure their organizations to reflect this; and

7) they ask big-picture questions about the work they do and its value.

Women entrepreneurs offer a productive opportunity to advance this feminine leadership style because they, being women and being acculturated to feminine values and communication styles, have a greater propensity for the feminine approach; and, being entrepreneurs, they have greater access to the freedom, power, and opportunity necessary to practice and therefore exert influence.

The barrier to the widespread acceptance of a participative, feminine leadership model seems to lie in the assumptions that participative leadership is too complicated, time consuming, and ambiguous. The problem lies in our bias against such a leadership model that, though perhaps no better or worse as models go, has the capacity for effective outcomes that should not be ignored or denied. Important to the discussion is the distinction between biology (sex: male and female), identity (gender: man and woman), and socialized perspectives (gendered characteristics or metaphors: masculine and feminine). An inclusive leadership model is not necessarily a female model. The qualities of participation, inclusion, and democracy have been associated with femininity, not only based on gendered stereotyping but also based on distinctly feminine culturally embedded values, beliefs, and assumptions (Coughlin and Thomas 2002; Helgesen 1995).

The leadership issue becomes gendered when we come to realize that, 10 years after Eagly and Johnson's (1990) meta-analysis on gender and leadership styles, the democratic style is rejected only when implemented by a woman; in male-dominated industries, women reported worse mental health when they utilized an interpersonally oriented leadership style, whereas men in male-dominated industries reported better mental health when they utilized such a leadership style (Gardiner and Tiggemann 1999). Women entrepreneurs rarely create businesses that scale up: just 1.8 percent of women-owned businesses crack the $1 million revenue mark, compared with 6.3 percent of men-owned businesses (Coleman and Robb 2012). However new technology is speeding the growth of female-owned firms, making it easier to reach $1 million in revenue or more to be obtained more quickly, so that percentage is changing (Macbride, 2012). Eagly and Karau's role congruity theory (2002) suggests that a bias exists against women in roles incongruent with their gender, causing feminine leadership principles to be only trusted if they are implemented by male leaders. The role incongruity lies in a woman taking on a leadership role, regardless of the leadership style the woman assumes, because leadership is perceived as a distinctly male domain.

More than 10 years have passed since this research was introduced and women still do not share the same opportunities in higher management as men. However, regardless of sex, leaders are considered more competent and efficient and are evaluated more favorably when they adopt stereotypically feminine leadership styles (Cuadrado et al. 2008). Herein lies a twist to the usual gender equity argument—while individual followers may regard the feminine leadership style favorably, predominant values, beliefs, and assumptions underpinning organizational and societal cultures continue to reflect masculine principles of command and control, and value male leaders, in general, more highly. The leadership challenge for women remains a cultural challenge related to gender role expectations. A leader, any leader employing any style, still appears to take the form of a man; however, thinking can change when women speak new values or when women strive to achieve old values in new ways. The security, certainty, and control that typify the masculine style of leadership can be achieved in different ways. The "skin in the game" that venture capitalists seek in an entrepreneurial proposal can be achieved in creative ways that reflect feminine values of inclusion, flexibility, and complexity. For instance, personal assets and collateral can be pledged (rather than time) as a demonstration of commitment.

Embedded in most organizational cultures is the assumption that hierarchism and judgment are fundamental to organizing. Bird and Brush (2002) have found that "the masculine-derived emphasis not only pervades (organizational) definitions and descriptions but also underpins the expected process of new venture creation, generally conceived as sequential, profit maximizing, and strategically and competitively focused," a process that "can be clearly laid out" in which "the entrepreneur searches for and evaluates an opportunity" (p. 42). Much of the research on entrepreneurial qualities was grounded in male samples between the 1970s and 1990s, a period when women's self-employment rates hovered around 6 percent (Ducheneaut 1997), which means that the earliest scholarly discourses around entrepreneurial leaders associated their style with the masculine characteristics and priorities of the research subjects. While it is true that women entrepreneurs are not discriminated against on the basis of their sex and/or gender, the culture of venture capital support demands a gruelling, relentless, and single-minded approach to business, an approach that conflicts with the values of family or community mindedness that many women uphold and strive to balance. Today, the greatest barrier to women may not be the leadership style, or the sex of the person delivering it, but rather the underlying assumptions, beliefs, and values of organizational culture in general.

It is at the level of organizational structure and communication that we see an opening for women entrepreneurs to create corporate cultures that align with their values and responsibilities outside of the workplace. Organizing can occur in different ways. If one drills down to the values fundamental to hierarchism and judgment, it is clear that stability, certainty, and excellence are the underpinning values at play. We propose that these values can be achieved just as effectively through feminine approaches of collaboration, support, and development. Note that we argue neither for one leadership style over the other nor for gender equality in management. Instead, we argue for the need to evolve from the taken-for-granted notions that currently dominate cultural assumptions about entrepreneurship and leadership—a model that assumes one style, mode, approach, or person must be judged as better than another or that business is a battleground as opposed to an ecological system. Until we can move away from a mentality of judgment and a worldview that sees only hierarchies of differential values, where one kind of leader is better than all the others, we may never fully embrace the human and social capacity that lies within a diversity of leadership styles or unique individual leaders. Generally, the last thing we as authors of this chapter want to do is to battle over which leadership model is best.

Instead, women need to employ tolerance, receptivity, dialogue, and equanimity so typical of the feminine participatory leadership model to facilitate an evolution in cultural assumptions and beliefs. Women do not need to fight for the feminine model of leadership; they merely need to live it. To do so, women need to speak and model their feminine values as a means to shifting organizational culture toward a feminine values framework. Energy could be focused on intentionally seeking, planning, and implementing communication strategies and channels for speaking women's values as feminine leaders and entrepreneurs. In living the values, beliefs, and assumptions associated with a feminine leadership and values-based organizational culture creation model, women have the greatest leverage for shifting culture (Schein 1985). While values, beliefs, and assumptions are the foundation of an organizational culture, it is through the communication of these values, beliefs, and assumptions that culture is enacted and built. The communication channels, artifacts, processes, and systems that women utilize to express feminine values offer the greatest amount of influence in their attempt to shift culture and the resulting practices.

Women Entrepreneurs as Game Changers

Women entrepreneurs have operated at the hub of a heretofore male-dominated economy and have more viscerally confronted the masculine cultural norms or "rules of the game." As Penelope Trunk (2010) points out in her blog post, "Women don't want to run startups because they would rather have children," while women entrepreneurs are numerous, venture-backed women entrepreneurs are few. Women typically are not interested in the same "rules of the game" (i.e., long hours and work–life imbalance) associated with and expected by venture backers. Until the rules of the game of entrepreneurship change, women do not want to play. Because they embody the cultural tension that exists between their feminine values and the masculine values of "the ring," they are uniquely poised to inspire the required shift in leadership models as they draw on their lived experiences as women to function as business professionals, venture capital seekers, and creative, game-changing innovators. We believe that women entrepreneurs are perfectly positioned to lead the shift in leadership and business culture.

The cultural change strategy we are proposing here is quite different from a liberal feminist approach that sees getting women into the existing game as paramount to engaging more women in entrepreneurship. The liberal approach focuses on narrowing the economic gap between men and women and is exemplified by how, following a 15-year stint with J.P. Morgan (during which she managed several global businesses for the financial services company), Stephanie Hanbury-Brown launched Golden Seeds, an investment firm that targets companies founded or led by women. Hanbury-Brown stated that she "wanted to support women entrepreneurs with a view of having women at the top of companies from the very beginning, to create a culture for women to get to the top, and for them to have a sustainable career at the top." While her initiative may well create unorthodox capitalization opportunities for women entrepreneurs, her efforts to help women "get into the ring" illustrates how women are assuming that grand game changers must operate within the masculine cultural norms—from, to, and at the top. Here, leadership is still conceived in masculine terms as *taking the reins, taking charge by taking over,* and *taking control,* and what it means to lead connotes values, beliefs, and assumptions grounded in an epistemology of control. Even more, feminine leadership models, such as servant leadership, open-space leadership, facilitative leadership, or participative leadership, are hamstrung by society's expectation of a fundamental need for control or power over, with one person directing others to do something. Women do not want to lead like a man, but they see no alternative.

As innovators, women entrepreneurs can be new kinds of leaders and lead in new ways, because their freedom to design organizational culture positions them as potential game changers. To change the game, women entrepreneurs need to design and build organizational culture utilizing their entrepreneurial role and process as their first channel and opportunity to communicate evolved leadership values. Being a game changer of this scale, a grand game changer requires women entrepreneurs to take on leadership roles. Women may be reluctant to take on leadership roles because being a leader in today's society means playing by the same work–life imbalanced rules of the game that women are trying to change. Women need to define the roles, design the game, and intentionally and strategically live and speak their values throughout. However, change may need to begin with first breaking free of our constrained conceptualization of leadership by envisioning a new kind of leadership, a leadership without reins or control, a new game altogether. We assert that power is necessary for women to lead, innovate, and create in our world. We also believe that power need not be conceived as power "over," but instead as power "to."

Facilitating our human capacity for power "to" is central to—though at this time, not made sufficiently explicit within—feminine leadership models. All women have the power to innovate, create, communicate, lead, change, grow, listen, imagine, support, and design the workplaces in which they will find the meaning and work–life balance they desire. Facilitating or leading within an organization founded on power "to" values is perhaps an even more productive path to optimizing human capacity than power "over." Once a new power "to" form of leadership is conceived, women entrepreneurs will be in a position to enact it. Before taking action, however, women entrepreneurs do need to understand the problem as a cultural one, one that is rooted in faulty conceptualization and one for which the solution lies in values-based communication and organizational culture formation.

The Default Cultural System and the Challenge of Cultural Change

Masculine organizations and organizational codes of leadership do not arise simply because it is men who have historically held leadership positions in those organizations. Indeed, the issue is more complex, because this overvaluing of one leadership style over another is a feature, not a flaw, of modern organizations and of the culture that produces them. The organizational cultures in which women entrepreneurs typically travel are themselves reflections of a system of thought that is associated with imperial values and the values of conquest and power "over" as a quality that signifies authority. The presuppositions of values associated with masculinity (domination, competition, and primacy of the individual) provide the matrix of our laws, philosophical and religious texts, and economic theories. They are found more subtly in common sense notions like "family values" (Lindsey 1994; Ting-Toomey 1999) and in the artifacts of popular and material culture that we consume and with which we interact on a daily basis (Hofstede 1998). If human beings have collectively assented to the normative notion that "might is right," then we are all, to some extent, responsible for perpetuating the myths and ideologies of paternalism through our goals, actions, and communication styles. The good news is that it is also within the power of human beings, and particularly the entrepreneur who is not as beholden to powerful institutional codes and structures, to challenge and reform paternalistic values and leadership styles. In a Darwinian society, imperial values are effective. We argue that the 21st century calls for an evolution of cultural thinking that strives for more elegant and sustainable approaches to leadership and human interaction.

As leaders, women entrepreneurs seeking a different way to envision, value, and organize the human processes of value creation must first understand and frame the key challenge they face. Our knowledge arises out of the concepts we use to make sense of our realities, so it is in our most basic guiding concepts that we can find the basis for the challenges that women (and men) face when they choose to lead through collaborative practice. It is true that *persistent systemic sexism* means that women's gendered bodies invite an even greater distrust and trivialization of collaborative practice than that of men collaborative leaders, but it is a deeper conceptual problem that forms the basis for both this trivialization of women in charge and the perception that collaborative leaders are not true leaders at all. Leadership as it is practiced in hierarchical organizations and politics is itself the product of a root conceptual problem that fuels all systems of domination, such as the Western tradition in which postpatriarchal leaders work and which they seek to transform.

Following Minnich (1990, 25), we argue that the root conceptual problem that practitioners of feminine leadership styles face is that pre- and post-Enlightenment Western knowledge arises out of the internalized and unexamined belief that it is logical and natural to divide humans (and all that is) into "kinds" whose immutable characteristics as a class are already given and determined by some nonhistorical, nonhuman authorities (e.g., Platonic forms, gods, nature). Through imperialism, colonialism, and global business linkages, this concept of humans (and all other beings and things) as irreducible kinds or classes of people has successfully been spread around the world. It is no coincidence that leadership as a concept is problematic for women in management and entrepreneurial positions. It is this root conceptual error of dividing people into sexed kinds and elevating only one of those kinds to normative status that gave rise to a cultural system that privileges a very few economically privileged men who then are taken to be not only the inclusive image of all leaders but also the ideal image of the leader. It is this root conceptual error of dividing all of humanity into hierarchies of differentially valued classes of people that gave rise to conceptual errors that conceal and perpetuate the root problem.

To tease out the conceptual foundations that drive the persistent delegitimation of feminine leadership styles, we draw on Minnich's identification of four logical errors that together create a worldview that allows us to see men as natural leaders, authority as a power "over" relationship, and the heroic leadership style as the only legitimate form of leadership: (1) faulty generalizations and universalization, (2) circular reasoning, (3) mystified concepts, and (4) partial knowledge that serves the dominant order and perpetuates the three previous errors (Minnich 1990, 104). When a masculine, hierarchized management style becomes accepted as the universal mode of governance and leadership, this in turn delegitimates other forms of leadership that have been demonstrated to be more appropriate to various kinds of organizations/groups, purposes, and desired outcomes. We have already mentioned the studies that show

how women who promote a more cooperative and collaborative communication and governance style, eschewing the ruthless competitiveness and short-term quarterly thinking, typically prized as a sign of true leadership, find it difficult to gain acceptance and respect for their leadership style. The repetition of the circular reasoning, which perpetuates this faulty generalization in business scholarship, trade organizations, popular culture, and everyday parlance, reinforces the cultural myth that even highly successful collaborative leadership models are an exception to the rule, even when they are widely practiced and surpass the expectations of masculinized organizations. The mobilization of this partial knowledge not only restricts the potential for equity within organizations but also stifles the creativity and innovation that is a central feature and outcome of collaborative, systems-based leadership models.

Understanding this problem of faulty conceptualization and reasoning gives women in business valuable insight into the reasons for the erroneous valuation of the masculinized heroic leader, whose chief role is autonomous decision making and sure-footed command "over," and as superior to, the collaborative "gardener" leader, whose skills lay in connecting and nourishing a human system. Once the trail of faulty reasoning is identified, it becomes clear why women entrepreneurs and collaborative leaders of both sexes are met with brick walls and lack of faith by investors. To wit, the feminine collaborative leadership style not only flies in the face of the validity of those root presuppositions of Western culture but also threatens to transform the organizational hierarchies of power that derive from and perpetuate those root presuppositions. If the problem lies in root conceptual errors that blind us to the reality of a diversity of leadership styles that work for different people in different situations, then one path to legitimating leadership styles that contradict the dominant model lies with women entrepreneurs who have the freedom to shape the culture of their own companies according to a rather different set of values.

Fostering Cultural Change

Fletcher (2004) notes that what has come to be known as "postheroic" leadership "re-envisions the 'who' and 'where' of leadership by focusing on the need to distribute the tasks and responsibilities of leadership up, down, and across the hierarchy. It re-envisions the 'what' of leadership by articulating leadership as a social process that occurs in and through human interactions, and it articulates the 'how' of leadership by focusing on the more mutual, less hierarchical leadership practices and skills needed to engage collaborative, collective learning." Similar to how Minnich has criticized the faulty conceptual thinking, Fletcher (2004) has noticed how our discourse of leadership has arisen from a false binary of a world made of leaders and followers, and how Western organizational discourse has conflated incorrectly assigned masculine qualities with leadership (also noting how postheroic leadership also is incorrectly gendered as being reflective of "natural" feminine traits). When women enact their postheroic leadership in masculine organizations, they are perceived as enacting their natural mothering skills, such that the perception is that the leader is not innovative and that the leader is expected to do all of the collaborating and knowledge work. Indeed, feminine leadership is in some ways an oxymoron within these interwoven discourses of gendered bodies and gendered practices. Fletcher warns that the "female advantage" that women leaders appear to have is not necessarily an advantage in the typical sense. Earning a berth in the organizational leadership realm for the feminine leadership style is not the outcome women seek. This strategy simply replaces one style for another within a larger gendered context. If this is the case, then what is to be done in this labyrinth of gendered subjects navigating gendered organizations that are themselves reflective and productive of an overall hierarchically gendered cultural system? We must address the gendered context.

By enacting feminine leadership, women entrepreneurs unsettle the gendered context that prescribes the "who, what, where, and when" of leadership. The shift to a postheroic leadership model not only leads to better business outcomes and overall work satisfaction but the very fact of women's postheroic entrepreneurship also contributes to the transformation of the presuppositions and language we draw on to think and speak about leadership and entrepreneurial endeavor. Like the "mystified concepts" Minnich refers to, the very enactment of postheroic leadership also does things to women, their reasoning, and the culture as a whole; only in this instance, women are alert to and cognizant of the effects they are aiming to materialize. On a cultural level, women entrepreneurs who are living their feminine values are reversing the damage of the presence of mystified concepts (e.g., leadership) that have not been as nourishing to themselves and to their businesses as they had been taught to expect. Though this decision to do things differently requires surrendering to complexity and the unknown, it teaches them. In turn, they teach others the wisdom of eschewing the myth of management as control and, instead, trusting the much more collaborative and open-ended process of taking time to visit with one another, telling each other's stories, asking for ideas and thoughts, listening to one another, and retelling new stories that integrate all those pieces in the form of an organization-authored strategy and operational protocols. The energy released can be immense and sustained, once people at the top and bottom of an organization see the singularity and unique contribution of each member as assets that contribute to the health of the organization.

In order to facilitate a cultural shift in the face of centuries of social and organizational communication practice that has led to these perceptions, it is important for women entrepreneurs to identify, articulate, and model the core values, beliefs, and assumptions one is attempting to communicate. Fletcher (2004) asserts the importance of acknowledging, recognizing, and naming the radical nature of the postheroic challenge as the first step in this process:

> This analysis suggests that to truly capture the transformational promise of post heroic leadership would require theoretical framings that acknowledge, recognize, and name the radical nature of its challenge and the gender and power dynamics inherent in it (e.g., Fletcher and Kaeufer 2003). This would mean acknowledging and further theorizing the way post heroic leadership challenges current power dynamics, the way it threatens the myth of individual achievement and related beliefs about meritocracy, the way it highlights the collaborative subtext of life that we have all been taught to ignore, and the way it engages displays of one's gender identity. Without such an explicit recognition, I suggest that the transformational potential of this new model of leadership is unlikely to be realized. (p. 650)

Indeed, naming the challenge helps us better understand the threat postheroism poses, and reveals what values are at stake. Postheroic or feminine leadership threatens most people's—especially, those who believe in the default cultural system—faith in individual heroics and achievement, which is unsettling for them because it shakes them and forces them to acknowledge their fundamental insecurity, uncertainty, and lack of control—something women and other marginalized groups have become quite good at doing, in fact.

By naming the challenge, women frame the challenge more precisely and productively. Women acknowledge that they neither have control and nor should they strive for power over anything or anyone; it is unsustainable and destructive to exert control over anything. However, they do have power "to"—the power to communicate, express, create, collaborate, inquire, and understand. In a masculine culture, the focus is on gaining control, thus causing control to become the goal rather than sustainability or some form of true innovation. Women entrepreneurs are perfectly positioned to both frame and confront the challenge that our troubled world system is posing because they are accustomed to facing these kinds of barriers. Also, they are now entering the world of business and innovation wielding completely different tools—tools of tolerance, collaboration, flexibility, and an ability to look beyond the lack of control.

The real advantage of the feminine leadership style is leveraged when women entrepreneurs employ feminine values to sustainably build culture—not lead or direct, but build. Culture is built by enacting values, beliefs, and assumptions, and it is circulated and reaffirmed through communication (Carey 1989). The first step is to identify the core values women wish to enact. The second step is to design a communication plan outlining the specific channels, processes, systems, and mechanisms they will utilize in order to communicate the values, beliefs, and assumptions they have defined. This attention to value articulation and communication processes allows them to effectively deal with the challenges postheroic leadership poses, which we are framing here as the requirement to learn how to have confidence and power without control and to develop the skills that are most important amid uncertainty. Of course, navigating uncertainty and lack of control demands core values, systems thinking, sustainable practice, integration, and collaboration, all of these gendered as feminine traits and skills that women have learned because of just such a lack of power.

For women entrepreneurs, the power to design their own organization offers just such a channel for building a new feminine culture, a forum in which women can speak and live their values, and a credible and powerful endeavor with which to impact social culture. Women entrepreneurs have the unique opportunity and capacity to lead the world into an evolved conceptualization of leadership and, with it, a new form of entrepreneurism grounded in feminine values and designed for more sustainable and truly social innovation. When women entrepreneurs create a culture of power "to," they will be able to thrive as entrepreneurs and game changers within a new environment of balance, creativity, innovation, and growth. Women entrepreneurs who enter the ring by living and communicating their feminine, postheroic values are themselves agents of cultural change and diversity, expanding the rules of the game overall and legitimizing alternative ways to shape sustainable careers for themselves, other entrepreneurs, and the employees who thrive within their organizations. Only the oppressed can free their oppressors (Freire 1993).

References

Bird, B., and C. Brush. 2002. "A Gendered Perspective on Organizational Creation." *Entrepreneurship Theory and Practice* 26 (3): 41–65.

Carey, J. 1989. *Communication as Culture*. New York and London: Routledge.

Coleman, S., and A. M. Robb. 2012. *A Rising Tide: Financing Strategies for Women-Owned Firms*. Stanford, CA: Stanford Economics and Finance (An Imprint of Stanford University Press).

Coughlin, J. H., and A. R. Thomas. 2002. *The Rise of Women Entrepreneurs: People, Processes, and Global Trends*. Westport, CT: Quorum Books.

Cuadrado, I., J. F. Morales, P. Recio, and V. N. Howard, trans. 2008. "Women's Access to Managerial Positions: An Experimental Study of Leadership Styles and Gender." *The Spanish Journal of Psychology* 11 (1): 55–65.

Ducheneaut, B. 1997. "Women Entrepreneurs in SMEs." Report prepared for the Organisation for Economic Co-Operation and Development (OECD) Conference on "Women Entrepreneurs in Small and Medium Enterprises: A Major Force for Innovation and Job Creation." Paris: OECD.

Eagly, A. H., and B. T. Johnson. 1990. "Gender and Leadership Style: A Meta-Analysis." *Psychological Bulletin* 108 (2): 233–56.

Eagly, A. H., and S. J. Karau. 2002. "Role Congruity Theory of Prejudice toward Female Leaders." *Psychological Review* 109 (3): 573–98.

Fletcher, J. K. 2004. "The Paradox of Postheroic Leadership: An Essay on Gender, Power, and Transformational Change." *The Leadership Quarterly* 15 (5): 647–61.

Fletcher, J. K., and K. Kaeufer. 2003. "Shared Leadership: Paradox and Possibility." In *Shared Leadership: Reframing the Hows and Whys of Leadership*, edited by C. Pearce and J. Conger, 21–47. Thousand Oaks, CA: Sage.

Freire, Paulo. 1993. *Pedagogy of the Oppressed*. New York: Continuum Books.

Gardiner, Maria, and M. Tiggemann. 1999. "Gender Differences in Leadership Style, Job Stress and Mental Health in Male- and Female-Dominated Industries." *Journal of Occupational and Organizational Psychology* 72 (3): 301–15.

Helgesen, S. 1995. *The Female Advantage: The Ways of Women Leaders*. New York: Doubleday Currency.

Helgesen, S. 2012. "7 Characteristics of Women Leaders," October 25. Available at: http://www.humanresourcesiq.com/business-strategies/articles/7-characteristics-of-women-leaders/.

Hofstede, G. 1998. *Masculinity and Femininity: The Taboo Dimension of National Culture*. Thousand Oaks, CA: Sage.

Lindsey, L. L. 1994. *Gender Roles: A Sociological Perspective*. 2nd ed. Englewood Cliffs, NJ: Prentice Hall.

Macbride, Elizabeth. 2012. "Women Entrepreneurs Smash an Old Barrier. New Technology Speeds the Growth of Female-Owned Firms, Making It Easier to Reach One Million in Revenue or More." *Crain's New York Business*.

Minnich, E. K. 1990. *Transforming Knowledge*. 2nd ed. Philadelphia: Temple University Press.

Schein, E. 1985. *Organizational Culture and Leadership*. San Francisco: Jossey-Bass.

Ting-Toomey, S. 1999. *Communication across Cultures*. New York: The Guilford Press.

Trunk, P. 2010. "Women Don't Want to Do Start-Ups. They Want Children," *Penelope Trunk* (blog), October 9. Available at: http://blog.penelopetrunk.com/2010/10/09/women-dont-want-to-do-startups-they-want-children/.

Chapter 5

Career Transitions in Marketing: From Corporate Life to Self-Employment

Clare Brindley, Carley Foster,
and Dan Wheatley

Marketing is a recently feminized industry, yet there is little knowledge about female careers in the profession, and the extent to which they reflect the nonlinear career paths of other women and are constrained by the complex demands of work life and family life. Drawing on an analysis of the UK Labour Force Survey (LFS) (Office for National Statistics 2008), in this chapter we attempt to update and extend the knowledge of women's careers in marketing, in particular, when and how women's employment changes. Despite the large number of women employed in marketing, female marketers are in the minority in senior marketing posts. Furthermore, women's careers in marketing are not homogeneous or linear, as indicated by a proportion of older women in self-employment who are more likely to have dependents, work less hours, and from home than employed women. It is proposed that self-employment offers the opportunity to achieve a better balance between domestic and work spheres, while responding to career constraints imposed on them by organizations; although it may not necessarily signify career progression for the individual involved. Self-employment appears to be a midcareer transition phase for women marketers.

Motherhood appears to be the key stimuli to this marketing career transition stage. The self-employed marketing career is a different career enactment from that of women marketers who are employed. However, self-employment is not a homogeneous career path. The research found two distinct cohorts of self-employed women: academically qualified women in managerial roles working longer than the average workweek and unqualified women who work shorter hours.

Introduction

There is much evidence that highlights the phenomenon of women and the glass ceiling (e.g., Broadbridge 2008) and the lack of women on corporate boards (e.g., Sealy, Vinnicombe, and Doldor 2009). However, there has been little work that has focused on a particular sector and that has tried to unpick the career path of women engaged in it to illustrate the nonlinear career paths of women. The aim of this chapter is to update and extend the knowledge of women's careers in one particular sector—that is, marketing—and to identify the timing and nature of transition stages in these women's marketing careers. A closer examination of women's careers shows that the industry women work in can disadvantage their career development, particularly those sectors which are dominated by men (Kusku et al. 2007; Lu and Sexton 2010). Recent data suggest that women are disadvantaged in their marketing careers. It is estimated, for example, that the gender pay gap for female marketing directors in the United Kingdom is £15,100 and £7,600 for female marketing managers. In 2012 male marketing directors earned £80,733 on average and women £74,241. So, the gap appears to be closing: in 2011, women earned £7,800 below the average salary but now the difference is £3,558 (Hemsley and Hoolahan 2012). Therefore there is a need for empirical work which aids our understanding of the careers of women working in marketing, particularly as research in marketing has a tendency to explore gender issues from the consumer's point of view rather than those "doing" the marketing work (Beetles and Harris 2005; Maclaren and Catterall 2000).

The aim of this chapter is to explore the broad career patterns of women working in marketing, and in doing so updates and extends existing knowledge. The LFS (Office for National Statistics 2008) was selected because it is the only current UK data set that reliably details the employment and career patterns of a large group of women working across different marketing occupations. The focus of the study is thus on the marketing profession, rather than adopting a sectoral focus, for example, marketing in financial services. The researchers' interest has been to investigate the timing and nature of transition periods in the marketing women's careers and the extent to which their career patterns are complex, patchworked, or frayed, as has been found to be the case in other industries and occupations (Mainiero and Sullivan 2005). In this chapter, we utilized data from the UK LFS (Office for National Statistics 2008) to illustrate the career trajectories of women marketers, using the following variables: employed/self-employed, full-time/part-time, total usual hours worked per week, qualifications, age, and number of dependent children.

Marketing as a Career

Debates continue about whether marketing is an art or a science but certainly it is now an integral management function of manufacturing, service, and third-sector organizations. Marketing has become increasingly professionalized, with those working in marketing gaining qualifications and thus entry into marketing professional bodies, such as the Chartered Institute of Marketing. Large proportions of professional qualifications are provided to women (Chapman, Conlon, and Muller 2008). Marketing encompasses a range of occupational roles as illustrated by the LFS data. These roles range from management positions, public relations, to telemarketing and market research positions. It is an external-facing function, charged with ensuring competitive advantage (CIM 2009) and is an attractive degree option for UK female undergraduates (HESA 2008). Indeed, as women hold the majority of jobs in the industry, it is a feminized industry. By *feminized* it is meant that more women than men are employed in the industry, and it is a term used by a range of researchers who refer to the employment patterns of a sector rather than the extent to which female traits are prevalent in the industry (Bradley and Healy 2008; Broadbridge 2008; Maclaren and Catterall 2000).

Women and Their Careers

Research suggests that women's career paths are different from men in that they do not conform to a hierarchical career trajectory. Traditionally, the term *career* has been used to describe long-term progression, a ladder, or linear promotion, within an occupation, or through a series of occupations involving increasing levels of responsibility at each stage (Evetts 2000). Women's careers thus have been described as multidirectional (Baruch 2004), or frayed (Peel and Inkson 2004, 544). Reasons for this have been explained by women's continued dual or even triple roles, as employees, mothers, and care providers (Hardill 2002; Perrons et al. 2005). The demands of balancing all these roles often coincide with transition periods in their careers.

Thus, masculine hierarchical career models fail to acknowledge the reality of balancing home and work demands (White 1995). Alternative models have been developed, such as the boundaryless career model, where paid and unpaid work, lateral and horizontal movements, and self-employment are recognized (Arthur, Khapova, and Wilderom 2005; Peel and Inkson 2004). Similarly, the development of patchwork or kaleidoscope career models have attempted to capture the complexity of female experiences of work, including the career transitions women may experience (Bateson 1990). These contemporary career models (Arthur 2008, 168) move away from the notion of a hierarchical career trajectory by highlighting how, for example, "women shift the pattern of their careers by rotating different aspects of their lives to arrange their roles and relationships in new ways" (Mainiero and Sullivan 2005, 111).

These models describe the turbulence inherent in women's careers, and it is not surprising to find career anchors that provide the individual with a sense of security and the opportunity to draw on her or his experience and knowledge of the industry (Peel and Inkson 2004; Schein 1978). Studies of women's careers have also highlighted how female career choices and success are influenced by their professional occupation (Crompton and Lyonette 2011), and this provides another rationale for focusing on the marketing profession.

In the seminal paper by Savage in 1988, he argues that an individual may utilize one of the three career strategies: (1) *organizational strategy* in which the individual pursues his or her career by moving upward through the structure of an individual (often large) organization; (2) *entrepreneurial strategy* in which a self-employed individual aims to become a small, and possibly large employer of labor; or (3) *occupational strategy* in which an individual continually invests in skills-based (usually occupation-specific) assets, often gaining experience via different employers. Labor market, household changes, and demographics have resulted in new career strategies, often transactional in nature and exemplified by change. Ackers (1998) and Fenwick (2006) describe a *portfolio career strategy* as individuals move between strategies, organizations, and even employment sectors at different times in their careers as other factors influence their career development. A *kaleidoscope strategy* is where an individual adopts a holistic approach, weighing up competing demands of home and work to achieve the best balance (Mainiero and Sullivan 2006). Increasingly, women are adopting an *entrepreneurial strategy* (Corden and Eardley 1999, 209).

So what does this mean for the careers of marketing women? A feminized industry does not mean that women achieve the majority of senior positions. Indeed, if one looks at the UK FTSE 100 index in 2008, there were only 17 female executive directors across a range of functions (Sealy and Singh 2010). This issue is compounded when one looks at marketing as a profession, as marketers are often overlooked for executive director positions, regardless of gender (Bennett 2009).

Like other women, women marketers often adopt an entrepreneurial career strategy as they seek greater flexibility and a better balance between work and home responsibilities (Drew 1998). As Anderson, Vinnicombe, and Singh

(2010) found, when studying women who had left senior roles within international management consultancy firms, flexibility and the desire to avoid high-pressure long-hour cultures were key to women's career decisions. However, there has been little work since the seminal research of Maclaren and Catterall (2000) that has specifically focused on women marketers. If one combines organizational structures and the conflict between work and home roles, as illustrated by Krider and Ross (1997) among women working in public relations, and the prevailing masculine culture (Broadbridge 2008), then the experience of women marketers needs unpicking. The strategies marketing women adopt during their career and the career trajectories they experience at different stages in their life are little understood. Subsequently, there is a lack of understanding of the feminization of the marketing profession and of the careers of women in this sector.

Empirical Evidence

Sources of Data

The UK LFS has been collected on a quarterly basis since 1992. The fourth-quarter 2008 LFS is used in the analysis presented in this chapter. The LFS provides a large cross-sectional sample of approximately 120,000 individuals suitable for investigating minority groups, such as women working in marketing occupations. Panel data such as that collected in the British Household Panel Survey (BHPS) could be argued as offering the potential to provide a more robust analysis. However, the BHPS comprises a significantly smaller sample size. The LFS also contains a panel element comprising five consecutive quarters, but this sample is again considerably smaller and therefore unsuitable for the analysis of minority groups, such as women marketers. In addition, the LFS provides a broad range of variables essential to researching patterns of work and occupation. The LFS is conducted through one-to-one interviews with telephone follow-ups. The first part of the survey collects data on household characteristics. The second part focuses on economic activity, and international definitions of employment, unemployment, and economic inactivity are used. The LFS gathers data on number of working hours, demographics, education, and job roles for those aged 16 and above in the household. The LFS data that are analyzed in this chapter focus on age, education, number of dependents, hours worked, and job roles of women employed in marketing. The analysis is presented firstly in descriptive form before the presentation of an exploratory two-step cluster analysis, and the subsequent statistical modeling uses logistic regression.

Descriptive Statistics

The fourth-quarter 2008 LFS provides a sample of some 1,849 women working in marketing occupations. Meanwhile, 1,315 men were similarly reported
working in marketing. In the UK Standard Occupational Classification (SOC)
systems' major occupation groupings, marketing women appear in SOC 1,
SOC 2, SOC 3, SOC 4, and SOC 7 roles (see Table 5.1). By analyzing the
LFS sample, we found that across all occupations, 7.9 percent of women report
being self-employed. In comparison, within the United Kingdom, some 18.3
percent of men are self-employed. Similarly, among all service sector occupations, some 7.7 percent of women report being self-employed, compared with
15.2 percent of men.[1] Comparatively, fewer women in marketing (and associated occupations)—approximately 5.5 percent—report self-employment.

Looking at the sample of women employed in marketing, there is a significant age difference between those who are employed and those who are
self-employed. The average age of the self-employed women is 46.1 years, compared to 39.5 years for the employed women.[2] Interestingly, these figures also
show that the marketing industry has a relatively younger workforce. Exploring
other demographics, no distinct differences are found in ethnicity, as around

Table 5.1 Breakdown of marketing occupations by gender (LFS 2008)

Occupation (marketing only)	Male (%)	n	Female (%)	n
Marketing and sales managers	50.7	667	15.5	286
Advertising and public relations Managers	3.7	49	2.6	48
Designer (advertising)	1.0	131	2.8	52
Buyer (advertising)	5.1	67	2.6	48
Marketing associate professionals	6.5	86	7.8	144
Filing and records assistants (marketing)	4.6	60	12.6	233
Market research interviewers	1.1	15	1.0	19
General office assistants (marketing)	18.3	240	55.1	1,019
Total	100.0	1,315	100.0	1,849

Source: UK Labour Force Survey, October–December 2008.

Note: x^2 tests confirm that the patterns observed in the proportions of men and women
by marketing occupation group are statistically significant (p value .000), and as such are
representative of the wider population.

5.5 percent of Caucasian women in marketing are self-employed, and similarly around 5.1 percent of non-Caucasian women. However, self-employed women, as well as being older than the average, also report greater household responsibilities and are likely to have more dependent children, both younger children under 16 (0.57 for employed, but 0.66 for self-employed), and young and older children under 19 (0.67 for employed, but 0.73 for self-employed).[3]

Reflecting on working patterns, in comparison with employed workers in the United Kingdom, total usual hours of work are longer among self-employed men, but shorter among self-employed women. Self-employed men report working, on average 43.0 hours per week, compared with 41.0 hours among the employed. Meanwhile, self-employed women report much shorter hours of 29.7 hours per week. In comparison, employed women report working 31.5 hours per week.[4] Within the marketing sector, total usual hours are reported as 33.0 hours per week among employed women, but just 26.7 hours per week among the self-employed following the broader trend among all occupation groups. Average hours among individual occupations are presented in Table 5.2.

The patterns in hours are led by the greater proportion of self-employed women working part-time equivalent hours (58.8%), compared with 34.3 percent of employed women working in marketing, and 52.0 percent of self-employed women across all occupations.[5] Furthermore, there is a significant difference in reported working hours between managerial and professional workers and associate professional and administrative and secretarial workers.

Table 5.2 Total usual hours among employed/self-employed women in marketing (Office for National Statistics 2008)

	Female		
Occupation (marketing only)	Employed	Self-Employed	n
Marketing and sales managers	41.1	32.5	286
Advertising and public relations managers	43.0	39.3	48
Designer (advertising)	32.1	35.7	52
Buyer (advertising)	38.5	50.0	48
Marketing associate professionals	34.2	22.8	144
Filing and records assistants (marketing)	31.8	19.7	233
Market research interviewers	17.1	39.0	19
General office assistants (marketing)	30.5	19.8	1,019
Total	33.0	26.7	1,849

Source: UK Labour Force Survey, October–December 2008.

Note: An ANOVA test confirms that the differences in hours are statistically significant $(F = 139.675, p$ value .000).

Managerial and professional workers report longer than average working hours, and the latter shorter hours. The number of women in the marketing industry working shorter hours may reflect the desire for flexibility and could be associated with the relative age of self-employed women working in marketing occupations. In addition, this result is indicative of the greater household responsibility women who are mothers often experience, and is a further feature of the sample of self-employed women in marketing from the LFS.

Place of work as reported by self-employed women marketers could reflect the need for financial prudence at start-up and/or reflect flexibility needs (Savage 1988). *Home working* could mean the home itself or within the grounds of the home. Of those employed as marketers, 11.8 percent mainly work from home, compared to 70.5 percent of self-employed women who mainly work from home. Both figures are above those reported nationally for all occupations.[6] Among the self-employed in the United Kingdom, 64.3 percent of women mainly work from home. In comparison, among those employed, just 4.0 percent of women mainly work from home.[7]

Qualification levels of self-employed women marketers appear at either end of a continuum. On average, self-employed women marketers are more highly qualified than their employed counterparts (38.2% of self-employed women in marketing occupations have degree/degree-equivalent qualifications compared with just 23.6% of employed women). Self-employed women marketers are also more highly qualified than the other self-employed women, 30.0 percent of whom reported a degree or equivalent in 2008. However, there is a marked division between those with degree level or equivalent qualifications (38.2%), and those with no qualifications (8.9%).[8] Those who have no qualifications is a relatively small group, this figure is almost double that of employed women working in marketing occupations (4.9%), and is marginally higher than the UK average for all self-employed women (7.1%). This qualification split is indicative of the range of roles self-employed women engage in and the marketing career paths they choose. While some women engage in managerial and professional occupations, including advertising designers and buyers, others work in associated marketing occupations including market research interviewing.

The descriptive statistics reported here support the findings already reported in the literature that the glass ceiling (Marshall 1989), industry experience/ qualifications, and work–life balance (Krider and Ross 1997) are having an apparent impact on women's careers in marketing. This is particularly evident in the move of highly qualified marketing women, who have reached a certain age, to self-employment. A decision was therefore made to further explore the data relating to self-employed women in marketing.

Comparisons between Self-Employed and Employed Women Marketers

In order to provide additional statistical evidence of patterns in self-employment among women in marketing, statistical modeling was performed in two stages: first using cluster analysis and then followed by a logistic regression model, informed by the results of the cluster modeling. A two-step cluster analysis was chosen. This technique is appropriate as an exploratory analysis tool as it automatically groups individuals based on their shared characteristics, allowing relationships to be observed that may have otherwise been difficult to observe. The two-step cluster analysis, using data from the LFS, produces six groups, or clusters, of individuals based on their occupation, individual, and household characteristics. The results of the cluster modeling are provided in Table 5.3.

The model clearly identifies self-employed women working in marketing occupations as they all fall into a single cluster, cluster 2. Interestingly, members of this cluster mainly work from home or use home as a base (91.1%), and the majority of women in this cluster work part-time (57.6%). These findings correspond with those of the descriptive analysis. Members of cluster 2 also report the second highest proportion of degree or equivalent qualifications (31.0%), although a number of women in this cluster have no qualifications (6.5%). This may reflect the spread of occupation groups found in this cluster, split between managerial (32.7%), associate professional and technical (16.9%), and administrative and secretarial (50.2%). Members of cluster 2 are also older, on average, than those in other clusters (45.0 years old), and are likely to have dependent children under 16, although those in cluster 5 are likely to have the highest number of dependent children under 16 (0.9 on average). The remaining clusters, automatically generated by the characteristics of those within, represent "young and educated" (cluster 1) women marketers who are the least likely to have dependent children, predominantly have degree-level education, and are the youngest cluster. Cluster 4 is comprised of a fairly even split of managerial and professional women marketers. Cluster 3 and cluster 5 are comprised of those women who are employed part-time. Those in cluster 3 report higher education levels on average, while those in the latter group are all in administrative/secretarial roles. Finally, younger women in administrative marketing roles, who are also less likely to have dependent children, are found in cluster 6.

The cluster analysis provides an exploratory, intermediate stage of analysis. This cluster analysis has confirmed a number of findings that were demonstrated in the descriptive analysis. Subsequent analysis is performed using a binary logistic regression model. The model uses the dependent dichotomous variable, "whether employed or self-employed," where self-employed = 1, and employed = 0. The

Table 5.3 Characteristic profile of clusters (Office for National Statistics 2008)

Two-Step Cluster Analysis

	Mean (continuous variables)		Percentage (categorical variables)		Highest Qualification						Major Occupation Group			
	No. Dep. Child. Under 16	Age	Self-Employed	Employed	Degree or Equivalent	Higher Education	GCSE A-Level or Equivalent	No Qualification	Part-Time	Work at Home	Manager	Assoc. Professor/ Technician	Admin. and Secretary	n
Cluster 1: young and educated	0.3	33.1	0.0	17.5	100.0	0.0	0.0	0.0	0.0	0.0	37.0	26.0	37.0	303
Cluster 2: self-employed	0.7	45.0	100.0	8.4	31.0	10.5	52.0	6.5	57.6	91.1	32.7	16.9	50.4	248
Cluster 3: part-timers	0.7	43.3	0.0	16.4	25.7	46.8	0.0	27.5	54.2	0.0	14.8	14.4	70.8	284
Cluster 4: Man./profs.	0.6	37.3	0.0	10.3	0.0	0.0	100.0	0.0	19.0	0.0	54.7	45.3	0.0	179
Cluster 5: P/T admin.	0.9	43.8	0.0	18.8	0.0	0.0	100.0	0.0	100.0	0.0	0.0	0.0	100.0	326
Cluster 6: young admin.	0.4	37.8	0.0	26.6	0.0	0.0	100.0	0.0	0.0	0.0	0.0	0.0	100.0	496
Combined	0.6	39.9	100.0	100.0	24.7	8.7	61.5	5.1	35.8	12.3	18.1	13.3	68.6	1836
p value	.000	.000	.000			.000			.000	.000			.000	

Source: UK Labour Force Survey, October–December 2008.

Notes:

p values for continuous variables are results of ANOVA tests. For categorical variables, the p values are results of x^2 tests. The reduction in sample size to 1,836 reflects the exclusion of nonresponses to questions.

regression analysis provides a statistically robust method for testing associations between this dependent variable and a range of independent variables, extending the more exploratory cluster analysis. The independent variables are consistent with those used in the cluster analysis and comprise a range of occupation, individual, and household characteristics. Ethnic group was not included in the regression modeling as it is a statistically insignificant variable. In addition, while the LFS provides excellent data on various aspects of working patterns, wages, and earnings, responses are problematic, especially for self-employed individuals, thus the data are not sufficiently robust to facilitate the investigation here. The parameter estimates (B) from the regression analysis are summarized in Table 5.4.

The model indicates that self-employed women working in marketing occupations are on average less likely to be working full-time equivalent hours (30 or more hours per week), and are more likely to work mainly from home. It is mainly those in managerial and professional occupations, including designer (advertising) and advertising and public relations managers that appear in this category. However, within this average, there are obvious significant clusters, in particular, some self-employed women are more likely to work long hours, over 48 hours per week. This heterogeneity is reflective of the descriptive analysis. Long hours may reflect the needs for start-up or growth businesses, while flexibility may be the reason for shorter hours. Obviously, long hours and flexibility may not be mutually exclusive, but the data indicate that there are differences in the hours worked.

Both the descriptive analysis and the regression results indicate a division in qualification levels of self-employed female marketers. They are either graduates or have no qualifications. This reflects the division between those who are freelancers/self-employed professionals (highly skilled) and those who work from home in lower-skilled marketing-associated occupations. Self-employed women are also likely to be older (although the coefficient suggests a weak relationship), and are more likely to have dependent children (although this variable is statistically insignificant).

The results of the descriptive analysis and two-stage statistical modeling indicate that self-employed women marketers fall into two categories: those that are highly qualified (and/or experienced), who report long working hours and identify themselves as working in professional/managerial roles, and those women who have no qualifications, work part-time equivalent hours, and have significant household responsibilities including caring for dependent children. Of course, it is also true that a number of women may fall somewhere in the blurred middle ground between these two groups and be pursuing a career, but become self-employed for the added flexibility perhaps because of caring responsibilities. Equally, gaining experience and contacts in the industry may be essential before self-employment is perceived as a potential route of employment. This again may be reflected in the average age of self-employed women in these marketing occupations.

Table 5.4 Logistic regression model: employed/self-employed women in marketing occupations (Office for National Statistics 2008)

	Binary Logistic Regression Model		
	Dependent: Employed/Self-Employed		
	Parameter Estimates		
	β	SE	Wald
Constant	−5.061***	0.456	123.151
Full-time	−0.587***	0.213	7.568
Mainly work from home	2.593***	0.179	210.443
Usually work over 48 hours in main job	0.447**	0.227	3.888
Minor occupation group: reference is marketing office assistants			
Marketing and sales managers	−0.016	0.260	0.004
Advertising and public relations managers	0.617	0.501	1.516
Designer (advertising)	2.565***	0.283	82.189
Buyer (advertising)	0.360	0.575	0.393
Marketing associate professionals	0.887***	0.308	8.297
Filing and records assistants (marketing)	−0.098	0.415	0.056
Market research interviewers	−2.681**	1.053	6.479
Highest qualification: reference is degree or equivalent			
GCSE, A level, or equivalent	−0.401**	0.175	5.234
No qualifications	0.356	0.339	1.103
Number of dependent children under 16	0.059	0.094	0.404
Age	0.038***	0.008	24.401

Source: UK Labour Force Survey, October–December 2008.

Notes:

Model diagnostics: $n = 1813$, p value = 0.000, R^2 equivalents of 16.1 (Cox and Snell R^2) and 39.0 (Nagelkerke R^2).

***, **, and * refer to p values less than 1 percent, 5 percent, and 10 percent, respectively.
Abbreviations: GCSE, General Certificate of Secondary Education; SE, standard error.

Findings

Since Maclaren and Catterall's (2000) seminal work, there has been little empirical research conducted, which explores the careers of women in marketing. Our analysis has updated and developed Maclaren and Catterall's (2000) research, providing a detailed insight into the employment of women in the marketing sector, and has concluded that the marketing industry remains feminized and reflects important gender roles. It should be noted that during the research, consideration was given to the use of the terms *women* and *female* and the connotations derived from their usage. The term *women* was used for those individuals who identified themselves as biologically female.

The LFS analysis concluded that a number of women in marketing adopt an entrepreneurial career strategy, often reflecting a career/life stage. A higher number of employed and self-employed women have qualifications, particularly in senior roles, which reflect the increasing professionalization of the marketing sector. Despite the feminization of the marketing profession, fewer women than men work in senior marketing roles (Chartered Institute of Marketing 2010). Continuing gender norms, burdening women with the majority of household labor, only exacerbate difficulties for women attempting to break the glass ceiling within corporate marketing, possibly acting as a driver for movements into self-employment. The analysis indicates that within marketing it is older women (often in their 40s), with dependent children, that are appearing in the self-employed category. The data, however, are unable to explain why women move into self-employment.

Tentative suggestions can be made in terms of the rationale driving movements into self-employment from employment, such as flexibility requirements, the impact of the glass ceiling, and the need for autonomy at work. Further research is required to explore the opportunities and challenges that attract women to become self-employed in the marketing sector. Questions remain over movements between career strategies, the factors influencing career decisions, and the permanence of movements into self-employment.

As Maclaren and Catterall (2000) argued, knowledge of women working in professions like medicine, teaching, and banking is evident, yet the experience of women working in marketing is largely anecdotal. This research enables women, educators, and professional bodies to explore their own experiences, advices, curriculum outputs, and the value of marketing qualifications to career paths. Moreover, little is currently known in relation to how the career aspirations of female marketers are reached or moderated over time. This has potential ramifications in terms of the higher education marketing curriculum and the embedding of small and medium enterprise marketing into qualifications. Although marketing remains a feminized sector, the lack of women in senior roles raises a number of challenges for the industry. Feminized industries generally report lower income levels than male-dominated industries (Adams, Hall, and Schäfer 2008). This lower income level is compounded when the lack of women marketing directors is also taken into account. Those starting out on their careers need to be informed of the inherent issues in the sector that they may have little control over, such as expectations in terms of motherhood that can impact upon their career trajectories (Gatrell 2011; Maclaren and Catterall 2000). Moreover, the dominance of large organizations within the marketing curriculum means that women's experience of self-employment in the sector is not readily available to those wishing to start a marketing career. The prevalent discourse is marketing is masculine and change is unlikely until there is a more balanced gender profile of those holding senior marketing roles (Beetles and Harris 2005; Maclaren and Catterall 2000).

Conclusions

This study finds that despite the presence of highly qualified women in the industry, fewer women than men continue to work in senior marketing roles. Furthermore, women's careers in marketing are not homogenous or linear as indicated by a proportion of older women in self-employment who are more likely to have dependents, work less hours, and from home than employed women. This move into self-employment, it is argued, represents a mid-career transition phase, which while offering a way of managing home/work demands and responding to career constraints imposed on them by orga-nizations, may not necessarily signify career progression for the individual involved.

The timing of the career transition stage from being employed in marketing to becoming a self-employed marketer appears to occur at the same time as these women become mothers. For these self-employed women, their market-ing career is enacted in a different way from those women who are employees. However, self-employment in marketing is not a homogeneous categorization, and marketing careers can thus be seen as complex. Self-employed women marketers can be split into two groups: those who have graduate-level qualifi-cations and who work for long hours in professional roles and those who have no qualifications, working in associate roles.

It is acknowledged that there are limitations in only presenting a quantita-tive analysis of the employment picture of women who work in marketing. However, the analysis of the LFS has gone someway to answer the criticism identified by Maclaren and Catterall (2000) that we know little about the women who work in marketing, by providing a macro-level update of wom-en's marketing careers. Our key findings have shown that compared to other sectors, marketing has a younger workforce and remains a feminized indus-try, but with a lack of women in senior marketing roles. In similarity with other professions, women's marketing careers are impacted by the competing demands of domestic and work lives. While the numbers of women and men working as advertising and PR managers are comparable, other senior mar-keting roles continue to be dominated by men with more women in assistant marketing roles. This finding reflects the lack of women in senior positions more generally, particularly at board level (Sealy, Vinnicombe, and Doldor 2009).

As our analysis has illustrated, women appear to experience a mid-career transition phase where they leave corporate marketing roles. Staying as marketers while moving from employment to self-employment may represent a "career anchor" or the "stitching," which holds these women's patchwork careers together (Peel and Inkson 2004; Schein 1978).

While these women may continue to use their professional qualifications, the professional bodies do not appear to offer specific engagement with these women at this particular career stage. Those women moving to self-employment are therefore again largely unsupported by the profession they are part of. Furthermore, it is posited that career guidance to graduates does not specifically address the portfolio nature of careers especially for women.

This snapshot of marketing careers in the United Kingdom will hopefully act as a catalyst for further studies that draw on international data on women's marketing careers. The topic would also benefit from interdisciplinary research that utilizes theories from the marketing, entrepreneurship, gender, economic, and career disciplines. The findings would be enhanced by a qualitative phase that explores why and how women move from a corporate marketing career to self-employment but remain as marketers. This would provide further data on the career trajectories of women marketers and how competing responsibilities can impact upon the entrepreneurial process and the career trajectories of female marketers. By adopting macroanalyses of the marketing profession, rather than at the sector or organizational level, this chapter contributes to Arthur's (2008) call for career research which moves away from a microview. The macroview of the profession, taken from the analysis of the LFS (Office for National Statistics 2009), shows that marketing is a feminized and professionalized industry, but this has not necessarily led to the feminization of power (Bruegel 2000). An earlier review of marketing careers by Maclaren and Catterall (2000) concluded the same; the analysis in this chapter shows that little has changed a decade later.

Notes

1. x^2 tests confirm that the patterns observed in the proportions of men and women, reporting being either employed or self-employed nationally (p value 0.000), and in the service sector (p value 0.000), are statistically significant, and as such are representative of the wider population.

2. An ANOVA test confirms that the differences in age are statistically significant ($F = 10.285$, p value 0.000).

3. ANOVA tests confirm the statistical significance between groups for number of dependent children under 16 ($F = 9.487$, p value 0.000) and under 19 ($F = 8.370$, p value 0.000).

4. An ANOVA test confirms that the differences in hours among all occupations ($F = 299.283$, p value 0.000) and among individual occupations ($F = 41.781$, p value 0.000) are statistically significant.

5. x^2 tests confirm that the patterns observed between part-time and full-time employed (p value 0.000) and self-employed (p value 0.012) women employed in marketing occupations are statistically significant, and as such are representative of the wider population.

6. x^2 tests confirm that the patterns observed in the location of work among employed (p value 0.000) and self-employed (p value 0.000) women in marketing occupations are statistically significant, and as such are representative of the wider population.

7. Ibid.

8. x^2 tests confirm that the patterns observed in qualification levels among employed (p value 0.000) and self-employed (p value 0.019) women are statistically significant, and as such are representative of the wider population.

References

Ackers, L. 1998. *Shifting Spaces: Women, Citizenship and Migration within the European Union.* Bristol: Policy Press.

Adams, L., P. Hall, and S. Schäfer. 2008. "Equal Pay Reviews Survey 2008." Manchester: Equality and Human Rights Commission. Available at: http://www.equality humanrights.com/uploaded_files/research/2_equal_pay_reviews_survey_2008. pdf.

Anderson, D., S. Vinnicombe, and V. Singh. 2010. "Women Partners Leaving the Firm: Choice, What Choice?" *Gender in Management: An International Journal* 25 (3): 170–83.

Arthur, M. 2008. "Examining Contemporary Careers: A Call for Interdisciplinary Inquiry." *Human Relations* 61 (2): 163–86.

Arthur, M. B., S. N. Khapova, and C. Wilderom. 2005. "Career Success in a Boundaryless Career World." *Journal of Organizational Behavior* 26: 177–202.

Baruch, Y. 2004. "Transforming Careers: From Linear to Multidirectional Career Paths—Organizational and Individual Perspectives." *Career Development International* 9 (1): 58–73.

Bateson, M. 1990. *Composing a Life.* New York: Grove Press.

Beetles, Andrea C., and Lloyd C. Harris. 2005. "Consumer Attitudes towards Female Nudity in Advertising: An Empirical Study." *Marketing Theory* 5 (4): 397–432.

Bennett, R. 2009. "Reaching the Board: Factors Facilitating the Progression of Marketing Executives to Senior Positions in British Companies." *British Journal of Management* 20: 30–54.

Bradley, H., and G. Healy. 2008. *Ethnicity and Gender at Work: Inequalities, Careers and Employment Relations.* Basingstoke: Palgrave Macmillan.

Broadbridge, A. 2008. "Senior Careers in Retailing: An Exploration of Male and Female Executives' Career Facilitators and Barriers." *Gender in Management* 23 (1): 11–35.

Bruegel, I. 2000. "No More Jobs for the Boys? Gender and Class in the Restructuring of the British Economy." *Capital & Class* 71: 79–101.

Chapman, J., G. Conlon, and P. Muller. 2008. "An Economic Impact Assessment of the CCPMO." Final report to the Consultative Committee for Professional Management Organisations. Available at: http://www.cipd.co.uk/binaries/economic_im pact_assessment_ccpmo_report.pdf.

Chartered Institute of Marketing (CIM). 2009. "The Future for Marketing Capability." Maidenhead: CIM. Available at: http://www.mbsportal.bl.uk/taster/subjareas /marketing/cim/133362futuremarketingcapability11.pdf.

Chartered Institute of Marketing (CIM). 2010. "Women in Marketing". Available at: http://www.cim.co.uk/Files/cim-women-in-marketing.pdf.

Corden, A., and T. Eardley. 1999. "Sexing the Enterprise: Gender, Work, and Resource Allocation in Self-Employed Households." In *Gender, Power and the Household*, edited by L. McKie, S. Bowlby, and S. Gregory. 207–25. Basingstoke: MacMillan.

Crompton, R., and C. Lyonette. 2011. "Women's Career Success and Work–Life Adaptations in the Accountancy and Medical Professions in Britain." *Gender, Work & Organization* 18 (2): 231–54.

Drew, E. 1998. "Changing Family Forms and the Allocation of Caring." In *Women, Work and the Family in Europe*, edited by E. Drew, R. Emerek, and E. Mahon. 27–35. London: Routledge.

Evetts, J. 2000. "Analysing Change in Women's Careers: Culture, Structure and Action Dimensions." *Gender, Work & Organization* 7 (1): 57–67.

Fenwick, T. J. 2006. "Contradictions in Portfolio Careers: Work Design and Client Relations." *Career Development International* 11 (1): 65–79.

Gatrell, C. 2011. "Managing the Maternal Body: A Comprehensive Review and Transdisciplinary Analysis." *International Journal of Management Reviews* 13 (1): 97–112.

Hardill, I. 2002. *Gender, Migration and the Dual Career Household*. International Studies of Women and Place series. London: Routledge.

Hemsley, Steve, and Roy Hoolahan. 2012. "The Marketing Week/Ball & Hoolahan salary survey 2012." Available at: http://www.marketingweek.co.uk/analysis/essen tial-reads/the-marketing-week/ball-and-hoolahan-salary-survey-2012/3033165. article.

Higher Education Statistics Agency (HESA). 2008. Available at: http://www.hesa. ac.uk/index.php?option=com_content&task=view&id=1897&Itemid=239. Accessed January 21, 2011.

Krider, D., and P. Ross. 1997. "The Experiences of Women in a Public Relations Firm: A Phenomenological Explication." *Journal of Business Communication* 34 (4): 437–55.

Küskü, Fatma, Mustafa Özbilgin, and Lerzan Özkale. 2007. "Against the Tide: Gendered Prejudice and Disadvantage in Engineering." *Gender, Work & Organization* 14 (2): 109–29.

Lu, Shu-Ling, and Martin Sexton. 2010. "Career Journeys and Turning Points of Senior Female Managers in Small Construction Firms." *Construction Management and Economics* 28 (2): 125–39.

Maclaren, P., and M. Catterall. 2000. "Bridging the Knowledge Divide: Issues on the Feminisation of Marketing Practice." *Journal of Marketing Management* 16 (6): 635–46.

Mainiero, L., and S. Sullivan. 2005. "Kaleidoscope Careers: An Alternate Explanation for the 'opt-out' revolution." *Academy of Management Executive* 19 (1): 106–23.

Marshall, Judi. 1989. "13 Re-visioning Career Concepts: A Feminist Invitation." *Handbook of career theory*: 275.

Office for National Statistics Social and Vital Statistics Division, and Northern Ireland Statistics and Research Agency Central Survey Unit. 2008. *Quarterly Labour Force Survey, 2008* [computer file]. Colchester, Essex: UK Data Archive [distributor]. doi: http://dx.doi.org/10.5255/UKDA-SN-6484-1. Available at: http://www.esds.ac.uk/doc/6484/mrdoc/UKDA/UKDA_Study_6484_Information.htm.

Peel, S., and K. Inkson. 2004. "Contracting and Careers: Choosing between Self and Organizational Employment." *Career Development International* 9 (6): 542–58.

Perrons, D., C. Fagan, L. McDowell, K. Ray, and K. Ward. 2005. "Work, Life and Time in the New Economy." *Time and Society* 14 (1): 51–64.

Savage, M. 1988. "Missing Link? The Relationship between Spatial Mobility and Social Mobility." *The British Journal of Sociology* 39 (4): 554–77.

Schein, E. 1978. *Career Dynamics: Matching Individual and Organizational Needs.* London: Addison-Wesley.

Sealy, R., and V. Singh. 2010. "The Importance of Role Models and the Demographic Context for Senior Women's Work Identity." *International Journal of Management Reviews* 12 (3): 284–300.

Sealy, R., S. Vinnicombe, and E. Doldor. 2009. "Female FTSE Index and Report 2009." Cranfield, UK: International Centre for Women Leaders, Cranfield School of Management. Available at: http://www.som.cranfield.ac.uk/som/dinamic-content/research/documents/FemaleFTSEReport2010.pdf.

White, B. 1995. "The Career Development of Successful Women." *Women in Management Review* 10 (3): 4–15.

Chapter 6

The Unique Management Skills of Women Entrepreneurs

Christine Janssen-Selvadurai

Over the past 20 years, women in the United States have been leaving corporate America in droves not only because they seek work–life balance but also largely for the simple reasons that they want independence and a meaningful, rewarding career (Heffernan 2007). They find the work environments of large organizations unfulfilling, boring, lacking potential, suppressive, and sometimes downright hostile (Kossek, Markel, and McHugh 2003; Moore, Moore, and Moore 2011; Orhan and Scott 2001). Frankly, they are tired of having their ideas and management styles marginalized, and they aspire to have more control over their lives (Heffernan 2006). They want to manage their lives, businesses, and careers their own way rather than being treated as inferior to men and their aggressive management styles (Heffernan 2007; Hytti 2010).

In the new millennium, women have actually been launching twice the number of businesses as men, with comparable success rates (Moore 2010; Moore and Buttner 1997; Moore, Moore, and Moore 2011). Recent statistics from the "2012 State of Women-Owned Businesses Report" prepared by American Express OPEN and *Womenable* reveal that there are more than 8.3 million women-owned businesses in the United States today. They employ approximately 7.7 million people and bring in revenues of over $1.3 trillion. Granted not all women business owners can be categorized as women entrepreneurs per se, but these figures illustrate the impact of women on business and the economy (Goldman 1994). They must be doing something right.

Of importance are the unique management skills and styles of women entrepreneurs because the way they manage business and people is often considered unorthodox, yet quite influential. Here we take a brief look at the perceptions of women's management styles, what is particularly noteworthy about women entrepreneurs, where their strengths and weaknesses lie, and what this all means for business moving forward.

Soft Skills versus Hard Skills

Historically, women have displayed feminine management styles, using such techniques as nurturing others and trying to gain consensus. On the other hand, some have tried traditionally masculine styles, using highly focused, aggressive "my way or the highway" tactics to fit in and adhere to traditional workplace norms (Griffin 2001). Esther Wachs Book, author of *Why the Best Man for the Job Is a Woman: The Unique Female Qualities of Leadership* (2001), claims that we are starting to see a more blended approach to management that is neither male dominated, nor female dominated; it is a bit of a hybrid. The good news is that soft management skills are finally being recognized as valid traits that play an important role in business, and this is particularly relevant for entrepreneurs.

As stated in Rochelle Sharpe's *Bloomberg Business Week* article entitled "As Leaders, Women Rule" (2000), "female managers' strengths have long been undervalued, and their contributions in the workplace have gone largely unnoticed and unrewarded." In addition, there have been skewed perceptions that women lack the necessary competencies and skill set to launch and build a business (Ahl 2002; Hytti 2010). This is a gross misunderstanding as we are now in the midst of a generation of women who are not only highly educated and have substantial professional experience but are also highly motivated and fully capable of running their own businesses (Brush et al. 2004). Above all, their experiences from a female perspective are influencing them to manage their businesses in different, nontraditional (i.e., nonmasculine) ways (Janssen-Selvadurai 2010).

Women's management styles and skills have long been referred to as the *soft skills* in business, and it is the men who possess the *hard skills* or the real know-how to manage businesses (Griffin 2001). These so-called soft skills tend to be either innate behaviors or skills learned on the job and they are linked to emotional intelligence and relational skills. Examples include human relations, organizing and planning, and communications. Hard skills tend to be teachable skills that are learned in a traditional classroom format or from a textbook. Such skills are more technical in nature and have more to do with intellect than emotions, that is, financial analysis and planning, strategy development, and technical analysis (Sharpe 2000).

Clearly, men and women can possess both masculine and feminine traits, but their individual strengths naturally rise to the surface. For example, men tend to be more strategic thinkers, good at negotiating, assertive/aggressive, dominant, individualistic, and profit oriented (Sharpe 2000). Women, on the other hand, possess strong communication and organizational skills, plus they are nurturing, compassionate, fair, and detail oriented (Davis and Long 1999). They are more concerned about what is best for the greater team or their customers, rather than feeding their own egos (Janssen-Selvadurai 2010). That said, more masculine traits such as leadership, conflict resolution, and negotiating are vital to all entrepreneurs in a competitive marketplace, but men and women simply have different ways of approaching these roles that affect how they make decisions and how they manage people.

Desire and drive aside, women entrepreneurs face unique challenges including stereotyping (Moore, Moore, and Moore 2011; Vongalis-Macrow and Gallant 2010), which can prompt their career choices and long-term career intentions. A topical study on gender and management styles revealed that women managers are perceived to be intuitive, grateful, sympathetic, understanding, modest, and aware of the feelings of others, whereas the perceptions of their male counterparts are decisive, assertive, hiding emotion, dominant, and comfortable about being aggressive (Ryan et al. 2011). Women often feel that they have to work harder than men to prove themselves to their clients, vendors, suppliers, and investors so they are taken seriously in business (Ashcraft 1998; Davis and Long 1999; Hytti 2010; Moore, Moore, and Moore 2011). And because most of the people in their value chain are likely to be men, women can find themselves at an immediate disadvantage (Buttner 1993). Unfortunately, the glass ceiling is alive and well.

Additionally, studies from 20 to 30 years ago disclosed that many women avoided certain career path choices, such as entrepreneurship, because their perceptions were that being an entrepreneur is a masculine, risk-laden endeavor (Heilman 1983). The image of an entrepreneur is *still* that of a man (Ahl 2002; Marlow 2002), and entrepreneurship is *still* considered a masculine career (Bosma et al. 2009; Hytti 2010; Gupta and Bhawe 2007); however, the number of women entrepreneurs has dramatically increased since the 1980s. Women today are less fearful of taking the road less traveled and are highly motivated to do so (Hytti 2010; Patterson and Mavin 2009). Currently, nearly one-third of all businesses in the United States are owned by women, according to American Express OPEN (Collins-Williams 2011), which signals the substantial—and continuing—growth of women entrepreneurs.

Women Entrepreneurs—Coming of Age

Managers across the board are expected to perform specific functions, such as planning, decision-making, organizing, staffing, communicating, motivating, leading, and controlling (Kreitner 2008). Women often tackle these roles and responsibilities differently than men, but women entrepreneurs take it up a notch because they are not only managers, they are also the face of a business that equates to greater responsibility and accountability. What is interesting is that their personal value systems are shaping the values they establish for their companies, and this in turn drives their management strategies (Chaganti 1986).

As women launch, manage, and build their organizations with a feminine touch, many of their personality traits and management skills are actually proving to be a competitive advantage for them. How so? Because building a business that fosters teamwork, integrity, and a people-centric strategy is precisely what employees, partners, vendors, and customers are looking for (Moore, Moore, and Moore 2011). For instance, consumers have high expectations and standards with respect to customer service and personalization, whereas employees demand greater work–life balance, flexibility, autonomy, empowerment, and meaningful work. Because of these exceptional people skills, women entrepreneurs are particularly gifted with respect to the following management skills:

- Communications
- Multitasking
- Networking and relationship management
- Collaboration
- Compassion
- Transformational leadership

Communications

Without question, all types of communication skills are needed in business. While the basics—public speaking, writing, and listening—are still immensely important, the expansion of technology has opened up more communication channels and thus required skills. Regardless of the vehicle, managers who listen to their employees and customers, who willfully share company details (i.e., financials, strategic plans, decision-making, staff changes), and who are outstanding writers and speakers are typically more respected and valued by peers and employees. Often overlooked as inconsequential or common sense, solid communication skills in the workplace—especially to/from managers—set the tone and culture of an organization and can be an underlying differentiator between companies that are successful and desirable to work at versus those that are not.

All too often, managers withhold information from their teams, which can hinder productivity and build distrust amongst people. Women entrepreneurs are more likely to keep everyone looped in and ask for input and ideas along the way. They encourage two-way communication versus a top-down dictatorship, they place a high value on openly communicating with others for clarity and understanding, and they are also open to hearing what others have to contribute to the conversation because they know that diversity of thought fuels creativity. Employees in turn tend to feel more appreciated and valued when they are included and listened to, which can impact productivity and loyalty (Moore, Moore, and Moore 2011).

Women also care about the details. Whether in an e-mail, on an invitation, in a blog posting, or marketing materials, they are articulate and thoughtfully choose their words, because they know that their reputation is strongly linked to their professional image, so they are certain to cross all t's and dot all i's. Irrespective of the channel or parties involved, women are approachable, understanding, and compassionate managers, who encourage open and honest communication. As a matter of fact, they often err on the side of overcommunicating. There are always exceptions to the rule, but women are probably better communicators because at the simplest level, they care about other people (Janssen-Selvadurai 2010).

Multitasking

When it comes to organizing, planning, and controlling, women entrepreneurs have a unique combination of strong entrepreneurial personality traits, organization skills, and common sense. They are masters at multitasking. From a management perspective, this is critical for entrepreneurs to manage their hectic lives and schedules—personally and professionally. It is no surprise that women are the ones who keep everyone and everything running smoothly, and because they have a keen eye for foreseeing future obligations and objectives, they plan accordingly to ensure the job gets done on time and according to high standards. How else would they be able to be a company's founder, marketer, PR specialist, bookkeeper, financial planner, sales representative, relationship manager, and fund raiser all at once (while also managing a household)?

In addition to having multiple roles and responsibilities, women entrepreneurs more often than not have several identities, especially, if they also have a family (Hisrich and Brush 1983). Indeed, they wear many hats. Sometimes one at a time. Sometimes all at once. And some women seem to constantly interchange identities depending on the task or situation at hand, resulting in a haberdashery with a high-speed revolving door (Janssen-Selvadurai 2010).

Networking and Relationship Management

Starting a business can be both isolating and overwhelming, and it only takes a short time to realize that entrepreneurship is not a solo effort. Professional relationships are critical in helping entrepreneurs build, launch, manage, and grow a business. Such relationships typically consist of former or current business contacts, peers, mentors, and role models, as well as clients, employees, and sometimes family members. These are the people who provide access, connections, guidance, leads, encouragement, financial assistance, resources, inspiration, validation, feedback, and reality checks (Janssen-Selvadurai 2010).

Women are credited as nurturing beings who depend on a variety of relationships for mutual support and growth, and this is evident in their professional as well as their personal lives. Recent research on women entrepreneurs in New York City (Janssen-Selvadurai 2010) has found that many women strongly believe they would have never gotten their businesses off the ground without dependable relationships and support systems. Relationships are not an optional part of their entrepreneurial journey, they are a necessity, and women are very good at cultivating new relationships while nurturing existing ones. Significant others and other women (especially fellow entrepreneurs) are some of the most prized relationships. Specifically, having the external support, validation, interaction, and advice of other entrepreneurs is critical to their growth, particularly from an emotional standpoint. They understand much of what the other is experiencing and are thus able to lean on each other for encouragement and knowledge sharing. After decades of being excluded from the "good ole boy" networks, women have taken networking to a new altitude and are thus able to build trustworthy relationships for the long haul rather than focusing on short-term, superficial transactions (Janssen-Selvadurai 2010; Sharpe 2000).

To support the growing presence and specific needs of women entrepreneurs, countless support/networking groups and events around the country have emerged, many of which were created and are led by women (see the next section Collaboration). It appears that many women rely on predominantly female support groups and organizations to build their businesses and clientele, but they also access other sources, such as Business Networking International or academic institutions to gain exposure and learn from other like-minded women and entrepreneurs. These groups and events also seem to reduce a lot of their fears and the isolation of launching a new business.

When it comes to identity, women are likely to define themselves according to their relationships and connections with people, whereas men typically identify themselves according to their job titles (Belenky et al. 1986; Gilligan 1982). It appears that this is a much more important part of their personal and professional lives than it is for men. Relationships, partnerships, support groups, and the like are a vital part of women's personal growth and success, as well as a significant source of inspiration. They provide an entity of belonging, understanding, and compassion that women strongly identify with. Women feel a part of something greater than themselves, and these relationships define who they are and where they stand amongst their peers. Thus the phrase: *your net worth is your network*.

Collaboration

Being a part of a community with similar goals and challenges has proven to be priceless for women entrepreneurs since they have a preference to work and learn in collaborative environments (Sharpe 2000). They strive to create work environments that support teamwork, transparency, and open and honest communication. By promoting interactive, open lines of communication, command, and control, behaviors are equalized and people feel free to be creative and take risks (Moore 2000; Moore, Moore, and Moore 2011). Developing such a culture enables people to focus on a shared vision and the greater good of the company rather than individual agendas, which often spark unnecessary internal competition. Not only is this a refreshing change from the typical masculine management styles but it also shows that women truly excel at creating such open and cooperative environments.

As a result of the growth of women business owners, two women in New York City, Amy Abrams and Adelaide Lancaster, saw an opportunity to create a collaborative workspace for women entrepreneurs and launched In Good Company (http://ingoodcompany.com) in 2007. It was created to be a working and networking community, as well as a learning resource, for women in the tristate area—a market that had been traditionally underserved. To date, they have helped hundreds of women entrepreneurs connect with their peers around the country to collaboratively help one another launch and grow their ventures.

The unique thing about how women entrepreneurs work together is that they truly enjoy supporting each other and serving others (Janssen-Selvadurai 2010). They like to partner with other women with complementary skill sets. They often barter with one another to show their support and to build credibility in the start-up phase. And while healthy competition is a good thing that sparks innovation and creative problem solving, women take the position that there are plenty of opportunities for all to succeed. One example of a truly supportive network for women entrepreneurs is Savor the Success (www .savorthesuccess.com). The goal or purpose of Savor the Success is to provide a community whereby women entrepreneurs can share public relations and marketing opportunities, network with peers, and learn from one another. There are countless educational and networking events hosted for and by members. By filling a massive void in the marketplace, founder Angela Jia Kim was able to attract over 20,000 members nationwide in less than four years.

Compassion

Women entrepreneurs are also driven by the impact they can have on others. They choose to become entrepreneurs not only for their own fulfillment and self-satisfaction, but also because they want to help others, whether that means empowering people on their staff or giving back to their communities or other women. Women entrepreneurs in particular launch businesses that they are passionate about and that serve the greater good. They create ventures that have a genuine purpose other than simply making a profit. While this sense of satisfaction by serving others can certainly be representative of women who are not entrepreneurs (Gerdes 2010), many women entrepreneurs create businesses specifically to help others. Building high-growth ventures with profit margins is secondary for them. This nurturing and compassionate role previously had no place in the world of business, but today it is a competitive advantage and it is literally recalibrating business values (Janssen-Selvadurai 2010).

When it comes to motivating and inspiring others, women also understand the value in utilizing nonmonetary rewards, such as opportunities for personal development, stretch assignments, and flexible schedules (i.e., working from home, virtually or in tandem with personal schedules) to keep employees happy and engaged. Women understand what is important to other women so as business owners, they know money alone does not necessarily equal happiness. Having this foundational understanding creates an open, nonthreatening, collaborative, and trusting environment to do business.

Having the desire to give back on a larger scale, many women are purposefully integrating a social component into their business models as well, launching social enterprises or giving a certain percentage of their profits to an organization or cause they believe in. A significant number of women entrepreneurs are leading the movement of social entrepreneurship worldwide. For example, Jacqueline Novogratz, the founder and CEO of Acumen Fund (www .acumenfund.org) left a lucrative career in international banking to launch a nonprofit venture capital firm to alleviate world poverty. Her forward-thinking business model enables people living in poverty to improve their lives by having access to capital, education, and other resources. Her motivation is not big profits; it is about helping people improve their own lives.

Transformational Leadership

According to transformational leadership theory, leaders can be transactional or transformational. Transactional leaders are driven by systems and processes, and operate according to a plan, whereas transactional leaders are visionaries who like to challenge the status quo and inspire others to do extraordinary things (Kreitner 2008). Women entrepreneurs are much more likely to be transformational leaders (Bass and Avolio 1994; Bycio, Hackett, and Allen 1995; Moore, Moore, and Moore 2011; Yammarino et al. 1997). Because of their emphasis on people, relationships, and collaboration, women also tend to be much more democratic than men when it comes to leading others. They value cooperation, encourage interactivity amongst team members, are respectful to individuals, and openly hold themselves accountable to the outcomes of their company and those involved (Buttner 2001; Eagly and Carli 2003; Moore and Buttner 1997; Moore, Moore, Moore 2011; Rosener 1990, 1997; Yammarino et al. 1997). This type of leadership is particularly important in a start-up setting, because it encourages employee learning and personal growth, creativity, risk taking, and of course, trust amongst key constituents (Brahnam et al. 2005; Moore, Moore, and Moore 2011).

With respect to perceptions of leadership styles between genders, a recent study suggests that women in leadership positions are considered to be effective if they are both strong and sensitive, whereas male leaders need only to display signs of strength (Vinkenburg et al. 2011). The ability to show concern and compassion for others should be considered a sign of good leadership, so it is perplexing that these acuities still exist in contemporary business. The reality is that transformational leadership skills paired with understanding and inspiration set women leaders apart from the norm.

Looking further back in time, Nieva and Gutek (1981) conducted a study over 30 years ago to explore individual women and their unique challenges, choices, decisions, and behaviors with respect to their careers. The end result was a book entitled *Women and Work: A Psychological Perspective*, and they found that "traditionally, women are seen as not possessing the necessary attributes for leadership. They are believed to be compliant, submissive, emotional, and to have great difficulty in making choices" (Nieva and Gutek 1981, 83). The truth is that the majority of studies that have explored leadership and gender differences since then have found that there is no significant difference between men and women leaders and their personality traits. However, more contemporary studies reveal that women may surpass certain leadership qualities when compared to men. According to a recent gender study conducted by Janet Irwin, a California management consultant, when compared to men, women are better at producing high-quality work, recognizing trends, thinking through decisions, and generating innovative ideas, and executing upon them (Sharpe 2000).

In addition to building a culture that encourages the free flow of information, women entrepreneurs are also good at fostering an environment based on trust (Mannix and Neale 2005). Trust is a key ingredient to leading others and building a strong ecosystem for one's business to thrive. This is especially true for new and small firms (Sako 1998). Women's leadership styles are likely to foster deep-seeded trust with partners, customers, and particularly employees. This trustworthy bond in turn improves productivity, loyalty, satisfaction, and engagement, and can also be a competitive advantage (Eagly, Johannsen-Schmidt, and van Engen 2003; Karakowsky and Siegel 1999; Moore, Moore, and Moore 2011). Since the cultural norms in many organizations do not necessarily breed trust, this renewed emphasis from women business owners is positively challenging the status quo.

Similar to leading, coaching is another example where women are making their mark. Somewhat of an extension of human resource management—which is dominated by women—increasingly more women are entering the field of coaching and launching their own independent consulting firms. There are various types of coaching, but most focus on guiding people in their careers and lives, especially during transitional times. Once again, women excel in this field because they are good at listening, counseling, making decisions, and helping others evolve.

Room for Improvement

Even though women definitely have the personality traits, ambition, and a unique set of valuable management skills to be entrepreneurs, generally speaking, they still fall short in a few areas that can impede their success. For example, many women entrepreneurs lack self-confidence, money management skills, hard negotiation skills, and sometimes the underlying tenet that one goes into business to make money, not just to follow a hobby or personal interest. Studies on career choice and motivation and the differences between men and women suggest much of the same (Ashcraft 1998; Buttner, Holly, and Moore 1997; Höpfl and Hornby Atkinson 2000; Morris et al. 2006), although they do not explicitly state that women are lacking in solid business skills. Here is what women need to focus on to strengthen their management arsenal:

- *Self-confidence.* Many women struggle with self-confidence or self-worth issues, but it is unclear what the underlying reason is for these inadequacies. It could be societal or family expectations; or it could be a reaction to past behaviors and experiences.

Nevertheless, it is still a perplexing issue given that women today—and particularly female entrepreneurs—are very educated, independent, assertive, and determined. Due to the endless challenges involved, entrepreneurial experiences actually have the ability to strengthen and/or weaken one's sense of self-confidence (Janssen-Selvadurai 2010).

- *Money management.* Since a significant number of women are pursuing lifestyle businesses versus high-growth, high-profit organizations, money management can easily get swept to the side for more interesting aspects of entrepreneurship. Even though women are detail oriented, they tend to eschew day-to-day bookkeeping and accounting responsibilities. It is not uncommon for entrepreneurs to hire independent consultants, financial planners, and small-business accountants for help with money matters, but one still needs to understand the basics when it comes to financial statements and cash flow. Whether through formal or informal training, women entrepreneurs need to become more comfortable with numbers and their finances.

- *Negotiating.* From a young age, women are programmed not to promote their own self-interest over others and instead assume they will automatically be recognized and/or rewarded for their hard work. The message: don't ask, don't be greedy, and don't be assertive. The result: women don't get what they want or rightfully deserve because they fail to ask or negotiate for things, such as higher compensation or favorable terms of a contract (Babcock et al. 2003). This is likely linked to issues of self-worth and self-confidence, but negotiation skills can be learned, continuously refined, and applied in so many circumstances throughout one's life. Women are certainly capable of learning how to negotiate, but the key is that they will also need to attain a certain comfort level and emotional chutzpah to see things turn in their favor. This skill alone could really strengthen the validity of and respect for women entrepreneurs.

New Norms

So what does this all mean for business going forward? Why should anyone care about the management styles of women entrepreneurs? By flexing the muscles of unique management styles that are second nature to them, women are establishing new norms in business. They are creating work environments that integrate their own personal values and thus emphasize open communications and transparency, collaboration, trustworthy relationships, and empowering others. It is evident that women are not just concerned about "what" gets done in the business, they are deeply committed to "how" things are done.

It is important to note, however, that these findings do not necessarily mean that women are better managers than men. The important takeaway is that men and women have differing management styles, and the more people-centric approach exercised by women is finally being acknowledged and appreciated. Women entrepreneurs no longer have to subscribe to masculine management skills and styles; they are building businesses and networks on their own terms—which is a positive, healthy approach to business. They seem to welcome the opportunity to challenge business as usual, and by doing so are cultivating new ways of doing business.

The bottom line is that in today's economy, feminine management skills and styles should be considered strengths, not weaknesses. They are a competitive advantage, not a hindrance. They are the foundation of all businesses, not tertiary nuisances. And as more women choose the path of entrepreneurship, we are going to see more collaborative, equitable, and dynamic work environments that are challenging the effectiveness of the traditional management skills and styles that have been valued in years past. The presence of women's preferred management styles has the potential to fundamentally change the way people do business and the landscape for employees, customers, and business partners alike.

Because if rules are meant to be broken, norms are meant to be transformed. Who better to lead the way than women entrepreneurs?

References

Ahl, Helene J. 2002. "The Making of the Entrepreneur: A Discourse Analysis of Research Texts on Women's Entrepreneurship." JIBS diss. series, No. 015. Jönköping, Sweden: Jönköping International Business School, Jönköping University.

Ashcraft, D. M., ed. 1998. *Women's Work: A Survey of Scholarship by and about Women.* New York: The Haworth Press.

Babcock, Linda, Sara Laschever, Michele Gelfand, and Deborah Small. 2003. "Nice Girls Don't Ask." *Harvard Business Review* (October 1). Available at: http://hbr.org/2003/10/nice-girls-dont-ask/ar/1. Accessed October 26, 2011.

Bass, Bernard M., and Bruce J. Avolio. 1994. "Shatter the Glass Ceiling: Women May Make Better Managers." *Human Resource Management* 33: 549–60.

Belenky, Mary F., Blythe M. Clinchy, Nancy R. Goldberger, and Jill M. Tarule. 1986. *Women's Ways of Knowing: The Development of Self, Voice, and Mind.* New York: Basic Books.

Bosma, N. S., Z. J. Acs, E. Autio, A. Coduras, and J. Levie. 2009. "Global Entrepreneurship Monitor, 2008 Executive Report." Global Entrepreneurship Research Consortium (GERA). Available at: http://www.gemconsortium.org/docs/download/264.

Brahnam, Sheryl D., Thomas M. Margavio, Michael A. Hignite, Tonya B. Barrier, and Jerry M. Chin. 2005. "A Gender-Based Categorization for Conflict Resolution." *Journal of Management Development* 55: 197–208.

Brush, Candida, Nancy Carter, Elizabeth Gatewood, Patricia Greene, and Myra Hart. 2004. *Clearing the Hurdles: Women Building High-Growth Enterprises.* New York: Financial Times/Prentice Hall.

Buttner, E. Holly. 1993. "Female Entrepreneurs: How Far Have They Come?" *Business Horizons* 36: 59–65.

Buttner, E. Holly. 2001. "Examining Female Entrepreneurs' Management Style: An Application of a Relational Frame." *Journal of Business Ethics* 29: 253–69.

Buttner, E. Holly, and D. P. Moore. 1997. "Women's Organizational Exodus to Entrepreneurship: Self-Reported Motivations and Correlates with Success." *Journal of Small Business Management* 35: 34–46.

Bycio, Peter, Rick D. Hackett, and Joyce S. Allen. 1995. "Further Assessments of Bass's (1985) Conceptualization of Transactional and Transformational Leadership." *Journal of Applied Psychology* 80: 468–78.

Chaganti, Radha. 1986. "Management in Women-Owned Enterprises." *Journal of Small Business Management* 24: 18–29.

Collins-Williams, M. 2011. "Iowa Missing the Mark with Women Entrepreneurs." *WCF Courier* (October 12). Available at: http://wcfcourier.com/business/columns/iowa-missing-the-mark-with-women-entrepreneurs/article_e2951ff0-f4d2-11e0-be87-001cc4c03286.html. Accessed January 1, 2012.

Davis, Susan E. M., and Dinah D. Long. 1999. "Women Entrepreneurs: What Do They Need?" *Business and Economic Review* 45: 25–26.

Eagly, Alice H., Mary C. Johannsen-Schmidt, and Marloes L. van Engen. 2003. "Transformational, Transactional, and Laissez-Faire Leadership Styles: A Meta-Analysis Comparing Women and Men." *Psychological Bulletin* 129: 569–93.

Eagly, Alice H., and Linda L. Carli. 2003. "The Female Leadership Advantage: An Evaluation of the Evidence." *Leadership Quarterly* 14: 807–35.

Gerdes, Eugenia P. 2010. "We Did It Our Way: Motivations, Satisfactions, and Accomplishments of Senior Academic Women." *Advancing Women in Leadership Journal* 30: 1–21.

Gilligan, Carol. 1982. *In a Different Voice: Psychological Theory and Women's Development.* Cambridge, MA: Harvard University Press.

Goldman, G. 1994. "Women Entrepreneurs." *Business Week* (April 18): 104.

Griffin, Cynthia E. 2001. "Be a Man! No, Wait . . . Be a Woman!" *Entrepreneur* (May 1). Available at: http://www.entrepreneur.com/article/39538. Accessed October 26, 2011.

Gupta, Vishal K., and Nachiket M. Bhawe. 2007. "The Influence of Proactive Personality and Stereotype Threat on Women's Entrepreneurial Intentions." *Journal of Leadership & Organizational Studies* 13: 73–85.

Heffernan, Margaret A. 2006. "Are Women Better Entrepreneurs?" *Forbes* (June 27). Available at: http://www.forbes.com/work/2006/06/26/women-entrepreneurs-heffernan-cx_mh_0626womenentrpreneurs.html. Accessed October 17, 2007.

Heffernan, Margaret A. 2007. *How She Does It: How Women Entrepreneurs Are Changing the Rules of Business Success.* New York: Penguin Group.

Heilman, M. E. 1983. "Sex Bias in Work Settings: The Lack of Fit Model." *Research in Organizational Behavior* 5: 269–98.

Hisrich, Robert D., and Candida G. Brush. 1983. "The Woman Entrepreneur: Implications of Family, Educational and Occupational Experience." In *Frontiers of Entrepreneurship Research*, edited by J. Hornaday, J. A. Timmons, and K. Vesper. 255–70. Babson Park, MA: Babson College.

Höpfl, Heather, and Pat Hornby Atkinson. 2000. "The Future of Women's Career." In *The Future of Career*, edited by Audrey Collin and Richard A. Young. 130–43. Cambridge: Cambridge University Press.

Hytti, Ulla. 2010. "Contextualizing Entrepreneurship in the Boundaryless Career." *Gender in Management: An International Journal* 15: 64–81.

Janssen-Selvadurai, Christine H. 2010. "On Becoming: The Lived Learning Experiences of Female Entrepreneurs." PhD diss. New York University.

Karakowsky, L., and J. P. Siegel. 1999. "The Effects of Proportional Representation and Gender Orientation of the Task on Emergent Leadership Behavior in Mixed-Gender Work Groups." *Journal of Applied Psychology* 84: 620–31.

Kossek, Ellen E., Karen S. Markel, and Patrick P. McHugh. 2003. "Increasing Diversity as an HRM Change Strategy." *Journal of Organizational Change Management* 16: 328–52.

Kreitner, Robert. 2008. *Foundations of Management: Basics and Best Practices*. Boston, MA: Houghton Mifflin Company.

Mannix, Elizabeth, and Margaret A. Neale. 2005. "What Differences Make a Difference? The Promise and Reality of Diverse Teams in Organizations." *Psychological Science in the Public Interest* 6: 31–55.

Marlow, Susan. 2002. "Women and Self-Employment: A Part of or Apart from Theoretical Construct?" *International Journal of Entrepreneurship and Innovation* 3: 83–91.

Moore, Dorothy P. 2000. *Careerpreneurs: Lessons from Leading Women Entrepreneurs on Building a Career without Boundaries*. Palo Alto, CA: Davies-Black Publishing.

Moore, Dorothy P. 2010. "Women as Entrepreneurs and Business Owners." In *Gender and Women's Leadership: A Reference Handbook*, edited by K. O'Connor. 443–51. Thousand Oaks, CA: Sage.

Moore, Dorothy P., and E. Holly Buttner. 1997. *Women Entrepreneurs: Moving Beyond the Glass Ceiling*. Thousand Oaks, CA: Sage.

Moore, Dorothy P., Jamie L. Moore, and Jamie W. Moore. 2011. "How Women Entrepreneurs Lead and Why They Manage That Way." *Gender in Management: An International Journal* 26: 220–33.

Morris, Michael H., Nola N. Miyasaki, Craig E. Watters, and Susan M. Coombes. 2006. "The Dilemma of Growth: Understanding Venture Size Choices of Women Entrepreneurs." *Journal of Small Business Management* 44: 221–44.

Nieva, Veronica F., and Barbara A. Gutek. 1981. *Women and Work: A Psychological Perspective.* New York: Praeger Publishers.

Orhan, Muriel, and Don Scott. 2001. "Why Women Enter into Entrepreneurship: An Explanatory Model." *Women in Management Review* 16: 232–43.

Patterson, Nicola, and Sharon Mavin. 2009. "Women Entrepreneurs: Jumping the Corporate Ship and Gaining New Wings." *International Small Business Journal* 27: 173–92.

Rosener, Judy B. 1990. "Ways Women Lead." *Harvard Business Review* 68: 119–25.

Rosener, Judy B. 1997. *America's Competitive Secret: Women Managers.* New York: Oxford University Press.

Ryan, Michelle K., S. Alexander Haslam, Mette D. Hersby, and Renata Bongiomo. 2011. "Think Crisis-Think Female: The Glass Cliff and Contextual Variation in the Think Manager-Think Male Stereotype." *Journal of Applied Psychology* 96: 470–84.

Sako, Mari. 1998. "Does Trust Improve Business Performance?" In *Organizational Trust: A Reader,* edited by Roderick M. Kramer. 267–93. Oxford: Oxford University Press.

Sharpe, Rochelle. 2000. "As Leaders, Women Rule." *BusinessWeek* (November 20). Available at: http://www.businessweek.com/2000/00_47/b3708145.htm. Accessed November 11, 2011.

Vinkenburg, Claartje J., Marloes L. van Engen, Alice H. Eagly, and Mary C. Johannesen-Schmidt. 2011. "An Exploration of Stereotypical Beliefs about Leadership Styles: Is Transformational Leadership a Route to Women's Promotion?" *The Leadership Quarterly* 22: 10–21.

Vongalis-Macrow, Athena, and Andrea Gallant. 2010 "Stop Stereotyping Female Leaders." *Harvard Business Review* (October 11). Available at: http://blogs.hbr.org/cs/2010/10/stop_stereotyping_female_leader.html. Accessed October 26, 2011.

Wachs Book, Esther. 2001. *Why the Best Man for the Job is a Woman: The Unique Female Qualities of Leadership.* New York: HarperCollins Publishers, Inc..

Yammarino, Francis J., A. J. Dubinsky, L. B. Comer, and M. A. Jolson. 1997. "Women and Transformational and Contingent Reward Leadership: A Multiple-Levels-of-Analysis Perspective." *Academy of Management Journal* 40: 205–22.

Chapter 7

Combining Motherhood and Entrepreneurship: Strategies, Conflict, and Costs

Eileen Drew
and Anne Laure Humbert

In *The Sunday Times* magazine (May 22, 2011) the front page heralds "March of the Red Ladies: How China's Women Seized Power." The article highlights the successes of a handful of self-made women, including Zhang Yin as the first woman to top China's rich list in 2006, out of a total population of 1.341 billion people. While lauding these achievements a subtext asks "What is the cost to their families, and would British women be willing to pay so high a price?" Indicators of massive wealth accumulation are interspersed with weekly hours worked (an average of 72 hours is cited but it was exceeded by one woman who worked 120 hours per week) and examples of the time sacrifices made (e.g., returning to their business within 2–3 weeks of giving birth and/or having their children reared by grandparents) to allow them the freedom to pursue a business lifestyle of long hours and long commuting times and international travel. Far from questioning the sanity of this lifestyle for men and women, the article pivots around the agonising cost of maternal absences and the sacrifices made by the successful women entrepreneurs who have managed to combine entrepreneurship with caring responsibilities (not solely confined to parenting).

This article is a classic illustration of what Smith (2009) has dubbed the *diva storyline*. Smith (2009, 149) argues that "Diva identity is socially constructed in the tabloid press and media and therefore, carries with it a judgemental stigma . . . in modern everyday usage it has expanded to include all outstanding female singers, celebrity film stars and now talented businesswomen." Bruni, Gherardi, and Poggio (2004, 259) reiterate this treatment stating that media coverage of women entrepreneurs reinforces the traditional gender stereotypes wherein only women are held accountable for seeking to balance work and domestic duties "under the assumption that their natural place—and their primary social responsibility—is the family."

Unlike in China, where one-third of self-made millionaires are females, the number of women entrepreneurs in Ireland, while increasing rapidly, represents only 15 percent of business start-ups. This is less than half of the European Union (EU) level of one in three. With the current slowdown in the growth of the Irish economy, particularly in services where women are well represented, rising female entrepreneurship will be vital to ensure that Ireland meets the Europe 2020 employment target of 75 percent for 20–64 year olds. O'Gorman and Terjesen (2006, 86) claim that low levels of entrepreneurial activity by women in Ireland "may be because females have less access to entrepreneurial opportunities, are less likely to have the skills and knowledge needed to start a business, and are less likely to have a recent entrepreneur in their personal network." According to Wilson and Tagg (2010), female entrepreneurs are judged and evaluated against a norm (established by a majority group "male standard"), which infers that female entrepreneurs are lacking or lesser than their male counterparts. For example, Lerner and Almor (2002, 122) found that female business owners need to invest more in strategic thinking and place less emphasis on quality and customer service, noting that "the owner of a small, life-style venture has to be competent in all areas and not excel in some while neglecting others." Gupta et al. (2009) stress the need to acknowledge "the invisible masculinity of entrepreneurship that so profoundly influences their assumptions, variables, theoretical and measurement models, and methodologies" and how gender influences the entrepreneurial activities of men and women.

The limited policy responses to address the underrepresentation of women among entrepreneurs in Ireland have been less than successful in achieving gender parity, since they still adhere to the belief that the answer lies in what Martin (2003) describes as "fixing the women," thus ignoring the major power imbalances that prevail in business life. To meet these, interventions are required to tackle the culture and context in which women entrepreneurs operate, including their current and disproportionate responsibility for parenting.

In this chapter, we present a response and challenge to the prevailing media discourse of entrepreneurial success which, in accordance with the male norm, conveys the expectation of demanding work styles as a given, but questions the accompanying costs and sacrifices only when these are made by women.

Commenting on the overreliance of entrepreneurial research using quantitative data and surveys involving small samples, Mirchandani (1999, 232) suggests that "more useful insight can be gained through the use of inductive methods of qualitative analysis whereby experiences and connections which are as yet 'unmapped' can be made visible." Hence in this chapter, we concentrate on in-depth interviews, conducted between 2005 and 2006, with eight women entrepreneurs who had dependent children. These interviews formed the final stage of the exploratory research into women's experience of entrepreneurship in Ireland, building upon the mainly quantitative findings of a national survey of women and men entrepreneurs. The objective of the overarching study was to investigate the experiences of male and female entrepreneurs in terms of their business and caring/domestic responsibilities. The survey findings reinforced those in the international literature, namely that fathers work significantly longer hours than mothers; the career trajectories of fathers are typically continuous, conducted via full-time work, while for mothers the usual pattern is more fragmented, reflecting absences for caring and adjustments such as part-time working (Drew and Humbert 2012). It was also evident from the quantitative and qualitative survey responses that it is mothers, rather than fathers, who feel responsible for child care arrangements and that this poses a major dilemma for them in pursuing entrepreneurship. The comments of survey respondents support the findings by Lee and Owens (2002) who noted that, despite a shift toward more interchangeable roles and egalitarian households, societal pressures and the socialization process ensure conformity to more traditional, socially constructed gender roles of father-breadwinner and mother-caregiver.

The research methods selected for this study reflect the views of Creswell (2003) and Saunders, Lewis, and Thornhill (2009) who advocate an alternative mixed methods approach to the traditional mono method choice in order to avoid the shortcomings of using one method alone. Qualitative methods are criticized for generally lacking direction and having limited comparability, while also demanding huge resources (e.g., financial or time considerations) from researchers. In contrast, quantitative methods are criticized for placing too much emphasis on the relationship between two variables, while not answering the "why" question. In other words, quantitative methods are performing well in terms of descriptive research, but less so in terms of analytical research in the social sciences. For example, the scope of questions available to quantitative researchers is itself limited by the types of questions that they can ask, the types of answers that are codified, and the meaning that the person analyzing the data will give to the answers (Remenyi et al. 1998).

Taking account of this, the authors sought to triangulate the research findings that sought to establish the realities of work–family interactions for mothers who are running small and medium enterprises involving a series of interviews. The open-ended responses to the earlier national survey of entrepreneurs pointed to the coping strategies used by mothers, the importance that they attached to their caring (as distinct from business) responsibilities, experience of conflict and of making sacrifices, and adherence to traditional gender roles reflecting societal expectations. The interviews analyzed in this chapter address a research deficit in exploring how women entrepreneurs reconciled their personal/family lives with running a business and how much their decisions and behavior were influenced by their own socialization.

The Irish Context

Since the 1960s, Ireland has experienced a major shift from a predominantly agrarian and newly industrializing country to a fast-growing service-led economy (Jackson 1993). Ireland's entry into the EU in 1973 marked a transition toward EU norms in terms of lower fertility rates, increasing female labor force participation, and higher levels of educational attainment by women.

In 1970, Ireland's fertility rate was 3.87 (Fahey 2001), the highest fertility rate in the EU, due in part to the strong influence of the Catholic Church over personal morals and on the political system: contraception, divorce, and abortion[1] were still illegal. Following the legalization of contraception, fertility rates dropped to levels comparable to other EU member states (1.93 in 1997). Since then, fertility rose to 2.07 in 2010 (CSO 2012). Alongside this change, births outside marriage rose to 34 percent of all births and there has been a rise in the mean age of women giving birth.

Over the last 50 years, Ireland experienced a feminization of education, most notably in secondary and tertiary rates of educational attainment. In 2011, women represented 57 percent of all third-level graduates (CSO 2012). The proportion of the female population aged 25–34 years with a third-level qualification is 51 percent compared with 39 percent for men. Furthermore, only 9 percent of young women leave the secondary school system early, while 14 percent of young men drop out of school before gaining a secondary qualification (Lunn, Fahey, and Hannan 2009).

Ireland's extraordinary economic growth since the mid-1990s (up to 2008) has been a major factor in women's rising labor market representation. By 2008, the female employment rate had met/exceeded the Lisbon target of 60 percent. However, by 2011, the level fell to 56 percent.

Attitudinal change in Ireland can be seen in the weaker adherence to traditional gender roles, the number of nonmarital unions/cohabitation, rise in births outside marriage, and an increase in legal separations and divorces, interpreted by some as reflecting an erosion of traditional family values (Commission on the Family 1998). The European Values Study (Halman, Inglehart, and Basanez 2007) shows the importance of a range of factors among the Irish population, notably that there is a very strong importance attached to family (91%), as well as to friends (61%) and work (51%), but less so to leisure time (40%). The survey demonstrates the importance of the family at the heart of Irish society, compared to other aspects of life, and stresses the traditional nature of Irish society. The study by Halman, Inglehart, and Basanez (2007) shows that, in 1990, a majority of respondents not only believed that a mother can be engaged in work outside the home and establish a secure relationship with her children (63%), and husbands and wives should contribute to household income (70%), but also, paradoxically, being a housewife can be just as fulfilling as paid work (72%).

More recent data from the same survey, collected in 2000 (Halman, Inglehart, and Basanez 2007), show that 68 percent of respondents believed that a child needs a home with both a father and mother. Only a minority believed that marriage is an outdated institution (22%) or that women should choose to have a child as a single parent outside a stable relationship (32%). Sharing household chores was seen as more important to a successful marriage (53%) in Ireland than in other countries surveyed. Furthermore, only 16 percent believed that women need children in order to be fulfilled.

These findings suggest that while major strides have been made by women in Ireland in accessing education and entry into a still highly gender-segregated labor market, these changes have to be viewed against a strong adherence to traditional expectations about gender roles in Irish society. This is exemplified by the importance attached to family and the high proportion (28% in 2011) of women outside the labor force who are engaged in "looking after home/family" (CSO 2012).

Review of Literature

Literature on gender and entrepreneurship is a relatively recent phenomenon, and until the late 1970s, the role of women entrepreneurs was rarely considered. Over the last three decades, female entrepreneurship has moved from being highly descriptive to much more analytical. As Carter and Shaw (2006) argue, the field is moving from looking at whether gender makes a difference to how it makes a difference. Thus, there has been a shift from attempting to include gender into existing theories of entrepreneurship toward developing new theories that acknowledge the presence of women in entrepreneurship (Chell and Baines 1998).

If existing studies of gender and entrepreneurship are scant, even less work has been done on Irish women entrepreneurs. Of the few studies that exist, some are based on weak sampling methodologies and/or small samples. Authors such as Stevenson (2003) and Greene et al. (2003) argue that there are few differences in the experiences of women entrepreneurs across countries, thereby suggesting that findings from the international literature should be pertinent to Ireland. However, as we show in this chapter, the Irish context is historically very different from the rest of the EU-15, therefore flagging up the need to exercise some care in adapting international findings to Irish entrepreneurship.

Gender and Entrepreneurship

Much international research has focused on the motivational factors behind decisions to become entrepreneurs. Most authors argue that entrepreneurial awakening is the product of social, cultural, and educational influences (Duchéneaut and Orhan 2000). A key strand of motivational literature concentrates on push/pull factors. "Push" factors force people to become entrepreneurs, while "pull" factors attract them. The combination of push and pull factors in each individual case may lead to the decision to become an entrepreneur. While some argue that this push/pull model reflects the majority of motivational factors (Duchéneaut and Orhan 2000; Orhan and Scott 2001), others argue that it is too simplistic in that it fails to take into account the dynamic nature of an individual's environment such as family background, family support, or economic outlook and its relationship with push/pull factors (Humbert 2007). Another major criticism of this theory is that while it provides a comparative analysis of entrepreneurial motivation between men and women, it only does so in the public sphere. As such, there is no recognition of the assumptions and expectations underpinning women's position in the private (domestic/family) sphere (Humbert 2007). Gendered power relations are mostly excluded from the discourse on women's entrepreneurship, and only a few studies that employ a feminist perspective have addressed the issue of identities of entrepreneurs explicitly (Essers and Benschop 2007).

Irish survey-based research shows that factors such as marital and family status and/or age are significant factors, particularly when interacting with gender, in determining the motivation for becoming an entrepreneur. Women entrepreneurs were found to be "much more likely than their male counterparts to cite wanting to achieve a better work/life balance, thereby reflecting the stereotypical view that it is women who ultimately have to juggle employment or entrepreneurship with caring responsibilities" (Humbert and Drew 2010, 190). This explicit adherence to the feminine attempt at reconciliation, particularly as mothers, reinforces the gender stereotyping of caring work and fails to acknowledge the role of fathers (Martin 2003).

An obstacle typically associated with women entrepreneurs is that they often have to confront hostile social attitudes and cultural biases when breaking into what is essentially a male business world. There is clear evidence that the socialization process of women, throughout their childhood in families and at schools, does not prepare them for the business world where female managers are in short supply (McClelland 2003; Stevenson 2003). Most literature states that family responsibilities are particularly problematic for women entrepreneurs (Still and Timms 2000; Rouse and Boles 2005) since women are traditionally perceived as being responsible for tasks related to the private sphere (Drew, Emerek, and Mahon 1998), and women entrepreneurs appear to be no exception (Rouse and Boles 2005). This aspect of gender and entrepreneurship is problematic in that there is a possible link between business performance and choices made in terms of work–life balance (Carter and Allen 1997; Chell and Baines 1998; Marlow 1997). This pattern is particularly strong in an Irish context where there is a lack of adequate child care facilities and structures (Coveney, Murphy-Lawless, and Sheridan 1998; McClelland 2003; Stevenson 2003). Irish evidence suggests that this holds in entrepreneurship also (Drew and Humbert 2010; Fleck 2010). As Jones and Spicer (2009, 112) state, entrepreneurship research needs to "recognise the social embeddedness of entrepreneurship, and the social relations that produce and maintain entrepreneurship, right down to the very idea of entrepreneurship."

Parenting, Work–Life Balance, and Entrepreneurship

International studies indicate that the differences between men and women exhibited in employment are largely replicated in entrepreneurship. It is clear that entrepreneurship can have a positive impact on gender equality (e.g., in allowing women to trade in traditionally male sectors) as well as negative ones (e.g., maternity leave is rarely available to women entrepreneurs) (Humbert 2007). Conceptually, entrepreneurship is essentially a male construct, which can often be detrimental in terms of how we think about women entrepreneurs. Ahl (2004, 59), in referring to an entrepreneurial imperative, argues that

> not only is the construct male gendered, it also implies a gendered division of labor. Being an entrepreneur—strong-willed, determined, persistent, resolute, detached, and self-centred—requires some time, effort and devotion to a task . . . leaving little time for the caring of small children, cooking, cleaning and all the other chores necessary to survive. Performing entrepreneurship in the sense described above requires a particular gendered division of labor where it is assumed that a wife (of if unmarried, usually a woman anyway) does the unpaid, reproductive work associated with the private sphere.

Despite the link between gender and family, research on whether gender equality is reinforced or undermined by entrepreneurship and research that links family responsibilities and entrepreneurship have been nominal. Baines, Wheelock, and Gelder (2003) examined flexibility in the management of small businesses in the United Kingdom. They observed that self-employment is often sought by mothers in order to reconcile paid work with child care. This finding is replicated throughout the literature on entrepreneurial motivational factors (Orhan and Scott 2001). The 30 entrepreneurial parents in the study by Baines, Wheelock, and Gelder (2003) were concentrated in highly gendered sectors, with men in construction and manufacturing, while women were in personal and health-related services. Men entrepreneurs were "minimally involved in bringing up their children because of the long hours they worked" (Baines, Wheelock, and Gelder 2003, 30). Furthermore, the study showed that domestic tasks were overwhelmingly the responsibility of women in two-parent households regardless of whether they were entrepreneurs themselves, or partners of male entrepreneurs.

Women now constitute a growing segment of the labor force in most industrialized economies (Rees 1992; Rubery, Smith, and Fagan 1999; Walby 1997) and particularly in entrepreneurship (GEM 2009; Humbert 2007). Nevertheless, there is much evidence that the input of employed mothers in domestic and caring work remains greater than that of fathers (Crompton, Lewis, and Lyonette 2007). While the adoption of flexible working policies has been steadily increasing within employment, this remains problematical in entrepreneurship, particularly for micro- or small businesses (Humbert and Lewis 2008). Struggling entrepreneurs may feel impelled to build/expand their businesses at the cost of nonwork activities such as caring and leisure.

Sheridan (2004, 222) argues that men's and women's differing working patterns are maintained by "a lifelong system of social control which begins with gender socialization and is continually reinforced and recreated by other institutions—the organisation and family—and ideologies." These differences are also present in entrepreneurship, as shown by Wynarczyk and Marlow (2010). Sheridan (2004) attributes the cult of "presenteeism" to the pressures that are differentially placed on men—to work long hours and be rewarded for doing so. These combine to form expectations that men will be ideal workers, thereby inhibiting men, especially fathers, from feeling able to access more flexible working practices. However, in the context of entrepreneurship, where there is arguably more control over time and space, the dynamics could be different and entrepreneurship might provide the opportunity for more work flexibility. However, this could be offset by other pressures (e.g., availability to clients) (Humbert and Lewis 2008).

Building upon the gender-differentiated working patterns stressed by Sheridan (2004), Brush, de Bruin, and Welter (2009, 12) flagged the importance of motherhood in addition to the original 3M's building blocks of market, money, and management: "At the centre is 'Motherhood', not only pointing to the importance of considering the role and position of a woman in the family but symbolizing the centrality of meaningful gender awareness and analysis to the whole framework as well." The authors refer to how motherhood, or family embeddedness, will affect how entrepreneurship develops, so that women with strong family obligations will be less likely to interact in business-related networks, "possibly affecting the growth prospects or even novelty of the venture" (Brush, de Bruin, and Welter 2009, 19).

International literature suggests that there continue to be major divergences in the working lives of fathers and mothers in employment in terms of working hours, patterns of working time, and consequent career paths, thereby raising questions about combining entrepreneurship and caring roles. In this chapter, we suggest that the prioritization of work by fathers versus caring by mothers, which is evident in employment, will also be present in some form in entrepreneurship and that the separation of the public/private spheres may lead to reconciliation and/or conflict. Thus, it would be anticipated that mothers will experience a greater degree of conflict in entrepreneurship, due to the caring responsibilities attributed to them. In the remainder of this chapter, we examine the discourses of women in Ireland who have chosen to combine motherhood and entrepreneurship.

Methodology

The methodological approach adopted for the study involved mixed methods of data collection commencing with a large-scale national survey of women and men entrepreneurs in Ireland. This generated a high volume of quantitative and also considerable qualitative data that reflected the views of entrepreneurs in Ireland. In the second stage of the research, there was a need to collect more in-depth interview data. Interviewees were selected through (women's) networking events and by writing to members of Kildare and Meath County Enterprise Boards' Women in Business networks. The 10 women entrepreneurs interviewed represented a range of different businesses. Particular attention was given to include women entrepreneurs who operated in a variety of business sectors, in different-sized businesses, with different methods of business creation (e.g., created versus inherited), and with contrasting family background and personal viewpoints.

The interviews were taped and transcribed, and the transcripts were anonymized, as agreed with the women interviewed. The women were asked about their motivations in becoming entrepreneurs to ascertain the importance of flexible working and reconciliation of work and family and personal lives. They were asked about the obstacles that they may have encountered, their degree of risk taking, management styles, and whether they saw themselves as role models for other women. The responses that are examined closely in this chapter relate to women's prioritization, or otherwise, of work-life balance arrangements for themselves and their employees and the links between their family/personal life and their businesses—whether they had experienced conflict and/or made sacrifices in these spheres. Interviewees were also asked if they thought that men would have experienced similar conflict, or not.

In order to avoid misinterpretation of the results, a short biography of each interviewee is presented in the next section. Due to ethical concerns and to ensure confidentiality, all names of interviewees have been changed.

Profiles of Interviewees

Orla is married and aged between 35 and 44. She has two dependent children who are both aged 13. She inherited the company (created in 1974) from her parents and currently runs it in conjunction with her siblings. The company employs more than 50 full-time employees as well as more than 50 part-time employees. The company, which she joined in 1989, trades in design, retail, and catering.

Lisa is married, aged between 35 and 44 years, and has two dependent children who are aged 4 and 10 years. She created the company in 1989 on her own. However, her husband joined her a few years later. She employs more than 50 full-time and more than 50 part-time staff. She works in human resources.

Catherine is cohabiting. She lives with her partner and his two children from a previous marriage, approximately 50 percent of the time. She has no children of her own. She is aged between 45 and 54 years. She created her company in 1989 and now employs less than 10 full-time and less than 10 part-time staff. She is involved in real estate.

Emily is married, aged between 45 and 54 years, and has two teenagers. She created her company in 1986 with her husband. She now employs between 21 and 50 staff full-time and more than 50 employees on a part-time basis. Her company trades in the media industry.

Teresa is married, aged between 35 and 44, and has one school-age child. She created her company in 2001. She employs no full-time staff and less than 10 part-time employees. She is involved in training.

Maura is single, aged between 35 and 44, and has one preschool child. She runs the family business in association with her father and brother. They employ less than 10 part-time employees and under 10 full-time employees. Their trading sector is manufacturing of agricultural and garden products.

Sarah is separated, aged between 45 and 54, and has four children, three of whom are teenagers and one is in college. Her business was created in 1983, and she is now the head of the corporation which merged with her business in

2001. She employs more than 50 full-time employees and less than 10 part-time employees. Her sector of trading is financial services.

Gemma is married, aged between 45 and 54, and has three children, two of whom are of school age, and one of whom is a teenager. She created her first company in 1989 as a partnership. She has since created another business. She employs less than 10 full-time employees and between 10 and 20 part-time employees. Her business sector is media and consultancy.

The profile of interviewees is presented in Table 7.1. The majority of women interviewed were from 45 to 54 years of age. They were, on average, older than

Table 7.1 Summary profile of interviewees ($n = 8$)

	Number of Respondents Grouped by Category
Number of dependent children	
1	2
2	4
3	1
4	1
Marital status	
Single/separated/divorced	2
Married/cohabiting	6
Age group	
35–44	3
45–54	5
Number of years in business	
6–10	1
11–15	1
16–20	5
21–25	1
Origin of first company	
Bought	0
Inherited	2
Created	6
Type of organization	
One main director	5
Partnership	3
Sector of trading	
Media	2
Design	1
Human resources	1
Real estate	1
Training/personal development	1
Manufacturing	1
Financial services	1

the women entrepreneurs in Ireland and the women entrepreneurs surveyed. This is due to the fact that women entrepreneurs with a long track record in business were targeted to participate in the interviews. As in the survey and other Irish studies (Goodbody Economic Consultants 2002; Valiulis et al. 2004), most women entrepreneurs were married or cohabiting. The vast majority had children, with an average number of two. Collectively, they were responsible for the care of 15 children, with family size ranging from one member to four members. The women interviewed had been in business for an average of 14 years, ranging from 1 year to 25 years. Most of their businesses were established by them. The key sectors in which the women traded were those in which women predominate: design, human resources, media, or training. The interviews were of approximately one hour's duration. The narratives of the eight women, who had a child or children, are reported in this chapter. Six women were married while one was single and another was separated.

Findings

Motivations

The main motivations of the women interviewed for becoming an entrepreneur were independence, aligned with being one's own boss or working for oneself; personal satisfaction and fulfillment; dissatisfaction with previous employment; unanticipated growth/success; taking over the reins of a family business; and family influences. Only one of the eight women—Catherine, having two stepchildren—mentioned more income as the motivation. She stated that she wanted to do business, "because it was the most profitable thing to do."

Two women mentioned wanting a lifestyle that was compatible with work–life balance, which had been flagged in the international (Duchéneaut and Orhan 2000; Goffee and Scase 1985; Marlow 1997; Moore and Buttner 1997) and Irish literature (Goodbody Economic Consultants 2002; Henry and Kennedy 2003; Valiulis et al. 2004). However, it is clear that the flexibility sought is entrenched with expectations of motherhood:

> My main motivation was probably because I am a mother and I very much wanted to be a mother. When my daughter was born, I stayed at home and didn't work. Now as she's getting older, I have more free time but I still want to be available in the hours that she is home. (Teresa, one child)

Teresa went on to state that she had been drawn into entrepreneurship rather than pushed out of the labor market. For her, entrepreneurship was a means to an end—motherhood and wanting to be with her child.

When asked if she felt that her entrepreneurial motivation was in any way affected by being a woman, rather than a man, Teresa stated that she had felt impelled to do entrepreneurship differently in conformance with the caregiver/breadwinner ideology, that being present at home is what ideal mothers do:

> I suppose my decision, it would have been [different for a man] . . . based on the fact that I am a mother and it had to suit my perception of being a mother, a mother at home. (Teresa, one child)

Teresa's business was established after the birth of her child, but another one of our interviewees, Lisa, felt that she had been able to act like a man, because she was not a mother at start-up. She stated that this would not have been the case if she had already been a mother when setting up a business:

> because it was something I wanted to do, nothing really to do with whether I was male or female. It may have been easier to do by virtue of the fact that I was single, I think it would be more difficult for me now, with two young children, to start out. That's my own perception. It's just a busy time when you have young children. (Lisa, two children)

The comments suggest that what matters so much is not gender among entrepreneurs but instead motherhood (as opposed to parenthood). The expectations and narrations of entrepreneurial experiences are deeply embedded with notions of what constitutes a good mother: the ideal mother.

Obstacles to Becoming Entrepreneurs

In support of the well-documented obstacles identified in the literature facing women entrepreneurs, the interviewees voiced their catalogue of impediments to business start-up and growth in terms of lack of experience/training, raising finance, retention and costs of labor, isolation, and sourcing materials. Also flagged was the issue of time constraints imposed by the business and how these impact on work–life balance. For Orla, who runs her business jointly with her siblings, this meant adjustments to the future growth of the business:

> Lifestyle would be the biggest reason why I don't . . . take some of the roads that have been offered to us . . . We're already very consumed by the company, and we don't want the lifeblood to be sucked from us or from the company. So, balance? . . . There are a lot of time demands. I would probably do 9 or 10 hour days. (Orla, two children)

Orla does not specifically refer to her role as mother, but Sarah described the contrary demands of business and family in terms of:

> I had to be very organised, huge amount of energy—which I do have. There were times when it wasn't easy juggling all the balls, you know. (Sarah, four children)

Sarah identifies this juggling act as particularly intense at the moment in her life when she had young children.

Work–Life Balance—For Themselves

In each of the interviews, women entrepreneurs were asked about how they prioritized their personal/family lives against their business and professional lives and how much importance they attached to work–life balance for themselves and their employees. Most were resigned to working long hours over protracted periods of time though they had evolved patterns of working time that allowed them to juggle with their business while still being available for their families (especially in the evenings). Typically, entrepreneurial mothers utilized compressed hours and/or "time off in lieu" and working from home, facilitated by Internet access:

> I tend to work flat out and long hours because I know something is coming up . . . social or family or whatever . . . [I] do it at the back end of Friday. (Sarah, four children)

> I suppose we [my partner and I] work full-time, but I suppose we would take a week off here and there, and a long week-end off, and that sort of thing. (Catherine, two stepchildren)

> I do 45 or 46 hours a week, so I work full-time alright, but I mean if I need the day off, I'll just take it . . . that's when I need my flexitime. (Maura, one child)

> I do work from home a number of days in the week so I can collect my children from school and I don't come into the office all the time. And email, and all those modern technological devices are fantastic to do that, and I . . . take a good chunk of the summer out to be with the children. (Emily, two children)

> I work from 9 until 6 and I don't tend to work late at night. Sometimes I work early in the morning. Certainly I like to be at home in the evening time when my kids are home. (Lisa, two children)

While women entrepreneurs could avail of some form of flexibility in their working hours they seldom availed of leave arrangements. Two women entrepreneurs stated

> Do you know how much maternity leave I took out on my children? Not that I would recommend it, I don't, the most that I took was a week. (Sarah, four children)

> I thought when I was pregnant that I would bring my baby in a basket and take her into my office . . . Little did I realise what it would do to my life. . . . I worked until three days before I had the girls and I was working completely full-time . . . But all I

had ever known was work. I don't know why, but I thought it was completely normal to go straight back to work, you know, very very quickly. (Orla, two children)

There is a very heroic subtext in the previous two comments. These women were very proud of having been able to ignore their motherhood status as much as possible, although with hindsight, they recognized that it was not without consequences for themselves, their children, or their family. What concerns us is the lack of recognition of the consequences this had to the image that they were projecting as entrepreneurs, and what we see as reinforcing gender roles in society and entrepreneurship.

Teresa felt differently, separating herself from the ethos of the ideal worker, and stated that work–life balance was important to her:

I think creating a balance that suits yourself and your family as well is important . . . As far as getting work–life balance here in our own situation, my work hours are between 9 and 3. And that's how I work, and at three o'clock it's family time. (Teresa, two children)

In summary, the women entrepreneurs interviewed regarded work–life balance practices as being important. However, few were availing of any themselves, except for a certain degree of flexible, often compressed, working time and/or working from home. Overall, these women worked to traditional patterns. There was a tension between those who embraced the culture of male ways of working and those who preferred more feminine practices with a shorter working day or taking time off during the summer school holidays.

Work–Life Balance—For Their Employees

Ironically, most women entrepreneurs said that they felt work–life balance practices were important for their employees. However, in reality the structure of their businesses was usually quite fixed and traditional in nature. Two women entrepreneurs mentioned that they offered work–life balance arrangements, provided these suited the needs of the business:

We would have flexi-hours, because we like to cover the office from 8 in the morning until 7 at night . . . We're flexible . . . if it suits the company. (Sarah, four children)

The business obviously has got to come first, and if I can match somebody's personal scenario into that, fine. (Gemma, three children)

Similarly, two women entrepreneurs did not offer work–life balance practices to their staff because of the difficulties such practices would generate.

Perhaps not surprisingly, Gemma equated flexible working practices with her female staff who had children:

> I actually have a lot of women who. . . . for family reasons, they've had to leave their jobs, but they want to keep their hand in. So I tap into that. (Gemma)

Orla cited the pool of expertise and responsibility necessary to ensure smooth operations:

> Well, I find personally that I don't like working with part-time people. Because they're not sufficiently with us as a team . . . There are other areas in the company that they can work in, but it's not for me in this area. (Orla, two children)

Two women entrepreneurs felt that smaller businesses did not have the necessary financial resources to make work–life balance policies available or to introduce them:

> A lot of the [public sector WLB] practices . . . don't really apply to small businesses. In fact, a small business does not have the luxury to do that. (Gemma, three children)
>
> [WLB] would be important to a fair extent. But you have to watch it, because there is a level where it becomes disruptive. (Catherine, two stepchildren)

The subtext of this disruption was often the (relative) cost of maternity leave and the flexibility required by mothers (not parents) to care for their children. When identified as an issue, offering work–life balance practices tended to be seen as a solution to problems arising from caring responsibilities:

> We do, flexitime is available here for those who want to take it, I would certainly always, as a mother myself, encourage that to be available. (Emily, two children)
>
> Well we did part-time for this girl, when she asked for it she got it, guys have no responsibilities, they are happy working their 39 hours. (Maura, one child)

Implicit in these comments is the view that work–life balance practices are required predominantly to meet the needs of mothers. This was noted among male and female managers in Irish public and private sectors (Drew and Daverth 2009), who mentioned the female staff who had availed, or were availing of, work–life balance practices.

However, Lisa pointed out that these should not be restricted to women only:

> Work/life balance is a good idea. Nowadays, it certainly is my experience here . . . It's not exclusively a female issue. I get very irritated . . . about the way it's portrayed in the media as being almost exclusively a female issue. (Lisa with two dependent children)

Women entrepreneurs generally felt that work–life balance practices were important for their staff. However, there was a feeling that implementing work–life balance practices was quite problematic, in relation to cost, practicality, reliance on a particular team, and feasibility of work–life balance options. Given the opportunity (and the resources), women entrepreneurs exhibited a degree of altruism toward their staff. Many identified with their employees, and particularly with those who were mothers with child care responsibilities, even though the majority of women entrepreneurs felt they could not, in practice, utilize work–life balance practices for themselves. Lisa concluded

> I think I have no option [about implementing work/life balance practices], that's the way things are going, I just have to get up to speed on it, and I just have to make sure we've got the management skills in place to manage people who are opting for various forms of flexibility. I think that's the way it's going to be, so we just need to be there, doing it. (Lisa with two dependent children)

These comments point to the need for new ways of thinking, not only about gender at work, but also parenthood and balancing of care and domestic work within the home.

Strategies

Delegation to Partner

A striking feature among interviewees was their home environment. Of the six married/cohabiting women entrepreneurs, five had husbands/partners who were involved full- or part-time in running the home:

> I should say though that I am in an unusual scenario, in that my husband would be full-time at home. He's been full-time at home for three years . . . But before he went full-time at home, he worked part-time at home. (Gemma, two children)

> [My husband] is self-employed, so that's extremely easy again. He can actually work at night. We've always had nannies . . . I went back to work when they [my children] were three weeks old, which was very very stupid, I wouldn't do that if it happened again, if I had that time again. (Orla, two children)

A further three interviewees' partners were involved with their wives' business ventures and could work from home:

> Likewise he [my husband] too tries to take two or three days, if we're here in the country, and not travelling, working from home and we both have separate offices at home. (Emily, two children)

[My husband] he's probably a little bit more flexible . . . So for example he will sometimes [be flexible], depending on what he's doing and what project he's on at a particular time. (Lisa, two children)

I mean that's what we worked out, that wherever possible there was usually one of us at home. He was in a work situation where I couldn't rely on him to be home or anything, and we decided that it wasn't for us and it wasn't what we wanted. (Teresa, one child)

This pattern was noted by Caputo and Dolinsky (1998) who concluded that the presence of young children increased the likelihood of women choosing self-employment as did the scale of child care that their husbands provided. From a feminist perspective, we find this pattern among women interviewees encouraging, as it seems that entrepreneurship could form a way of challenging the status quo at home and at work.

Delegation to Nanny/Crèche

Another strategy for entrepreneurial mothers was to enlist the help of professionals in the form of nannies and day care:

We've always had very very high quality nanny. . . I struggled with it an awful lot when I was younger, what effect it would have on my children? Was I with them enough? (Orla, two children)

I tend to rely on the crèche to do [my son's] homework and I know it's going to be an issue for me in a year of two . . . Well you see it's hard . . . there isn't a partner in my life, so I feel it's all on my shoulders to do it. (Maura, one child).

Sacrifices and Sources of Conflict

It was evident before asking specifically about their experience of conflict in their work versus business lives that two mothers had experienced dilemmas arising from their own personal expectations and desires, even though they had supportive male partners, dilemmas that were fuelled by very essentialist notions of what it means to be male or female:

I think it's harder for women, because I think women take more responsibility for the running of the home. No matter how good their partner is, and no matter how supportive, I still think, it's so engrained in us, so much part of our nature . . . I think we are by nature, organisers and planners . . . I think [women] can keep a lot of balls in the air . . . I have a very supportive husband, who did, when I was very busy . . . did do a lot of the home management, but I think, even now, I make all the decisions about schools and I make all the [school] contacts. (Emily, two children)

When I was younger and I had the children, it [gender] had a much bigger effect on me. I had a feeling of being pushed and pulled by my emotions, and whether or not I was doing the right thing with my children. These are things that I don't think that my brothers suffered. (Orla, two children)

These comments clearly demonstrate that, as women and mothers, Emily and Orla felt torn between the demands of business while still believing in a strongly prescribed maternal role in the care of their children. More positively, Emily saw herself as a decisive organizer/planner who could apply these skills in the home and her business.

Only one of the women entrepreneurs stated that she had experienced no conflict between her family and her professional life. Rather she had sacrificed her social life. Lisa, with her company listed among the top 50 Irish businesses in 2005, felt particularly passionate about her business and her entrepreneurial status. She saw the two aspects of her life as intrinsically linked:

I would think family life is part of my work life, my work life is part of my family life, they blend quite a bit, my children are very aware of what I do, I get them involved in what I'm involved . . . I grew up in a family business, and that was all around me, we didn't separate our family life from our work life . . . So I don't really experience a conflict . . . I don't do the sacrifice bit, not at all. In fact, if anything, I would really say that they complement each other. I find, having children is just marvellous. It's a great enjoyment . . . I think . . . if I had sacrificed anything, I'd say I sacrificed a social life . . . I'm sure if that was really important to me I wouldn't sacrifice it, but it's not as important to me as my children and work. (Lisa, two children)

Other interviewees had experienced a conflict between their family life and their work life in relation to time spent with their children, caring responsibilities, the need to multitask, and, finally, society's expectations of them. Three of the women entrepreneurs felt that they had sacrificed time with their offspring due to their business:

I suppose you sacrifice when the children are smaller, not being around enough. That's the choice! . . . But I think my children thought they would have suffered more if I was at home! I wouldn't have been very happy. But would I like a little bit more time? Yes. (Sarah, four children)

I don't know that there is such a thing as a perfect balance. I would regret, if I had any regrets, I would regret not having more time with my children when they were younger, these early pre-school years . . . There was a conflict . . . for a period. And I had a lot of travelling . . . and I go down to collect [my son] who was then maybe five, and the teacher said 'Oh I always know when you're away because he's always upset in the classroom', and you know you just hate that . . . Would I do it again? I don't know. I felt I had no choice at the time. (Emily, two children)

I think every woman, every mother wonders, you know, am I doing enough and all the rest of it. And then, when I look at my kids, and they're kind of pretty well adjusted . . . they're all very independent, independently minded, and that's a combination of both parents. And I really wonder, how many times do men ask that question? Never, I'd say. (Gemma, three children)

Spending time with children was closely followed by issues associated with caring and managing the home as sources of conflict for women entrepreneurs. Entrepreneurial mothers experienced high levels of guilt, uncertainty, and insecurity. Emily believed that the psychological responsibility for the home and the children was the hardest part she had to deal with. She also felt that women assume greater responsibility for the well-being of their children and the smooth running of the home. She concluded that when women choose not to execute their traditional feminine roles, they have a large amount of guilt to deal with:

[The conflict] is completely, solely, and exclusively female. I don't believe [my husband] would have it on the same emotional level that I would have . . . I think it is the female, I think it is the mother role, the responsibility, and it is also about the fact that we take the responsibility more for what happens within the home. The ups and downs of a five years old's life, and his/her worries/concerns. (Emily, two children)

Sarah indicated that this conflict had been one of the root causes of the breakdown of her marriage:

I definitely think that if I was a man, I wouldn't have to double job, which I think I do, because I still run the home. Through my marriage . . . my job was also in the house and there was no allowances made for that . . . if I had been another man, then I would have just sat down, not worried about the cooking and the cleaning and the whatever. I have plenty of help and I pay for help, but my children would prefer if I cook the . . . I still do a lot myself [even though] I have a full-time nanny and a housekeeper. (Sarah, four children)

Overall, these findings reinforce the notion that women are expected to do well in all areas of their lives and to juggle many things within that (Hochschild 1997):

Yes because, as a woman, you're fulfilling two, three roles, so there was conflict. There's the job, there's the wife and there's the mother . . . trying to be everything to everybody is very difficult. (Sarah, four children)

I think women are good at keeping things, many things, on the go, men are less good at that. (Gemma, three children)

It can also be argued that the kaleidoscope model outlined by Mainiero and Sullivan (2005, 106) could be used to describe the complex work styles of the mothers interviewed in which "women shift the pattern of their careers by rotating different aspects in their lives to arrange their roles and relationships in new ways." This rotation extended into juggling with time zones (Emily's working pattern when based with her children in the United States) and even breast-feeding, always in the perceived best interests of their children. However, the workload adjustments also took their toll:

> *Men have been brought up to believe, by society, to believe that they needed to work and they needed to support their family, and be the breadwinners. Women have a choice. And the thing in a way, makes me out to be much more of an 'uncaring bitch' of a mother because my choice was to work, and to work full-time. (Orla, two children)*

> *In the early years, when I was travelling long days, and I would have worked from about 10 in the morning until about 12 at night. In some cases, I remember standing at the kitchen sink and getting the bottles ready ... and I was expressing my milk, and trying to breastfeed and during the day putting him into the crèche ... All those kind of things were very very tough because it's a whole other area. And then, the whole hormonal emotional thing after you have baby, and then there is the practical fact that they don't sleep at night. So you're not getting your sleep either. And you don't have a moment to yourself at weekends. So I think you have to train like a marathon runner to be a working mother of young children—physically and emotionally. (Emily, two children)*

It is evident throughout the interview narratives that the mothers were highly conscious of society's expectations of them. The majority felt that they experienced a great degree of conflict because they were taking on two very different and divergent roles. First, by being successful businesswomen, they were, to some extent, adopting the traditional male breadwinner model. However, because of their status as women, and as such for many, mothers and wives, they also felt they were expected to fulfill their role as carers. Furthermore, there was a tendency among women to punish themselves for experiencing a conflict. There was a general sense of guilt, regret, and resignation, particularly surrounding the welfare of their children.

Discussion

This analysis reiterates the predicted juggling faced by women who choose to pursue a career while having children, by highlighting the time pressures and tensions that can often lead to stress and guilt. Without exception, the mothers interviewed felt primarily responsible for their business (even when involved with a partner) *and* their children. Yet the strategies employed to facilitate this did demonstrate that fathers' involvement could be of critical importance. More predictably, mothers drew upon professionals to provide domestic and caring work within the household and most had adapted their work styles to allow them to spend time with their children. Though conscious of the fact that men would have done it differently, none of the mothers interviewed had challenged the culture of entrepreneurship itself, though some had stepped back from the imperative to grow their business when this could have jeopardized the delicate balancing act of providing care alongside running an enterprise.

The interviews highlight the conflicting tensions that women entrepreneurs face in combining parenthood with running a business. For men entrepreneurs, the prevailing corporate world and family discourses do not imply any incompatibility in work and lifestyles—there is no implicit tension and conflict. In strong contrast, the Irish women entrepreneurs, like their Chinese counterparts, are subject to "conflicting images and behavioural scripts" (Deetz 2003) from family and corporate discourses, which leave them needing to perform against impossible odds, and to doubtful acknowledgement—damned if they succeed as entrepreneurs (hence implicitly abandoning their children) and damned if their business fails (citing the domestic division of labor as the overriding factor). The women interviewed were at pains to elaborate on how they had addressed "the time with their children" dilemma by adjusting their schedules, working from home, and compressing their working day to allow them time to spend with their children. However, they had seldom taken maternity leave away from their businesses.

On a more positive note, there is some indication that entrepreneurship provided the women interviewed with the tools necessary in shaping their work environment to suit their needs. For example, it was possible for some women to work the number of hours they chose and/or from home, without encountering penalties for not conforming to the prevalent long-hour culture in employment. Furthermore, some also felt that entrepreneurship had allowed them to work within an environment supportive of the people in it.

Feminist research has sought to address the gendered divisions in the labor market *and* in the domestic sphere (Drew 2000), pointing to the fact that gender roles are not immutable but socially and culturally constructed. The challenge ahead will be to reexamine and redesign the social context for entrepreneurship to take account of the allocation of child care and domestic responsibilities in order to forge an alternative model in which otherness is incorporated. As Deetz (2003, 43) states, "Developing a sense of *care*, as an appreciation of *otherness*, is central to reclaiming a form of democracy appropriate to the modern age." Only an alternative model can ensure that it is not only mothers who shoulder the dual burden of work and care for the needs of family members, while fathers limit their role to that of providers.

Research and Policy Implications

Across EU states, the adherence to gender-specific roles associated with caring leads mothers, rather than fathers, to seek solutions, by adopting flexible working practices and availing of maternity/parental leave. In employment, this is precisely the mechanism that leads to an undervaluing of women's contributions as employees, and legitimizes their societal role as the primary carers. While most employees have only minimal power and autonomy over their working environment, it is possible for them to fashion, to some degree, their own caring arrangements that take place in a nonemployment environment. Entrepreneurship, while providing an equivalent source of income, also offers an alternative course of action to individual men and women. In theory, entrepreneurship could provide a mechanism to rethink gender roles, which imply a dichotomy between work and caring, by creating opportunities to integrate these activities. Unlike the employment sphere, in which specific working hours or patterns of leave allocation are, to a large degree, determined by the organization, entrepreneurship could facilitate alternative time and task allocations by men and women. This would have important implications for parents who wish to reduce the time spent in paid work in order to be more involved in unpaid caring and domestic work. Entrepreneurs, as distinct from employees, could command the freedom to do gender differently through making adjustments to their working patterns that would be more difficult in regular employment. However, effecting structural changes in a business enterprise would be limited by the prevailing social and cultural factors and constraints, most notably in gender role expectations. Martin (2003) argues that to redress gender inequalities, not only are major structural changes required (in how work is undertaken and adherence to hierarchy and the divisions of labor), but also other feminist goals would need to take precedence over organizational objectives such as efficiency or profitability. However, in the context of business endeavor, Martin acknowledges that such goals may make it harder for feminist organizations to survive, particularly in the long term.

Gender roles are under challenge, not least from the feminist movement. Women now take on many roles that were traditionally reserved for men such as leadership in politics and business, while men have sought a more active role in fathering. However, international research suggests that despite growing support by men and women for more parental involvement on the part of fathers, this is not reflected in practice. Das Dores Guerreiro and Pereira (2007, 204) argue, from a Portuguese perspective, that "male participation in household tasks is generally low, quite specialized and very often perceived as extra help," while U.S. researchers such as Kimmel (2004) and Griswold (1998) point to fatherhood as an evolving role with varying degrees and forms of involvement by fathers with their children. In Europe, the prevailing role of 20th-century fathers remains being the breadwinner (Crompton, Lewis, and Lyonette 2007; Drew, Emerek, and Mahon 1998) in an asymmetrical relationship with a housewife/carer partner.

Future Research

The interview data are limited in number, which restricts the generalizability of the findings. However, the narratives provide a rich source of information on the ways that entrepreneurial mothers had adapted their working lives around the needs of their families—rather than vice versa. They underline the expected internalization of social expectations about their roles as primary caregivers. Without further follow-up research it would be difficult to conjecture whether this represents a temporary transitional state or a more permanently embedded adherence to gendered parenting roles. The women interviewed were all of Irish ethnicity and had been socialized into a national ethos in which family is of paramount importance and into the implication that a "woman's place is [still] in the home with her children." Cross-country comparisons are needed along with studies of women from different ethnic backgrounds who are now better represented among a more ethnically diverse Irish population. Further, diversity and gender balance could be introduced for future interviews with the inclusion of fathers in similar sectors and sized businesses and likewise women who are in lesbian partnerships.

Note

1. Contraception and divorce have been legalized. In 2013, the Protection of Life During Pregnancy Act was passed. It defines the circumstances and processes within which abortion in Ireland can be legally performed where pregnancy endangers a woman's life, including through a risk of suicide.

References

Ahl, H. 2004. *The Scientific Reproduction of Gender Inequality: A Discourse Analysis of Research Texts on Women's Entrepreneurship.* Copenhagen: CBS Press.

Baines, S., J. Wheelock, and U. Gelder. 2003. *Riding the Roller Coaster: Family Life and Self-Employment*. Bristol: The Policy Press.

Bruni, A., S. Gherardi, and B. Poggio. 2004. "Entrepreneur-Mentality, Gender and the Study of Women Entrepreneurs." *Journal of Organizational Change Management* 17 (3): 256–68.

Brush, C., A. de Bruin, and F. Welter. 2009. "A Gender-Aware Framework for Women's Entrepreneurship." *International Journal of Gender and Entrepreneurship* 1 (1): 8–24.

Caputo, R., and A. Dolinsky. 1998. "Women's Choice to Pursue Self-employment: The Role of Financial and Human Capital of Household Members." *Journal of Small Business Management* 36 (3): 8–17.

Carter, N., and K. Allen. 1997. "Size Determinants of Women-Owned Businesses: Choice or Barriers to Resources?" *Entrepreneurship and Regional Development* 9 (3): 211–20.

Carter, S., and E. Shaw. 2006. "Women's Business Ownership: Recent Research and Policy Developments." Report to the Small Business Service. London: Department of Trade and Industry Small Business Service.

Central Statistics Office (CSO). 2012. *Women and Men in Ireland 2011*. Dublin: Stationery Office.

Chell, E., and S. Baines. 1998. "Does Gender Affect Business 'Performance'? A Study of Microbusinesses in Business Services in the UK." *Entrepreneurship and Regional Development* 10 (2): 117–35.

Commission on the Family. 1998. "Strengthening Families for Life, Main Report, July." Dublin: Stationery Office.

Coveney, E., J. Murphy-Lawless, and S. Sheridan. 1998. *Women, Work and Family Responsibilities*. Dublin: Larkin Unemployed Centre.

Creswell, J. W. 2003. *Research Design: Qualitative, Quantitative, and Mixed Methods Approaches*. 2nd ed. Thousand Oaks, CA: Sage.

Crompton, R., S. Lewis, and C. Lyonette, eds. 2007. *Women, Men, Work and Family in Europe*. Hampshire: Palgrave Macmillan.

Das Dores Guerreiro, M., and I. Pereira. 2007. "Women's Occupational Patterns and Work-Family Arrangements: Do National and Organisational Policies Matter?" In *Women, Men, Work and Family in Europe*, edited by R. Crompton, S. Lewis, and C. Lyonette. 159–82. Hampshire: Palgrave Macmillan.

Deetz, S. 2003. "Disciplinary Power, Conflict Suppression and Human Resource Management." In *Studying Management Critically*, edited by M. Alvesson and H. Willmott. 23–45. Thousand Oaks, CA: Sage Publications.

Drew, E. 2000. "Reconciling Divisions of Labour." In *Gender, Economy and Culture in the European Union*, edited by S. Duncan and B. Pfau-Effinger. 87–111. London: Routledge.

Drew, E., and G. Daverth. 2009. "Living to Work . . . or Working to Live? The Role of Managers in Creating Work–Life Balance in Ireland." Briefing paper. Dublin: Irish Congress of Trade Unions. Available at: http://www.ictu.ie/download /pdf/20090113104912.pdf.

Drew, E., and A. Humbert. 2010. "Squaring the Circle? Work and Family Issues among Owners of Small Business Enterprises in Ireland." Proceedings of the 33rd Institute for Small Business and Enterprise Conference, November 2–4. London. Available at: http://www.tara.tcd.ie/bitstream/2262/64128/1/ISBE%202010.pdf.

Drew, E., and A. Humbert. 2012. "'Men Have Careers, Women Have Babies': Unequal Parental Care among Irish Entrepreneurs." *Community, Work & Family* 15 (1): 49–67.

Drew, E., R. Emerek, and E. Mahon, eds. 1998. *Women, Work and the Family in Europe.* London: Routledge.

Duchéneaut, B., and M. Orhan. 2000. *Les Femmes Entrepreneurs en France, Percée des Femmes dans un Monde Construit au Masculin.* Paris: Seli Arslan.

Essers, C., and Y. Benschop. 2007. "Female Entrepreneurs of Moroccan or Turkish Origin in the Netherlands." *Organization Studies* 28 (1): 49–69.

Fahey, T. 2001. "Trends in Irish Fertility Rates in Comparative Perspective." *The Economic and Social Review* 32 (2): 153–80.

Fleck, E. 2010. "To Grow or Not to Grow: Challenges and Choices for Women Entrepreneurs." Proceedings of the 33rd Institute for Small Business and Enterprise Conference, November 2–4. London.

Global Entrepreneurship Monitor (GEM). 2009. "GEM Ireland 2008 National Report." Dublin: Enterprise Ireland.

Goffee, R., and R. Scase. 1985. *Women in Charge: The Experiences of Female Entrepreneurs.* London: Allen & Unwin.

Goodbody Economic Consultants. 2002. "Entrepreneurship in Ireland." Report to Forfás. Dublin: Goodbody Economic Consultants.

Greene, P. G., M. M. Hart, E. J. Gatewood, C. G. Brush, and N. M. Carter. 2003. "Women Entrepreneurs: Moving Front and Center: An Overview of Research and Theory." *USASBE White Papers, United States Association for Small Business and Entrepreneurship.*

Griswold, R. L. 1998. *Fatherhood in America: A History.* New York: Basic Books.

Gupta, V., D. Turban, S. Wasti, and A. Sikdar. 2009. "The Role of Gender Stereotypes in Perceptions of Entrepreneurs and Intentions to Become an Entrepreneur." *Entrepreneurship: Theory and Practice* 2 (March): 397–417.

Halman, L., R. Inglehart, and M. Basanez. 2007. *Changing values and beliefs in 85 countries: Trends from the values surveys from 1981 to 2004.* European Values Studies. Leiden, Netherlands: Brill.

Henry, C., and S. Kennedy. 2003. "In Search of a New Celtic Tiger: Female Entrepreneurship in Ireland." In *New Perspectives on Female Entrepreneurs*, edited by J. Butler. Hong Kong: Information Age Publishing.

Hochschild, A. 1997 *The Second Shift*. New York: Metropolitan Books.

Humbert, A. L. 2007. "An Exploratory Study of Women Entrepreneurs in Ireland." Unpublished PhD thesis. Trinity College Dublin.

Humbert, A. L., and E. Drew. 2010. "Gender, Entrepreneurship and Motivational Factors in an Irish Context." *International Journal of Gender and Entrepreneurship* 2 (2): 173–96.

Humbert, A. L., and S. Lewis. 2008. "I Have No Other Life than Work—Long Working Hours, Blurred Boundaries and Family Life: The Case of Irish Entrepreneurs." In *The Long Work Hours Culture, Causes, Consequences and Choices*, edited by R. J. Burke and C. L. Cooper. Bingley: Emerald Publishing.

Jackson, P. 1993. "Managing the Mothers: The Case of Ireland." In *Women and Social Policies in Europe: Work, Family and the State*, edited by J. Lewis. 72–91. Aldershot: Edward Elgar.

Jones, C., and A. Spicer. 2009. *Unmasking the Entrepreneur*. Cheltenham: Edward Elgar.

Kimmel, M. S. 2004. *The Gendered Society*. New York: Oxford University Press.

Lee, C., and R. G. Owens. 2002. "Men, Work and Gender." *Australian Psychologist* 37 (1): 13–19.

Lerner, M., and T. Almor. 2002. "Relationships among Strategic Capabilities and the Performance of Women-Owned Small Ventures." *Journal of Small Business Management* 40 (2): 109–25.

Lunn, P., T. Fahey, and C. Hannan. 2009. "Family Figures: Family Dynamics and Family Types in Ireland 1986–2006." Dublin: Economic and Social Research Institute. Available at: http://www.fsa.ie/fileadmin/user_upload/Files/Familly_Figures.pdf.

Mainiero, L., and S. Sullivan. 2005. "Kaleidoscope Careers: An Alternate Explanation for the 'Opt-Out' Revolution." *Academy of Management Executive* 19 (1): 106–23.

Marlow, S. 1997. "Self-Employed Women—New Opportunities, Old Challenges?" *Entrepreneurship and Regional Development* 9 (3): 199–210.

Martin, J. 2003. "Feminist Theory and Critical Theory: Unexplored Synergies." In *Studying Management Critically*, edited by M. Alvesson and H. Willmott. 66–91. London: Sage.

McClelland, E. 2003. "A Cross Border Exploratory Study of Internationalising Female Entrepreneurs in Ireland." Paper presented at the Promoting Female Entrepreneurship Conference. Dundalk Institute of Technology.

Mirchandani, K. 1999. "Feminist Insight on Gendered Work: New Directions in Research on Women and Entrepreneurship." *Gender, Work and Organization* 6 (4): 224–35.

Moore, D. P., and H. E. Buttner. 1997. *Women Entrepreneurs: Moving Beyond the Glass Ceiling*. New Delhi: Sage.

O'Gorman, C., and S. Terjesen. 2006. "Financing the Celtic Tigress: Venture Financing and Informal Investment in Ireland." *Venture Capital: An International Journal of Entrepreneurial Finance* 8 (1): 69–88.

Orhan, M., and D. Scott. 2001. "Why Women Enter into Entrepreneurship: An Explanatory Model." *Women in Management Review* 16 (5): 232–43.

Rees, T. 1992. *Women and the Labour Market*. Routledge, London.

Remenyi, D., B. Williams, A. Money, and E. Swartz. 1998. *Doing Research in Business and Management: An Introduction to Process and Method*. London: Sage.

Rouse, J., and K. Boles. 2005. "The Big NES Survey 2004: An Evaluation of the Experiences of New Entrepreneur Scholars." *Manchester Metropolitan University Business School*. Available at: http://www.nesprogramme.org/index.htm. Accessed January 4, 2012.

Rubery, J., M. Smith, and C. Fagan. 1999. *Women's Employment in Europe: Trends and Prospects*. London: Routledge.ss

Saunders, M., P. Lewis, and A. Thornhill. 2009. *Research Methods for Business Students*. 5th ed. Harlow, England: FT Prentice Hall.

Sheridan, A. 2004. "Chronic Presenteeism: The Multiple Dimensions to Men's Absence from Part-Time Work." *Gender, Work and Organization* 11 (2): 207–25.

Smith, A. J. 2009. "Representations of Transgender Young Adults in Multiple Medias, or The Transgender Success Story." PhD diss., University of Texas Libraries.

Stevenson, L. 2003. "Facilitating Women's Entrepreneurship." Organisation for Economic Co-Operation and Development workshop on "Entrepreneurship in a Global Economy: Strategic Issues and Policies."

Still, L. V., and W. Timms. 2000. "Women's Business: The Flexible Alternative Workstyle for Women." *Women in Management Review* 15 (5/6): 272–82.

Sunday Times Magazine. 2011. "Red Ladies: Enter the Dragons." May 22: 20–26.

Valiulis, M., E. Drew, A. L. Humbert, and G. Daverth. 2004. "Springboard for Women in Business Initiative: Women in Entrepreneurship." Report to Wicklow Chamber of Commerce.

Walby, S. 1997. *Gender Transformations*. London: Routledge.

Wilson, F., and S. Tagg. 2010. "Social Constructionism and Personal Constructivism Getting the Business Owner's View on the Role of Sex and Gender." *International Journal of Gender and Entrepreneurship* 2 (1): 68–82.

Wynarczyk, P., and S. Marlow, eds. 2010. *Innovating Women: Contributions to Technological Advancement*. London: Institute for Small Business and Entrepreneurship/ Emerald Books.

Chapter 8

Women Who Launch: Making the Transition from Employee to Entrepreneur

Bett Mickels

Women are making the transition from corporate employee to business owner in large numbers. Women are reevaluating what success, excellence, and quality means for them in the workplace. Coaches and advisors for entrepreneurial women see a new surge of energy taking place with female entrepreneurs more than ever. Some women no longer feel satisfied with their role in corporate America regardless of the level of responsibility. Women have the business savvy, motivation, and skills to be successful in business. Many women have already launched a business or are looking at the option to launch a business and leave their corporate positions.

In this chapter, we explore why women leave corporate positions to launch a business. A common reason women launch a business is because of a reduction in force (RIF) or reorganization. A growing number of senior women leaders are leaving corporate positions in what is called the executive flight. Women are reshaping the workforce, as women of all ages regard their lives at work as the extension of family, personal, and business values that continue to change. As women launch new businesses in record numbers, they are gaining new personal perspectives. Women who launch new businesses experience self-discovery during times of business successes, challenges, and failures. Launching a business is empowering women in ways women felt could not be achieved by remaining in corporate positions.

Women's transition from corporate careers to business ownership is a trend expanded outside of the United States. In this chapter, we present an international observation of women launching businesses, to provide an understanding of how women's entrepreneurship differs between countries and cultures. The differences and commonalities of women launching businesses in Malaysia, Afghanistan, Taiwan, Nigeria, and Australia will be examined.

As women transition from the titles of employees to entrepreneurs, they experience newfound benefits as well as difficulties. The loss that women experience regarding benefits and corporate perks is tangible resources lost and not quickly recovered. Launching a business takes priority for some women over the security of employment, salary, and benefits. Women who launch experience doubts, confusion, and at times, second-guess their decision to leave a corporate environment.

Six stories from women who launched businesses after departing from corporate positions are included in this chapter. The reader will learn about what it takes to build a career outside of a corporate environment. In this chapter, we provide the types of support and advice women received when launching a business. Women shared what they needed, what they learned, and skills they acquired or bought during their business launch.

Support is available in a variety of sources to women who launch. Government-sponsored initiatives, national and local associations, and professional groups are available for women who launch. A personal relationship with an experienced women entrepreneur is how many women shorten the entrepreneurial learning curve. Support resources available for women who launch are provided in this chapter.

Throughout the chapter are original stories of women who launched a business. You may be inspired by the challenges, transitions, and accomplishments found in their personal experiences. Some women left a successful career to launch a business searching for life balance, control, and a revival of passion. Women leveraged acquired corporate experience into their new business. Skills and knowledge needed for entrepreneurs and how women compensated for skills they did not possess are examined in this chapter. Friends and family often encourage women to avoid disruption in life and career (Johnson 2012). But many women found that a career disruption resulting in a move from employee to entrepreneur was just what was needed. Career disruption is increasing because younger and more technically advanced workforce is entering corporate organizations. Global competition for corporate jobs is also increasing career disruption.

A trend reveals that women are starting more businesses, particularly home-based microbusinesses. The majority of these businesses employ fewer than five people. "Women will create over half of the 972 million new small-business jobs expected to be created by 2018 and more and more are doing this from home offices across the country" (McNeil 2012, 230. The Resource Center for

Women Owned Business Research 2008–2009 study reports that 10.1 million organizations are owned by women (more than 50%), 13 million people work for women-owned organizations, and women-owned businesses accounted for $1.9 trillion in sales in 2008. In the next section, we will explore why women launch businesses.

Why Women Launch?

Today's women have fewer barriers to entry when starting a business than those in the previous decade had. The Internet, technology, and a global marketplace are just a few of the reasons why business start-up costs are down. Prior to the power of Internet search engines and low-cost communication methods available to connect with people around the world, the marketing and communication budget for a start-up business kept many women from taking the risks associated with start-ups.

One reason why women are exiting the corporate workplace is the invisible glass ceiling. Daniel (2004, 60) says that women are "voting with their feet and making a loud statement that the corporate environment—with its hierarchy and closed networks—just does not fit." In an entrepreneurial environment, women are finding what they have always longed for—an environment that is inclusive, motivating, and respectful of women differences and uniqueness (Daniel, 2004).

Numerous researchers have cited reasons why women have been successful in launching a business. According to Daniel, special success skills that women possess are communication skills, people skills, web thinking, consensus building, nurturing skills, and relationship building. There were factors that did not differ between male and female entrepreneurs in the areas of sales, profitability, and employee development.

Male-gender-driven protocol provides barriers for women. Starting a business is the dream of many women because they desire to have more control over their lives. Some women are driven intrinsically as well as competitively and look for a balance to their busy days. Other women find self-employment as a means to provide the basics—food, clothing, and shelter—for their families. There are many reasons for starting an entrepreneurial business. Sometimes there are no other financial alternatives for women to support themselves and families except starting a business.

Some women have no choice but to begin a business after an RIF or reorganization. It may be difficult to find a comparable position in another company after being laid off. Women may have fewer interview skills if they have moved through corporate positions based on relationships they forged.

Felena's Story

Felena launched her business after being laid off three times from marketing and advertising positions over an eight-year period. After her third layoff she decided that rather than finding another *job*, she would create her own business in marketing. Marketing and advertising consulting was a natural fit for a business because of her expertise in corporate marketing positions.

Felena did not want prospective clients to think she was a woman working alone out of her home. She missed networking with other women and struggled with where to take clients for meetings. The coffee shop down the street was often crowded and noisy, and working from home was isolating.

Many women use the skills learned in their corporate positions to launch their businesses. Felena commented, "With an MBA and a solid background in marketing from my previous corporate positions, I was able to launch my consulting practice. I could help companies see issues from an objective angle, a 30,000 foot view." Over an eight-year period, Felena helped small service companies grow their business through a marketing niche she created.

Felena started her first marketing consulting business as most entrepreneurs do with an employee of one—herself. Felena would often catch herself inflating her business when she was out networking. She would refer to her business as *we* rather than *I*. It sounded more impressive and professional, and she did not want to appear to be a one-women business. Felena determined that if she is having this difficulty with her transition from corporate employee to businesswoman, there must be other women in the same situation. Understanding her business start-up transition needs led to the development of a successful women-only office space and networking business in San Diego called Hera Hub.

Hera Hub provides a coworking office space for female entrepreneurs so women can meet with clients and collaborate with other women entrepreneurs. Felena supports women entrepreneurs challenged with appearing professional, prominent, and powerful to prospective clients. The location is more than an office; it is a haven where women support women. Felena comments, "I started my business without a mentor or advisory board. At Hera Hub it is amazing for me to see how much women are willing to help each other." Find out more about Felena and Hera Hub at www.herahub.com.

Felena's Story (End)

Many of the women we talked to stated that they felt the need to launch a business because of a loss of control over their time, a lack of balance with family and loved ones, and a misfit with values. Abarbanel (2008) found during inter-views with women entrepreneurs who are reshaping the workplace that the Internet, a volatile economy, and stage of life shifts contributed to transition-ing from corporate career to business ownership. Freedom and flexibility were found as the most common reasons women launch business as espoused by such organizations like Ladies Who Launch.

A study entitled *The Top Women-Led Businesses in Massachusetts: Lessons from 2000 to 2004*, sponsored by Babson College and the Commonwealth Institute, cited a desire for greater personal achievement and more challenging work as reasons women leave corporate positions (Abarbanel 2008). In the next story, an executive vice president in a large financial institution shares the reasons for her leaving a corner office at a major corporation.

Ruth's Story

Ruth worked in corporate America in both New York and California in a career that spanned 30 years. She watched firsthand the financial crash that unfolded starting in 2008 while reporting directly to the chief financial officer of a large national financial institution. Ruth never saw herself as an entrepreneur, but rather as a loyal company employee. When her long-standing boss of 10 years decided to retire very suddenly, it forced her to take a closer look at her own situation. As Ruth calls it, she had her "face-in-the-mirror moment," where she finally put a name to feelings she had long been having. She identified herself as disengaged, and decided to make a significant career decision.

Ruth explains, "I would sit in my corner office for the first half hour of the day staring at my computer. I did not want to talk to my colleagues." Ruth was concerned her team and peers might see her disengagement. She owed them more than that. It became clear to Ruth that with the organizational changes underway, the firm really did not need her role, and she decided it would be a good time to leave.

Some of her friends and work acquaintances were experiencing similar feel-ings in their jobs, but did not label themselves as *disengaged*. Many of them, Ruth included, worked for a bully boss at some point in their corporate lives and came to the realization that they did not want their lives to be dictated by someone else anymore. As Ruth says, "Leaving was the only way to get some control back in my life." For at least a year she was thinking about leaving and was mulling over ideas about what comes next. She was fortunate to retire from her employer and decided now was the time to begin a new challenge.

Ruth started her business to focus on an area she is passionate about, which is training and coaching managers to be the best they can be. She believed that frontline managers are often overlooked and not given the resources needed to do their jobs. Her desire was to train these managers in areas such as coaching and feedback, situational leadership, and legal aspects of management. Her new business did not go completely according to plan. Instead, she spent a majority of her time working directly with managers and their teams as a coach and mentor. Her first consulting contract was not awarded based on slick advertising or marketing. Ruth was handpicked by someone whose new firm she took a chance on 14 years earlier when he launched a business start-up. The two forged a great working relationship, and when he heard years later about her company, he hired Ruth to coach his new human resource manager.

Ruth comments, "Marketing my new business is the hardest thing I have ever done. I am not a sales person. I do not even like marketing myself. I am not great at touting my horn. This is the hardest part for me." She surprised herself at how large of a network she built as an executive vice president. She could rely on these relationships to support her during her business start-up. She admits that relationship networks do not always translate into paid consulting business. Ruth has completed a number of pro bono jobs and speaks at several conferences each year to build her business. She has faith that at some point, this type of networking and relationship building will pay off.

Ruth believes that an advantage of launching her own business is the control she now has over her life. Creating her company has reignited her passion for the kind of work she does. Her belief in being passionate about what she does came from her dad. He always told her that passion about her work is the secret to success. He did not retire until he was 72 because he loved what he did. He served as a great role model for Ruth. An outcome of starting her own business is that Ruth quickly realized how creative she actually was. Starting this business allowed her to go through a period of self-discovery that was enlightening.

According to Ruth, the disadvantage of owning your own business is like being on a never-ending roller coaster ride. Rejection is not something she was accustomed to in her executive role. As a consultant, you have to prove yourself over and over to new people all the time. Many times you will not get the consulting contract or something you thought you firmed up falls apart at the last minute. Handling the emotional highs and lows of selling your services is something new that she is learning, but Ruth would not change a thing about her new engaged career.

Ruth's Story (End)

As many women trade in corporate America for entrepreneurship, women are becoming major players in the traditional and e-business market environments

(Delaney 2003). Women are not afraid to support and encourage other women entering the entrepreneurial field. Women supporting women is one element that is less common in more competitive male-dominated environments. In the early decades leading up to the Internet and technology revolutions, women were more willing to forgo personal and professional goals for workplace security.

Women seek freedom, work-life balance, flexibility, and opportunities to leave a legacy (Delaney 2003). Women are concerned about being a mother who is available, a friend who comes when needed, a daughter who can care for her parents, and a businesswoman who can find recognition, money, and opportunities in her business. In the next section, we will explore women all over the world who launch businesses.

In a survey of executive women who already left or were considering leaving their corporate positions, a study conducted by the University of North Carolina found that the number one reason women left corporate employment was to do something that mattered to them (Helgesen and Johnson 2011). Primarily, personal meaning and satisfaction motivate women's career decisions. In a corporate world driven by profits, and a shareholder-pleasing marketplace, it is not surprising that many women are taking the entrepreneurial route (Helgesen and Johnson 2011).

International Women Who Launch

Around the world, women are leaving employment positions at a similar trend as those seen in the Americas. Although the trend is somewhat similar to the United States, the reasons women leave and the challenges they encounter differ. Many researchers in countries around the globe are researching and studying this workplace movement trend as it unfolds. Xavier et al. (2011) found of Malaysian women entrepreneurs who transitioned from corporate careers to business ownership with similar reasons and rationale for corporate flight as their American counterparts. Relevant factors that led Malaysian women to launch businesses leaving corporate positions were needs for achieving personal growth, independence, and economic payoff (Xavier et al. 2011).

Specific personal skills were predominant in Malaysian women entrepreneurs. These skills included communication skills, specifically listening, and self-discipline. The specific entrepreneurial skills that were strongly indicated by the women studied were "showing confidence, leadership skills, creative thinking in problem solving, being efficient and effective in executing plans, entrepreneurial/business knowledge, being analytical, balancing skills between personal and business life, and flexibility i.e. ability to change" (Ahmad and

Xavier 2011, 220). There were no real differences among any of the major ethnic groups in Malaysia.

Holmen, Min, and Saarelainen (2011) researched Afghan entrepreneurial women during the start-up and operations of their businesses. They divided the factors for women starting a business into push factors and pull factors. Push factors were compelling reasons in which women had little choice but to begin a new business. This could be the result of unemployment or underemployment. The overwhelming push factor was the generation of income.

Pull factors were related to the desires of women who began a business. Major pull factors for Afghan women were the desire for autonomy and independence. A difference that the researchers discovered was that the need for achievement was not found as a push or pull factor for Afghan women—a noticeable difference from the women of the United States and other international countries. An unexpected finding from the Afghanistan study is that many women begin a business to help other non-family members. This shows a greater need to help, support, and care for those in the community. Support of community employment is a significantly different motivation for launching a business than what researchers found of women in other countries.

Afghan women entering business ownership had little desire for personal achievement (Holmen, Min, and Saarelainen 2011). The main start-up problems for Afghan women included financial and operational problems, which are common to U.S. women entrepreneurs. Afghan women faced other negative factors. Other start-up problems not as prevalent with their U.S. counterparts are personal security, mobility constraints, lack of social acceptance, and negative feelings toward female entrepreneurs (Holmen, Min, and Saarelainen 2011).

In some countries, female entrepreneurs gravitate to specific industries. In Taiwan, for example, the industry of choice for female entrepreneurs is the service industry where 86 percent of all service entrepreneurs are females (Li-Min et al. 2012). There are several reasons for women starting businesses in this area, including specific industry experience of the Taiwanese women and the market social capital that is available to women in this industry. Women recognize the service industry as an opportunity for success based on their personal experience, ability, and judgment.

In Nigeria, women face additional roadblocks because of deeply ingrained traditions in the country's policy, values, and legal environment (Madichie 2009). Some Nigerian men feel threatened by women, which increases discrimination in certain fields. The government tolerates religious and customary practices that adversely affect women (Madichie, 2009). Ironically, a key entrepreneurial driver in Nigeria is support from males. In some areas of the country, Nigerian women feel just as capable and respected as their male counterparts. Many women see progress being made for women entrepreneurs.

In comparison, we looked at the examples of women entrepreneurs from Malaysia, Afghanistan, Taiwan, and Nigeria. Here is an Australian woman's story explaining the development of her global franchising business.

Kim's Story

Kim is a women entrepreneur from Australia who made the decision to start a business after 22 years working for a nonprofit organization. Kim grew her business in five years into a global franchise enterprise. Kim was motivated by a desire to make financial and spiritual differences in her community and in countries around the world.

Kim is an award-winning businesswoman, who is based in the Sunshine Coast of Australia. She is the founder and co-owner of SEA English Academy, a business that has grown over the last five years into a string of international franchises. Kim is driven by a passion for high-quality education and equally by the desire to make a positive impact through her business. She is a high-profile businesswoman who seeks to leverage her experience and success to make a difference in her community and in all the nations.

Kim likens being in business with jumping into a *Learjet* after being on a slow train. For her the destination remains the same: to deliver high-quality English language training, open up opportunities to bless communities around the world, and help to mobilize those who have a heart for mission to those places. However, the vehicle to reach that destination has radically changed. Kim reflects, "Before we started I couldn't imagine the impact we could have or how we could grow as a business. But all of a sudden I realised that with my business card in hand, there was no need for caution. Wherever I went I could say 'this is who I am, I am a businesswomen!'"

Kim started the business on a shoestring with initial start-up costs kept to an absolute minimum and provided largely by business partner Ingrid's salary. They did not have any money for advertising their first course, so they put on free monthly information nights about what the Teachers of English to Speakers of Other Languages course involves, getting their contact details into as many places as possible. Kim says, "Ingrid is great for me, she is a very detailed person and an implementer, whereas I am much more of a visionary and an entrepreneur. We make a great business team."

At first, developing the franchise business slowed everything down a bit. "We needed a framework in order to multiply," says Kim, "We had to document everything and somehow capture the culture of the company into something written down and systematised." Although it slowed them down, this process was exactly what was needed for the business to continue to flourish. Kim shares, "To minimize that risk, we have really focused on building a strong brand, with a strong culture and values. But sometimes things just don't work out and from these experiences we have learnt much more about the kind of people we are looking for in our franchisees." The motto of SEA English Academy is "Inspiration—Education—Destination."[1]

Kim's Story (End)

Researchers and leaders outside of the Unites States are determining if there is enough support for female entrepreneurs. In the developing and high-unemployment country of Tunisia, it was found through a survey that the existing support systems and services were inadequate for servicing female entrepreneurs (Drine and Grach 2012). Many countries are designing specific systems for female entrepreneurial support. Some policy makers are less concerned about the differences between male and female entrepreneurial support policies. These agencies are more concerned about increasing employment in their countries regardless of gender.

Transition from Employee to Entrepreneur

In the 1970s, women left their homes in droves to enter the workforce. Women today are leaving the workforce they fought so hard to get in. Unlike women from generations past, women today are opting to leave the workforce not to stay at home but to be as job-creating entrepreneurs (McNeil 2012). Women transition from corporate positions to business ownership to align their intrinsic values with their work.

The original motivation for women leaving corporate careers to begin their business was not initially satisfied by their transition. Early months and even years after a corporate career transition can be filled with self-doubt, second-guessing, and the harsh reality of no steady income. Research suggests that after a female entrepreneur's business evolves, the personal and professional development that the women underwent supersedes the concerns they had regarding their original motivation to leave their corporate position (Patterson 2009).

Many women entrepreneurs worked extremely hard at corporate objectives and believed they could work just as hard (or even harder) in their business. Some women saw several professional and personal friends make the transition and thought they could do it too. These entrepreneurs were people they could go to for support. Leiber (2007) solicited more than 150 stories from women who were previously on CEO corporate tracks and then transitioned to a start-up business. Many women transition out so they can do things their way and have a say in how things get accomplished (Leiber 2007).

The next story shows how one woman used the skills she acquired in her current retail management position as a jumping-off point for her first business. One way that women launch is by expanding on the skills they like to possess in their corporate position and use those same skills to launch a business.

Andrea's Story

When Andrea was questioned about starting her business she stated, "I simply used what I learned in my corporate position to start my business." This provided an avenue to do what she always wanted to do, which was her love for writing. Andrea comments on why she left her corporate position, "I had to get out of the retail management world. There was too much work and not enough appreciation." As her responsibilities grew in her corporate retail position, her leadership and organization skills increased. Andrea organized employees in a fast-paced, multidisciplined retail environment. Andrea decided to launch a business based on the skills she liked most about her corporate position. She enjoyed organizing and leading employees in a chaotic retail world so they could be more effective. Andrea used the skills she gained over many years of increasing higher-level retail positions to start her business.

Andrea launched Professional Organizer in the early 1980s. She decided to help individuals and businesses organize their homes, offices, and lives. Transition to her business was a natural fit because Andrea was able to use skills she was already using in retail management. She saw a connection between what she got paid to do for her employer and what she could do in her business. Her skills in using resources, systems, processes, and disciplines were the same skill set she used at Professional Organizer.

Andrea helped and taught clients to clean off work areas so they could focus on the specific project they were working on. This included handling papers only once, and using tools and technology for difficult or complex activities. She used her expertise in the organization of things, thoughts, and papers, and to be more effective in less time. These are skills clients were willing to pay for, and her business flourished.

The launch of Professional Organizer became a foundation for her writing passion. While teaching clients and organizations on productivity, she realized many people commented on their need for coaching and support with their businesses in the areas of writing, editing, and publishing.

Andrea used her corporate skills to transition to her business as the owner of Professional Organizer. She used a different motivator, her passion, to launch a second business called WritersWay. She knows what she is good at and where she needs support. She says, "Writing is easy! Publishing is getting easier! Marketing is a challenge! Selling is a learned art!" In WritersWay, Andrea works with individuals and entrepreneurs to get their writing completed and polished for books, e-books, articles, blogs, press releases, or websites. "A win-win for women entrepreneurs is for us to support and recommend each other," explains Andrea. She recommends consultants in her network to clients for specific works she does not do, such as fiction books. Other business entrepreneurs in her network send clients to WritersWay.

Andrea has found a way to incorporate another passion of hers, which is teaching. She created the company The Ebook Academy, an educational portal that provides live and online training in writing, publishing, and promoting e-books. You can reach Andrea at Andrea@WritersWay.com (www.Writers Way.com).

Andrea's Story (End)

According to Sullivan (2001), most successful business entrepreneurs acquire their needed entrepreneurial skills while working for others. Sullivan interviewed Moore, the author of *Careerpreneurs: Lessons from Leading Women Entrepreneurs on Building a Career without Boundaries*. Moore interviewed more than 100 women who started a business after an extensive career, and called these women careerpreneurs. Moore found several areas of expertise that women were already familiar with when they began their start-up businesses. Moore comments that "when they started their businesses, they were already familiar with product diversity, quality, service, operations, cost control, focusing on the customer and all the other important elements in their fields or they were in business with someone who was [familiar with these issues]" (Sullivan 2001, 158).

There are many kinds of financial and administrative problems that entrepreneurs face when starting up a business. Women tend to overcome these difficulties by using a skill found more predominantly in women than men. Women are more prone to develop informal and permanent relationships because of the dual role they play—as businesswomen and the primary role they play in the family (Paoloni and Demartini 2012).

As a member of the labor workforce, women make long-term relationships with many of the people they work with, including peers, supervisors, corporate leaders, and the people who report to them. Women rely heavily on the relationships they have built in the past, many at their most recent corporate organizations. In the next story, a woman explains that she landed her first consulting contract because of a former professional relationship she built 10 years earlier. This is a powerful example of the importance of relationships for women who launch businesses.

Olivia's Story

Olivia worked with an associate named John from one of the large consulting firms. John and his brother had an idea and they sold it to Olivia while she was in a corporate position. These two gentlemen were smart, and Olivia liked the idea they were presenting. She supported the idea, and the project was successful. John never forgot that Olivia supported him when he needed a break. He was intrigued when Olivia launched her new business. John often commented on how he would like to hire Olivia as a consultant, but he had a good management team and did not need her expertise. Suddenly John had an emergency need for a human resource lead. Olivia was asked to consult to an internal promote who would be moving into a human resource director position. This was a turning point for Olivia and her business. She had a significant coaching project, and other consulting prospects followed. Olivia shares, "I got the consulting work because of the relationship I formed with John when he needed support."

Olivia's Story (End)

Many women leave corporate positions in their 40s and 50s compared with men who stay until their 60s to start a new business (Rosener 2003). Men more often start new businesses after retirement. If women wait until their 40s or 50s to start their first business, they have had time in the workplace to acquire skills and resources. This allows women to leave their positions with more potential for success and less risk.

Women leave corporate positions with financial security, achievements, self-confidence and esteem, and professional networks that can jump-start their businesses (Rosener 2003). Many women define themselves based on their values and what is important to them. Less often Rosener found that women compare themselves to a corporate job or title, company size, money, or how many people report to them.

Corporate working careers and entrepreneurship are not mutually exclusive (Sullivan 2001). In designing careers many women have incorporated both into their span of working years. Many women that were interviewed spent the first, second, or third decade of their career in a corporate setting acquiring the knowledge, confidence, and risk taking that were needed to launch a business because they had to or because they could. Some women were supported during their launch. Others, like Felena, show that determination and fortitude alone can forge a new business.

Transferability of corporate acquired skills by women to entrepreneurial opportunities was the subject of research by Terjesen (2005) in the United Kingdom. Women develop human capital and social capital throughout their careers. Human capital is the knowledge obtained during years of working experience, and social capital is assessed by who you know and the relationships that were built. Siri concluded that some human capital and social capital were embedded or embodied. Embedded capital was tangible and was useful in areas outside of the specific arena in which the capital was obtained. This made the human capital and social capital mobile, and they could generate values outside of the corporate environment and were useful during transitions to entrepreneurial activity. Other human capital and social capital that were more industry or organization specific were called embodied human capital and social capital. Embodied capital was less transferrable and less valuable in entrepreneurial opportunities.

Most women business ventures were started with two to five partners (Terjesen 2005). Less than half of the women who were interviewed in the UK research started a business by themselves. Women start businesses with a husband, a family member, or work colleagues. Work colleagues are often sorted and sifted based on competency or financial investment. Many women benefitted from family member business start-up expertise or experience, including business plans and strategy.

With so many women leaving corporate positions for entrepreneurial positions, corporate human resources and talent management executives are looking for ways to stop top talent from leaving the organization. When women leave companies, problems are created for the future. For many companies the pipeline for women moving into senior positions is shrinking. As women leave to start a business, organizational leaders are rethinking their old-fashioned attitudes toward male-dominated protocol. The UK government is concerned about the loss of women in key organizational roles that it is looking at the endorsement of flexible working (Hanson 2007). Hanson believes there is a fundamental cultural issue because men work in an organization in a way that is second nature to them but unnatural for women. A male-dominated competitive model has women reevaluating their priorities and looking for ways to leave. Organizational leaders will need to be more innovative and take more risks to reduce the loss of corporate women leaders. In a talent-starved knowledge economy, only inflexible and short-term thinking would disregard the need for major changes in the workplace (Hanson 2007).

Advice and Support for Women Who Launch

A strong foundation of resources devoted to supporting female entrepreneurs exists. These resources are in the forms of professional associations, entrepreneurial mentors and sponsors, websites, books, conferences and events, and financial grants and loans. If you conduct an Internet search for resources for women entrepreneurs, you will be inundated with resource links of support. If you conduct a search for resources for men entrepreneurs you will again be inundated with resource links for women resources. The same scenario happens when you search resources for female entrepreneurs and resources for male entrepreneurs.

There are less Internet resources for men starting a business than those for women. Women enjoy supporting other women. Women are less apt to provide business start-up resources that support entrepreneurial men. Men are less programmed to seek out support because it can be looked upon as a sign of weakness.

The difference in resources geared for women versus men entrepreneurs may signify one of the reasons why women launch. Women may be encouraged to launch because of the ample support for them who do. It is instinctive in most women's belief systems to intuitively help others launch.

Mary's Story

After being laid off from one of the Big Four accounting firms, Mary realized that her livelihood was gone after a short meeting with a human resources representative. "When you are laid off, it is difficult to think about what you will do," Mary confides as she sips her coffee and thinks back of her successful years in not one, but two Big Four accounting firms. She proved to herself and others that she could complete an education and work for a prestigious accounting firm. Without the Fortune 500 organization on her current business card, she wondered how to gain confidence back that she acquired during her corporate positions.

"Confidence is the most important skill to take with you to a new business," Mary explains in a soft but strong voice. Over her years as a federal and multistate tax consultant, Mary enhanced her business skills. She developed expertise in professional writing, communication skills, executive meeting leadership, research, advanced computer skills, and business protocol.

Mary's first launch at becoming an entrepreneur did not end in a soft landing and escalating bank account. She spent one full year working six to seven days a week on a start-up with a few close business partners. Each week and month she believed her hard work was building equity and freedom that she would never realize working in a Big Four firm. After one full year (365 days) with full commitment to a new business, she accepted the reality that the business would not get established and worse yet would never be profitable. One year after a devastating reduction in force termination she had little money to show for her first year in business.

She spent a year working in a start-up that never posted a profit but she never lost her confidence. Mary realized she did not know enough about marketing herself or her ideas, much less a new brand. She was never concerned with marketing in her Big Four firm because there was always more than enough work to do. The marketing departments at these firms were responsible for that. She decided she would find, buy, or learn how to market her new company.

Mary realized how important relationships are for women in the workplace and equally important in starting her business. She was placed in her Big Four positions based on relationships with organizational leaders. Although her technical competence was strong and competitive, it was not her competency that led to her promotions. Each promotion was because of a business colleague with whom she had established a strong working relationship. She sees relationships as a key foundation for women who launch businesses. Mary works with women who start and establish businesses. Mary comments, "It is amazing what relationships can do for you personally and for your business."

Mary's advice to women looking to launch a business is to get out of your comfort zone. What surprised Mary is that she found her hidden talents. Either these talents blossomed or were always there and never utilized or needed. She developed strong networks and relationships in her corporate positions, and these networks were part of her support system. Mary summarizes her transition commenting, "I needed to switch my brain into entrepreneurial mode."

One surprise for Mary is how long it is taking to launch her business. She advises women to be prepared to spend the first year with limited income. Through a mentoring program called Experienceship, sponsored by a local business owner, Mary was connected with experienced entrepreneurial women who helped her transition to an entrepreneur. Even with the length of time needed to launch her business, she decided to stay positive. "Of course, it is scary." Mary admits, "I know many women in their 40s and 50s who are unhappy but stay at their job because of a lack of confidence." Mary exclaims, "This is what is holding women back. Just jump off the cliff!"

Mary did not continue in her tax career after leaving a corporate position because she never truly loved that career. She was not interested in attending tax courses, pursuing tax law content improvement, or new tax initiatives. Mary adds, "I like to work when I am engaged about what I am doing. I do not want to be like so many women who stay just for the money."

Mary's Story (End)

The next story from one woman's personal experience provides specific advice for women who launch businesses. This story includes recommendations on what women should do before they quit their corporate positions.

Judy's Story

Judy was an executive with a large global insurance organization. She found herself in a financial position to pursue her entrepreneurial spirit. Judy transitioned to her own business of investing in and selling real estate. Judy believes women launch new businesses for flexibility and freedom. "I never considered myself a corporate employee and wanted to start my business sooner than I actually did," says Judy. However, she recommends women get at least 10 years of corporate experience before launching a new business.

She noticed a significant difference in the corporate objectives she was responsible for and the new objectives she was creating for her business. In a corporate environment, objectives drive initiatives, and internal leaders determine the best way to execute those initiatives. Judy says, "In an entrepreneurial environment, objectives are financially driven. It is much more personal. An entrepreneur's money comes from her personal bank account."

Judy recommends preparing for a new business financially and administratively. Before leaving a corporate position apply for credit cards in your corporate name. After you lose your corporate income it is more difficult to qualify for the line of credit needed to start a business. She also recommends getting the business structure set up. New start-up administration tasks take focus away from precious start-up marketing time.

Judy advises to get as much done as possible on a business plan and sales projections before leaving your corporation. Talk to as many people as you can in the business you are looking to start. Ask people in your field of business interest for realistic viewpoints of exactly what they want through to launch their business. Judy says that women should focus on acquiring business skills and building relationships before launching a business.

Judy does miss some of the brainwork necessary in her corporate position. She does not miss hurrying to work every morning and loves working from home. Judy likes the flexibility that having her business has given her. She can structure her work around other personal and professional activities that are important to her.

Judy's Story (End)

Stories from Judy and Mary provide advice for women who will launch businesses from corporate positions. One common thread in the interviews with women who launched has been the ongoing commitment and passion for women to support other women who launch businesses. The following resources were compiled as a starting point for women who are planning to launch a business:

NAWBO—National Association of Women Business Owners
Propels women entrepreneurs into economic, social, and political spheres of power worldwide.
Website: http://www.nawbo.org

Women 2.0
Mission is to increase the number of female founders of technology start-ups. Women 2.0 supports entrepreneurs with a network, resources, and knowledge to take their start-up from an idea to launch.
Website: http://www.women2.org/

Astia
Propels women's full participation as entrepreneurs and leaders in high-growth businesses, fueling innovation and driving economic growth.
Website: http://www.astia.org

Count Me In
Mission is to promote economic independence and the growth of women-owned businesses.
Website: http://www.makemineamillion.org/

Hatch Network
Mission is to give women a business school of their own—a place to learn to start and grow a business of any size.
Website: http://hatchnetwork.com/

Savor the Success

Mission is to pool together resources to offer affordable PR tools for women entrepreneurs both online and offline.

Website: http://www.savorthesuccess.com/

Ladies Who Launch

Mission is to make entrepreneurship accessible to every woman.

Website: http://www.ladieswholaunch.com

Women Initiatives

Mission is to build the entrepreneurial capacity of women to overcome economic and social barriers and achieve self-sufficiency.

Website: http://www.womensinitiative.org

eWomenNetwork

Mission is to connect and promote women and their businesses worldwide.

Website: http://www.ewomennetwork.com

Conclusion

Women are transitioning from employee to entrepreneur in the United States and countries around the world. A new surge of interest in women launching businesses is building. Women are using the skills, relationships, and knowledge they acquired while working in all types of industries from small business to large multinational organizations. Women are reshaping the workforce. There is a large amount of support for women who launch businesses from other women entrepreneurs, family and friends, and government agencies.

Internationally, there are similarities and differences in why women launch businesses. Women around the globe share the need for more control and balance to their busy lives as mothers and employees. Contrasting to women entrepreneurs in the United States, women in some foreign countries were faced with negative feelings toward female entrepreneurs. A lack of social acceptance, personal security, and mobility constraints were start-up problems experienced by some international women.

Interviews from six women who launched businesses revealed their personal stories. There was not one common path that led these women to launch a business. Each story was as unique as the women who told it. An analysis of the interviews revealed some common characteristics of the women. There was an inner calling, either forced through lay off, or inspired through revelation that the risk of a start-up business was worth it. The interviews and research showed many examples of women supporting other women during the startup phases of launching a business.

As women find success and relief as business entrepreneurs, strong consensus among researchers is that women will continue to launch new businesses. Younger females may bypass the corporate world altogether in search of a more natural blending of family life and work and the nurturing characteristics of business women (Daniel 2004). Over the past 20 years, women have increased the education and formal training they have, which will play an important role in preparing women to launch their business in the future.

Note

1. Jo Plummer, full article available at http://www.businessasmission.com/story-glo balfranchise.html.

References

Abarbanel, K. 2008. "Women Entrepreneurs: Reshaping the Workplace." *Interbeing* 2 (2): 31–34.

Ahmad, Syed Zamberi, and Siri Roland Xavier. 2011. "Preliminary Investigation of Yemeni Women Entrepreneurs: Some Challenges for Development and Barriers to Success." *International Journal of Entrepreneurship and Small Business* 13 (4): 518–34.

Daniel, T. A. 2004. "The Exodus of Women from the Corporate Workplace to Self-Owned Businesses." *Employment Relations Today* (Wiley) 30 (4): 55–61. doi:10.1002/ert.10108.

Delaney, L. 2003. "Escape from Corporate America." *Across the Board* 40 (2): 38.

Drine, I., and Grach, M. 2012. "Supporting Women Entrepreneurs in Tunisia." *European Journal of Development Research* 24 (3): 450–64. doi:10.1057/ejdr.2011.13.

Hanson, S. 2007. "Why Women Leave?" *Director* 60 (11): 50–53.

Helgesen, S., and Johnson, J. 2011. *The Female Vision: Women's Real Power at Work.* 1–7. San Francisco: Berrett-Koehler Publishers, Inc.

Holmen, M., T. Min, and E. Saarelainen. 2011. "Female Entrepreneurship in Afghanistan." *Journal of Developmental Entrepreneurship* 16 (3): 307–31.

Johnson, W. 2012. "Disrupt Yourself." *Harvard Business Review* 90 (7/8): 147–50.

Leiber, N. 2007. "She Did It Her Way." *Businessweek Online*: 11. March 15, 2007.

Li-Min, C., L. Chun-Chu, H. Chien-Min, and T. Hui-Ching. 2012. "An Evaluation Model of Female Entrepreneurship in the Service Industry—Human Capital,

Social Capital and Opportunity Recognition Perspective." *International Research Journal of Finance and Economics* 85: 55–67.

Madichie, N. O. 2009. "Breaking the Glass Ceiling in Nigeria: A Review of Women's Entrepreneurship." *Journal of African Business* 10 (1): 51–66.

McNeil, Rita C. 2012. "Leveraging the Power of Diversity in Workplace Learning Strategies." *Handbook of Research on Workforce Diversity in a Global Society: Technologies and Concepts*: 225–43.

Paoloni, P., and P. Demartini. 2012. "The Relational Capital in Female SMEs." *Journal of Academy of Business and Economics* 12 (1): 23–32.

Patterson, N. 2009. "Women Entrepreneurs: Jumping the Corporate Ship and Gaining New Wings." *International Small Business Journal* 27 (2): 173. doi: 10.1177/0266242608100489.

Rosener, J. B. 2003. "Females in Executive Flight." *Orange County Business Journal* 26 (44): 51.

Sullivan, S. E. 2001. "Careerpreneurs: Lessons from Leading Women Entrepreneurs on Building a Career without Boundaries [book review]." *The Academy of Management Executive (1993–2005)* 15 (1): 157–59.

Terjesen, Siri. 2005. "Senior Women Managers' Transition to Entrepreneurship: Leveraging Embedded Career Capital." *Career Development International* 10 (3): 246–59.

Xavier, S., A. Ahmad, S. Perumal, L. Nor, and J. Mohan. 2011. "The Transition from Corporate Careers to Business Ownership: The Case for Women Entrepreneurs in Malaysia." *International Journal of Business Administration* 2 (3): 148–59. doi:10.5430/ijba.v2n3p148.

Chapter 9

The Dilemmas of Women Entrepreneurs

Yenni Viviana Duque Orozco
and Maria Carolina Ortiz Riaga

When addressing topics related to female entrepreneurship, a global issue arouses the interest of researchers and scholars. The growing incursion of women in the workplace has reduced their private—family and domestic—time, and has transformed it into public and productive time. As a consequence, women have been forced to construct other identities, to identify themselves with new roles. Specifically, in the case of women entrepreneurs, there are dilemmas and conflicts in reconciling the different roles they must assume as mothers, wives, homemakers, and entrepreneurs. The way in which these dilemmas have been solved seems to directly impact the size of female-owned firms (Anna 1999).[1]

In this chapter, we present the results of the research that addresses the case of women entrepreneurs in Colombia and documents the ways in which they have reconciled their family and organizational commitments, and the strategies used for this end.

Conceptual Elements

To conduct this study, we chose the conceptual framework developed by Dyer (1993). He has developed an entrepreneurial career model based on four dimensions:[2]

Career Choice

This dimension formulates three factors that influence the decision of becoming an entrepreneur:

- *Individual factors*. Factors on which certain issues have been traditionally studied, such as the need for control, motivation for achievement, the ability to take risks, and tolerance for uncertainty. Other scholars find these psychological factors insufficient and have added other categories of analysis such as cognitive processes and social cognition phenomena.[3] Additionally, some gender studies have suggested key differences in the orientations and motivations of men and women (Demartino and Barbato 2002; Kourilsky and Walstad 1998).[4] Although these factors cannot fully explain the entrepreneurial choice, it is clear that they play an important role in the business career choice and cannot be left out.

- *Social factors*. Earlier studies dealing with entrepreneurs have shown that many of the entrepreneurs came from social groups that could be described as deprived (Kets de Vries 1977).[5] Suffering from negligence, abandonment, and economic difficulties has motivated individuals to take control over what they saw as an unfair and hostile world. One way of taking control was to create their own businesses.

  Family is an important social actor in several ways. On the one hand, the entrepreneur exhibits the influence of parents who were business owners or independent workers. On the other hand, family support is a key element in areas such as providing the financial resources necessary to start a business venture.

  In addition to family support, some studies have mentioned the support of the community in the success of business activities, such as the support provided by social labor networks and local businesses (Aldrich and Waldinger 1990; Stevenson 1987).[6] As a result, Dyer (1993) proposed the influence of role models in the community as an important factor in entrepreneurial activity.[7]

- *Economic factors*. Factors that may be related to the lack of employment opportunities and labor discrimination, which drive entrepreneurs to search for new alternatives to start a business; to the national economic growth that creates business opportunities; and to the access to financial aid and networks of raw material that increments the creation of new business endeavors.

Career Socialization

Career socialization refers to the experiences people have had throughout their lives. Aspects such as childhood work experiences that assign responsibility at an early age, work experience after graduation, training, or previous initiatives associated with business start-ups give people the confidence to start their own firms.

Career Orientation

Career orientation occurs in two stages. The first stage is the acceptance of an entrepreneurial role and the assumption of the role in whole or in part, that is, many entrepreneurs create their own businesses while keeping their regular jobs. The second stage is what one might call the "specific entrepreneurial role." Some begin their careers because they enjoy developing new technologies, others because they find it interesting to build organizations and own their own business. Others prefer to take risks and start new projects but are not interested in managing them. The relationship between different socialization experiences and the reasons for taking the entrepreneurial role has also been explored in some studies.[8]

In a gender study, it was found that the orientation women give to their business careers has a profound impact on their lives (Goffee and Scase 1985).[9] The women studied varied in their career orientation depending on how they perceived their roles in relation to their families and work. Women who prioritized their family tended to organize their business around the family needs and activities. Those who prioritized their business worked away from home and were "married to their business." Their family needs were subordinated to their business. In this vein, the roles adopted by entrepreneurs and the dilemmas and conflicts they face depend on their orientation.

Career Progression

Career progression describes the kind of roles taken by entrepreneurs over the time. A dynamic perspective is proposed, one that highlights the changes in the interaction of people with their context from a historical perspective. Some common roles in the life of an entrepreneur can be business owner, husband/wife, father/mother, community leader, and manager. Depending on how far entrepreneurs have progressed in their careers, they can assume different roles as a result of changes in their families, businesses, and personal lives. Dyer conducted a research, exploring the life stories of 100 entrepreneurs, and from this information, some dilemmas that they may face arise, depending on the time of their lives they are at. Dyer identified the dilemmas that may exert a decisive influence on career progression in the personal, family, and business areas.[10]

Current Context of Female Entrepreneurship in Colombia

According to data from the Global Entrepreneurship Monitor (GEM) 2010 report, in Colombia, the total entrepreneurship activity indicator for men has been greater than that of women over the five years before 2010 by an average of 8.22 percent. The gender gap has closed significantly, from 11 percent in 2006, to 4.6 percent in 2010; nevertheless, this reduction is better explained by a decrease in the rate of new business activities undertaken by men, which has been declining since 2008.

The study proposes two types of motivation to create a company: by chance or by necessity, and found a similar pattern for both sexes: the range of people aged between 18 and 44 years were motivated to start a new business by opportunity in a higher percentage, while people aged between 45 and 64 years were motivated by need; nonetheless, the percentage of women who were motivated by need was greater. With regard to educational level, a higher percentage of women did not finish high school (41%), although there was also evidence that as educational level increased, so did the percentage of individuals who were motivated by opportunity.

The study also found that women who are early-stage entrepreneurs had lower income levels than men, while women who were established entrepreneurs outnumbered men in higher income ranges. The business background rate was very similar in men and women, which led to the conclusion that there is no possibility of setting up this feature as a distinctive factor of entrepreneurship according to gender.

GEM also measured Colombians' attitudes and aspirations about entrepreneurship, and states that women had a greater fear of failure rate than men, although they had positive attitudes that related to the belief that entrepreneurship is a desirable career choice and that there was good media coverage of successful entrepreneurs' cases.

With regard to the potential for innovation, women felt that their companies offered products or services with little innovation, either by the perception of their customers or because there were many companies that offered them in the market. The potential for internationalization of new businesses was also lower than those of men.

The study also consulted the opinions of national experts in order to have information on the socioeconomic conditions and institutional environment surrounding the business. The evaluation of these experts on the existing support for women entrepreneurs is positive, especially, the consideration that women have the same level of knowledge and skills for entrepreneurship that men do, that entrepreneurship is a socially acceptable career for women, and that women have equal access to opportunities for starting a business as men have. The recommendation made by experts deals with the need to strengthen and improve social services to support women so they can continue working even after starting a family.

Methodology

We used the previous framework to analyze the career progression issue in a group of 59 women with higher education and ownership of their firms, selected through a convenience sampling. They were selected from the database provided by the Counseling for Women's Equality (Alta Consejería

Presidencial para la Equidad de la Mujer) study, and the study was conducted in the three major cities in Colombia: Bogotá, Cali, and Medellin.

For information gathering, a survey was applied. The instrument consisted of 43 closed questions based on Dyer's framework.[11] This instrument collected general information related to family, academic background, and previous work experience. Also, it inquired about business-related aspects: the sector in which the business operated, size, number of employees, partners, financing methods, years in the market, business development difficulties, and female entrepreneurship perceptions.

This was followed by semistructured interviews with all the 59 women, on the grounds that social reality does not have an objective nature, but is inseparable from the participant subjects themselves and their expectations, intentions, value systems, and so on. Each interview lasted approximately one hour. The study focused on each of the entrepreneurs to know how they perceived reality and their own actions, how they read situations, what their intentions were, and what meanings they assigned to their intentions. The discourse analysis technique was employed because it offers the possibility to investigate the nature of the participants, and allows, based on certain data, valid inferences that can be applied to a specific context (Andréu 2008).[12] The analysis of the information was supported by the software Atlas.ti.

Regarding sociobiographical traits by age, women entrepreneurs were mainly distributed between ages 25 and 54 years (see Table 9.1); on average, 60 percent of the women interviewed had children. Table 9.2 shows that the group of female entrepreneurs interviewed in Cali and Medellin held a bachelor's degree and most did not go beyond undergraduate higher education. However, this

Table 9.1 Age ranges of women entrepreneurs

City	18–24 Years	25–34 Years	35–44 Years	45–54 Years	55–64 Years
Medellin	1	3	6	9	0
Cali	1	6	5	6	1
Bogotá	0	8	6	5	4

Table 9.2 Educational level of women entrepreneurs

City	Undergraduate	Specialization	Master	PhD
Medellin	15	3	1	0
Cali	16	3	0	0
Bogotá	12	6	4	1

Table 9.3 Economic sector

Business Activities Sectors	*Bogotá*	*Cali*	*Medellin*
Handicraft production	5	12	7
Health and Social Services	0	1	1
Education	0	1	0
Photography-related activities	0	0	1
Foodstuff production	5	0	3
Software consultants	0	0	1
Business consultancy and support activities	4	1	1
Publishing activities	0	0	1
Specialized animal breeding	1	0	0
Retail activities	3	1	2
Manufacturing industry	5	1	4

trend changes in Bogotá, with 48 percent of female entrepreneurs surveyed in the capital having masters or specialization[13] graduate degrees.

Table 9.3 shows in detail the sectors in which the interviewed women develop their business activities. The categories were taken from the International Standard Industrial Classification of All Economic Activities. The result shows that Medellin and Bogotá had the highest variety of subsectors, Cali had a significant concentration of production and manufacture of handicrafts—activities that are considered to be primarily female.

Dilemmas of Women Entrepreneurs: Business and Family

According to Dyer, approaches in the career progression dimension and the emergence of dilemmas posed at the beginning, middle, and end of the business career describe the different situations faced by women in this study.[14]

In this section, we discuss the dilemmas faced by women principally and the ways to reconcile their business with the roles traditionally assumed in their capacities as wives, mothers, and homemakers.

Multiple studies report that one of the main motivations for women to create an enterprise is the search for greater labor flexibility that allows them to balance work and family life (Brush 1990; Hup and Richardson 1997),[15] and studies such as those by Cooper and Artz (1995) show that the higher levels of satisfaction recorded among women entrepreneurs correspond to the psychological benefits that they find by being able to reconcile work and family life better than a wage-earning employee.[16]

Stress and tension are aspects that go along with the business activity in the three stages of an entrepreneurial career. Sandín (2003) recaps the findings of several authors who state that stress is associated with life changes.[17] It is evident, for example, when a woman believes that she has a role overload and therefore, feels that the demands of the environment exceed her capabilities. It also occurs when there are conflicting demands between different roles, for example, between family and work demands. In these cases, as Sandín (2003) states, the individual feels unable to meet the demands and expectations of one role, without neglecting the demands of another.

Stress is also present because of role restructuring, that is, due to alterations associated with changes in the life project. This leads to variations in expectations and in interaction patterns assumed long before. Stress disappears as people readjust their expectations and their interactions. In the same way, Vega (2006) states that one of the tensions that people in modern societies must resolve is to reconcile the demands of work with personal time, where family plays a prominent role.[18]

The firm and the family are the two most significant networks which women in this study belong to. How are these two areas made compatible? That is going to be answered through the comments given by the interviewed women.

Balancing the Role of Being Entrepreneurs and Homemakers

The results of our study show that women resolve the dilemma of balancing the role of entrepreneur and housewife through time management. The solution, according to them, is organization. However, organization itself represents an additional time demand. So, for example, to determine how schedules are managed and established and how much time is spent on each task adds to an already long day devoted to work, family, and home. To determine how schedules are managed, and established how much time is spend on each task, involves very long days to be able to devote time to work, family, and home. On many occasions, at night, after they had finished their duties at home, they went back to work a bit to compensate for the time they did not devote to the company. This was combined with the fact that as the majority were small-business owners, they did not have the possibility of hiring another employee to replace them in certain tasks, thus ending up performing multiple functions.[19]

It can be demonstrated in the following excerpts from the interviews with the women in this study, which recurs in other cases too:

> So I think it's about discipline, about separating things. What is the home schedule? Which is the work schedule? And what is the house schedule again? Then up until 7 a.m., at the latest, I do home chores, early, so my household is taken care of. And from there I commute to work and it is up to 5 1/2 to 6 pm, almost playing no role in the house, I just come to lunch, if my child is home we have lunch together and this is the time we set up to continue working. In fact, no client of mine knows that I have an office at home.
>
> EM6

> It is very difficult. Although I've always thought that women bear the most burden. Men focus on work, on making money and no more. We women focus on producing more money, on work, on having a child in a home, on the groceries, things like that. Then, it is much more difficult because your burden is heavier. And because we are in no position to say, well, if I hire someone to help me around in the house then it will work. So one becomes sort of a juggler, making 10 thousand things at the same time.
>
> EC5

> It is terrible, terrible. I tell you, time is not enough for me. I have an excess of orders and I start going crazy because the children's time suffers. I have to take them to school twice a week. And on top of that my husband, and on top of that … Anyways. It's all about setting schedules. When my kids were little, I spent their first year with them, completely devoted to them. Completely devoted to them and with the last one, I painted from home. And I started to detach myself little by little, and the school gives me more room; the child arrives home at four in the afternoon and by that time, I've had enough time for the business. And at night I have to get strength so, I drink Red Bull to take care of my husband. And that's it, I have managed to get used to it, but it is very difficult.
>
> EC6

In this testimony also appears the concept more often expressed, "it's difficult." It is difficult because of the responsibility acquired, and because of the struggle to reach a satisfactory balance between all the activities women must perform. Even the possibility of having more children is sacrificed because of the lack of time to respond appropriately.

Balancing the Role of Being Entrepreneurs and Mothers

The combination of having a mother's and entrepreneur's role is resolved in several ways:

- Working in a business that allows time to manage to be home with the children, so work activities do not interfere with their maternal role. It is common that the place of residence is close to the company in order to be on top of the child care. It is also common to run the company from home.

- Working part-time to be with the children when they arrive from school or when they are needed at home.

- Organizing task scheduling, so they can spend time with their children and continue with the activities of the company. A time and a place are set apart to keep track of their children, struggling to make them independent, responsible, and task oriented, so that maternal control is carried out only at certain times. This allows time for them to work in the company.

- Having a support network that includes grandparents, maids, and other relatives is helpful to take care of children while women are working.

- Taking their children to the workplace is also a common practice.

These results show the importance of time management, therefore, the proximity of home to the workplace is vital to reduce the commuting time between home and the workplace; the proximity should be even more when it comes to cities as Bogotá, where the average commuting time is between 60 and 90 minutes.

With regard to family environment, family support networks provide a balance between work and personal life. Having a family that helps with household chores is important to meet the responsibilities that both roles require. In this regard, other studies support that family coresponsibility is one of the factors that facilitates the reconciliation between work and family life (Greenhaus and Parasuraman 1999).[20]

One aspect that stands out is the fact that most of the women interviewed stress out that their priority is family. The fact that in all the cases the reconciliation between the different roles assumed by women is experienced as a problem relates to a continuous tension between the desire to consolidate a company that demands time and effort and their responsibilities as mothers and family members, an aspect they have chosen as the most important in their lives.

This explains why female-owned firms are smaller: they do not have the possibility to devote more time for growing their business because they employ much of their efforts on traditional female roles. Studies such as those done by Aponte (2002) support this. Aponte says that women's perception of increased responsibility at home care makes them less willing to devote time to their own business; therefore, they are only willing to take on a moderate level of risk.[21]

Striving to fulfill the role of mother and the business role makes the time dedicated to the company decrease. Women who established large and medium enterprises did not exercise their role as mothers; they were single or widows, or in a particular case, a woman had her son 15 years after getting married. The entrepreneurial option, in most of the studied cases, had been chosen after marriage; therefore, business activities were developed after having assumed the role of wives and, sometimes, mothers.

On this, Romero (1993) states that as long as women are required to be in charge of most of the housework, their productivity will automatically decrease; increasing the competitive disadvantage with men and supporting greater social inequality. The problem, according to Romero, lies in "although the idea of labor equality is spreading and being internalized, the natural consequences that men should do half of the housework—is less spread and makes it very difficult to achieve one without the other."[22]

However, studies by Collins-Dodd, Gordon, and Smart (2004) show that entrepreneurs who started a business with the aim of reconciling family and work achieved better financial performance in their businesses than those who did so to attain greater independence. It would be worthwhile, then, to pay greater attention to variables such as the family structure that supports women entrepreneurs, the children's age, and support networks, among others.[23]

This entrepreneur summarizes the feelings of many other women like her:

> So there are a lot of things, women are allocated many roles, but we as women were created with that purpose and we women were created to be the harmony in everything, to be very smart, to know how to handle that and to want to. You have to want things. And now I want to do it all, I want to be a good mom, I want not to make mistakes, I hope God gives me the best tools to provide a life with all the elements to my little girl, I want to be a good wife, a good partner, because being a good woman is not only to care for them, and to love them, but being a partner in everything, in building a future, in building a home, in raising a daughter, being by their side through everything and even more with a man who has been incredible to me, I see how he is with my mom, that is a very good family member, I want to continue growing next to him, he makes me a better person, he is a truly great man, so at the moment this is what I want to do. So I think it's about willingness and wanting to do it even if we are made for that.
>
> EC11

It is important to notice that from the role of an entrepreneur and mother emerges a sense of guilt for their children, as can be seen in the following:

It's not easy, not easy to build a business in Colombia; it is not easy to leave your children to build a business. Sometimes I think: am I being selfish? But then many of us women are selfish, because how else can we work and raise children. Or are we to go back to ancient times where they are engaged in raising children only and the children leave and then what are women to do? There are, then, so many things; they are so many that one fights internally.

EC11

And how it was solved? The following statement is an example of the way how they solved the dilemma between business and children, the rest of the cases have related and close answers:

You have to be a magician. This has to make magic and being everywhere. No, seriously. For me, my family has always been the most important thing and after I was a mom. It has always been … I mean, I never wanted to be a mom for the title. Also, because I will be a mom only once in a lifetime. Then it had to be well done. Then the first years I was always with him and now I'm working outside home, I have tried to work here until he comes home from school. I almost never get to do it, but I try. I try to leave by 4:30 or 5:00. And beyond that my time is for him and for my husband. And all the remaining free time is for the family. And the times that the family is asleep, the rest of the time for Fotocolombia.com at night. I mean, I am working around the clock. So, when you're independent and you have a virtual business, because if in China it's 8 in the morning, and they mind if they are visiting the site and is not updated, they don't mind if here it's 10 at night. As a virtual business, there are no closing hours.

EM8

It is very hard. With the other partner we split the time. I work in the morning until two in the afternoon. She gets here and I go do my duties as mother with the children and the whole story. In the evening I send mails, I reply requests, I mean; I go back and make up for working in the house. Then when you realize, it's twelve o'clock at night and you are still in front of the computer answering emails or in my case designing. It is very hard. And say that while the company comes forward and produces enough revenues to pay for another employee and a messenger, we do absolutely everything. I think that's why many of us fail along the way.

Well, one last thing. Some of us, I at least I have the support of my husband, but I see that some of us don't even have that. To the contrary, it is the source of conflict. They get things like "look, you neglected the children." So there is a big lack of support in that regard.

EM12

It might be assumed from the various testimonies that one positive aspect is the autonomous development of children. Although women entrepreneurs establish balance between work and family life, trying to devote time to both roles, most of them reported that their children learned to cope alone, to be more independent, and to understand and support the work of their mothers. When children became older, some were linked to business activity and were an important support, helping as needed, but no prospects of carrying the business on. Others were completely oblivious to the activity their mothers carried out.

Balancing the Role of Being Entrepreneur and Wife

How is it, then, the relationship with their husbands vis-à-vis their business roles? Some female entrepreneurs were supported by their partners in taking care of the children and sharing responsibilities at home. In other cases, they received direct support in the management of some aspects related to the proper development of the company. In addition, some husbands offer support by providing respect and understanding for the time and space that needs to be devoted to the management of the business.

On the other side of the spectrum, conflicts in the relationship arose related to the husband's lack of belief regarding the business. In other cases, the man freed himself from financial responsibilities, because there was economic support from the activity carried out by his wife. However, when crisis occurred, there were complaints, and women were blamed for the economic problems the family faces. There can also be problems that stem from the management of shared authority: for men it is sometimes difficult to accept that women assume management.

In the studied group, there were 14 female entrepreneurs whose husbands were their business partners. When the husband is the business partner, several situations are manifested:

- They share all aspects of the company, everything they do, and they do it together.
- They complement each other appropriately. Based on the individual characteristics they possess, they assign tasks according to their personal strengths to run the business successfully.
- They try to differentiate the familiar spaces from the workplace, always being careful not to take discussions, misunderstandings, and fights to the other environment. Also they try to build individual spaces because of the fear that by sharing everything all the time, both at work and in the family spheres, the relationship may become stressful.

- Even though the husband has a separate company, he is actively involved in the development of his wife's company.
- Business development forces the husband to be involved in it, although initially there is little conviction about the idea.
- Despite being partners, the woman controls the financial aspects and leads the business.

Conflicts arise because sometimes it is difficult to agree, in spite of the fact that each one has identified their own strengths. This is coupled with the difficulty of managing the different roles in different spheres, that is, efforts are needed not to confuse the family life with the activity of the company.

Taking advantage of existing resources implies for some entrepreneurs starting their business at home. This results in the loss of some familiar spaces. The following testimony is that of an entrepreneur who started a business with her husband:

> We started like this. As newlyweds we didn't have a dining table. So we said let's make that room the reception, we named the dining room reception hall. And the kitchen, coffee area, so to speak. In a moment we'll show the little signs and this is how we started. In other words, the only thing we owned was the bedroom. That's it. All the rest became an office. And then we started to further get into that dream of having our own business, from our own home.
>
> A lot has been gained and things have also been lost. A lot has been gained in the financial side, we do not have to pay rent, we have broken even with the market we have now, but a lot has been lost in our personal life, so to speak, since our space has been invaded by people, many people coming in and out the selection process, some interviews. So sometimes it's even six, six thirty and we are not done yet. So that part has been lost. But we have gained a lot.
>
> EM11

The intimacy of the couple is also affected by the business activity when the husband is the partner:

> It has been pretty hard and we have been in that development and personal growth process. The advantage is that we have had communication and dialogue. We are working 24 hours together; we're seeing each other 24 hours a day. At this point what we are doing is managing some spaces and times. One of the main problems we had been having that, for example Alex (husband) was working up until to 9 and a half and I was free. Then I would demand him that time. And there were days when I worked until 9 1/2, 10, 11 at night, just like him and he was free. So we weren't managing spaces in that respect. So what we started doing was this: Well, let's work

Monday through Friday and Saturdays and Sundays are for us as a couple. If a mandatory activity that demands our Saturday comes up, and that's it. We work until 6 pm, then we stop and thereafter we do not talk about work.

And something that Alex and I have done is, since we have a group of friends who are also professionals and what we do many times is that we are together Monday to Friday; I mean, sometimes we do not see each other because he is downstairs in the commercial area; then what we do on the weekends is that he goes out with his friends, he has his space, and I go out with my friends and we met at night or something like that. Because otherwise, we start to invade each other and then we no longer have anything to talk about. We go out to eat and well, what we speak of, what do we say? Because we know everything, he knows what's going on with me, he knows if I have a problem with another company or he goes and faces it, because the positions here, Alex is the manager and I am a psychologist because there have to be roles. And the role here although we are two and we are both the owners, it should be handled this way. So when we see that, well, we were together every day, all week, we struggle with the weekends to create spaces to be alone or he goes to see his family or we struggle to breathe a little not seeing each other. Compared to other couples that never see each other in the week, then in the weekend they are inseparable. So it's like the opposite. We have done that to have a better relationship and to be able to live together.

EM11

In another case, the concern was evident in the difficulty of managing a family business, self-regulating themselves to avoid the problems of working with family, and trying to set out spaces so that the business did not absorb the people who were working on it. In this testimony, the entrepreneur raised concerns about the issue of family business:

But it seems difficult to me because there are many conflicting opinions and you become more relaxed because it's your family. You have people outside your family, I mean, if you work in a company X, you have a boss who is showing results to other people, to shareholders, instead here, you have to be responsible for what you do, to yourself, with yourself, then it is very difficult.

Beyond that, managing the schedule, the obligations, requirements, too. So you become sort of the judge and the plaintiff. It's very complicated, very complicated! Because you have a responsibility with yourself, with others, which is not so easy because if you work in a company it is like this: I work my schedule and I'm gone, I fulfill my obligation and I'm gone. But here you are here all the time, with the children, with the husband, with everything that surrounds it, with the workers. You are working all day, the day does not end. Yesterday we got home at 10 pm.

EM3

This confronts us with the problem of family businesses. For Gallo and Amat (2003), a business family is one that owns a family business fully or partially and that, additionally, exerts a strong influence on the company and for that reason, the sustainability of the latter depends largely on the family characteristics, their beliefs, values, patterns of interaction, and the behavior of its members. Gallo and Amat (2003) state that the family business mechanics are influenced by the individual motivations and the dynamic interactions between the family members.[24]

In our research, the women interviewed agreed that when there was a family business, the family usually revolved around the business. Children saw how their parents got involved with the company. Even when the family was gathered, the company was the main focus of interest and sometimes occupied spaces destined for other activities, such as weekends.

Conclusions

This study presents evidence that in Colombia there is a heterogeneity of female businesses and entrepreneurs who face not only the typical tensions of entrepreneurs, such as market dynamics, economic policy, opportunities, and threats presented by the local, national, and global contexts in which they operate, and so on, but also the tensions that arises from their gender, in which familiar, cultural, economic, and social factors interact defining their actions, not only in regard to instrumental rationality reference but that are also based on a world of values, emotions, and everyday reasoning regarding these factors.

About the balance between family and work, there are two aspects to take into account. First, the child care and household, where family support is the key for balancing personal life and work. Second, the relationship, in which establishing time to share with their husbands as a couple more than parents is one of the most used strategies. Support networks, such as family, husband, and those closest partners, become the most important support for women to develop as entrepreneurs, but this in turn can be a barrier to grow when they play together the roles of mothers, daughters, wives, and businesswomen.

Although we did not present in this chapter the results on the institutional support provided to women in the cities studied to start a business, it is important to mention that programs to support women's entrepreneurial activity must consider the roles women assume at different stages of their business and personal life in order to generate alternatives to ease the personal burden, while supporting business growth.

Notes

1. A. Anna, G. Chandler, E. Jansen, and N. Mero, "Women Business Owners in Traditional and Non-Traditional Industries," *Journal of Business Venturing* 15 (1999): 279–303.

2. G. Dyer, "Toward a Theory of Entrepreneurial Careers," *Entrepreneurship Theory and Practice* 19, no. 2 (1993): 7–21.

3. K. A. Eddleston and G. N. Powell, "The Role of Gender Identity in Explaining Sex Differences in Business Owners' Career Satisfier Preferences," *Journal of Business Venturing* 23 (2008): 244–56.

4. R. Demartino and R. Barbato, "An Analysis of the Motivational Factors of Intending Entrepreneur," *Journal of Small Business Strategy* 13, no. 2 (2002): 26–36 and M. Kourilsky and W. Walstad, "Entrepreneurship and Female Youth: Knowledge, Attitudes, Gender Differences and Educational Practices," *Journal of Business Venturing* 13 (1998): 77–88.

5. M. Kets de Vries, "The Entrepreneurial Personality: A Person at the Cross-Roads," *Journal of Management Studies* 14, no. 1 (1977): 34–47.

6. H. H. Stevenson, "General Management and Entrepreneurship" (Working paper, Harvard University, 1987) and H. Aldrich and R. Waldinger, "Ethnicity and Entrepreneurship," *Annual Review of Sociology* 16 (1990): 111–35, cited by G. Dyer, "Toward a Theory of Entrepreneurial Careers," 8.

7. G. Dyer, "Toward a Theory of Entrepreneurial Careers," 8.

8. K. Vesper, *New Venture Strategies* (Englewood Cliffs, NJ: Prentice-Hall, 1980) and C. B. Derr, "Entrepreneurs: A Career Perspective" (Paper presented to the Academy of Management meeting, Boston, MA, 1984), cited by G. Dyer, "Toward a Theory of Entrepreneurial Careers," 13.

9. R. Goffee and R. Scase, *Women in Charge* (London: George Allen and Unwin, 1985), cited by G. Dyer, "Toward a Theory of Entrepreneurial Careers," *Entrepreneurship: Theory and Practice* 19, no. 2 (1993): 7–21.

10. G. Dyer, "Toward a Theory of Entrepreneurial Careers," 15–18.

11. Ibid., 401–16.

12. J. Andréu, "Las Técnicas de Análisis de Contenido: Una Revisión Actualizada," http://public.centrodeestudiosandaluces.es/pdfs/S200103.pdf (accessed November 2008).

13. Specialization is a graduate program that is aimed at the professional qualification and development of skills that enable the improvement in the same occupation, profession, or discipline, or in related or complementary disciplines.

14. G. Dyer, "Toward a Theory of Entrepreneurial Careers," 14–17.

15. C. Brush, "Women and Enterprise Creation: Barriers and Opportunities," in *Enterprising Women: Local Initiatives for Job Creation*, ed. S. Gould and J. Parzen

(Paris: Organisation for Economic Co-Operation and Development Publications and Information Centre, 1990) and A. Hup and P. Richardson, "Business Ownership as an Economic Option for Middle-Income Educated Urban Women in Bangladesh." *Frontiers of Entrepreneurship Research* (Babson Park, Wellesley, MA: Babson College, 1997).

16. A. C. Cooper and K. Artz, "Determinants of Satisfaction for Entrepreneurs." *Journal of Business Venturing* 10, no. 6 (1995): 439–57.

17. B. Sandín, "El Estrés: Un Análisis Basado en el Papel de los Factores Sociales," *International Journal of Clinical and Health Psychology* 3, no. 1 (2003): 141–57.

18. G. Vega, "Familia y Empresa," in *Actualizaciones para el Management y el Desarrollo Organizacional*, ed. L. Marchant (Valparaíso, Chile: Universidad de Viña del Mar, 2006).

19. We will include excerpts from the interviews that illustrate the dilemmas faced by women. After each fragment appears the code that was assigned to each interview to make the analysis.

20. J. H. Greenhaus and S. Parasuraman, "Research on Work, Family and Gender: Current Status and Future Directions," in *Handbook of Gender and Work*, ed. G. N. Powell (Thousand Oaks, CA: Sage Publications, 1999).

21. M. Aponte, "Factores Condicionantes de la Creación de Empresas en Puerto Rico: An Enfoque Institucional" (Doctoral thesis, Universidad Autónoma de Barcelona, 2002).

22. M. Romero, "El Empresariado Femenino en España. Riesgo Económico e Identidad Femenina" (Thesis for the PhD degree in Sociology, Universidad Complutense de Madrid, 1993).

23. C. Collins-Dodd, I. M. Gordon, and C. Smart, "Further Evidence on the Role of Gender in Financial Performance," *Journal of Small Business Management* 42, no. 4 (2004): 395–417.

24. M. A. Gallo and J. Amat, *Los Secretos de las Empresas Familiares Centenarias* (Vizcaya, Spain: Ediciones Deusto, 2003).

References

Anna, A., G. Chandler, E. Jansen, and N. Mero. 1999. "Women Business Owners in Traditional and Non-Traditional Industries." *Journal of Business Venturing* 15: 279–303.

Aldrich, H., and R. Waldinger. 1990. "Ethnicity and Entrepreneurship." *Annual Review of Sociology* 16: 111–35.

Aponte, M. 2002. "Factores Condicionantes de la Creación de Empresas en Puerto Rico: Un Enfoque Institucional." Doctoral thesis. Universidad Autónoma de Barcelona. Available at: http://www.tesisenred.net/bitstream/handle/10803/3946/mag1de1.pdf?sequence=1.

Brush, C. 1990. "Women and Enterprise Creation: Barriers and Opportunities." In *Enterprising Women: Local Initiatives for Job Creation*, edited by S. Gould and J. Parzen. Paris: Organisation for Economic Co-Operation and Development Publications and Information Centre.

Collins-Dodd, C., I. M. Gordon, and C. Smart. 2004. "Further Evidence on the Role of Gender in Financial Performance." *Journal of Small Business Management* 42 (4): 395–417.

Cooper, A. C., and K. Artz. 1995. "Determinants of Satisfaction for Entrepreneurs." *Journal of Business Venturing* 10 (6): 439–57.

Demartino, R., and R. Barbato. 2002. "An Analysis of the Motivational Factors of Intending Entrepreneurs." *Journal of Small Business Strategy* 13 (2): 26–36.

Dyer, G. 1993. "Toward a Theory of Entrepreneurial Careers." *Entrepreneurship: Theory and Practice* 19 (2): 7–21.

Eddleston, K. A., and G. N. Powell. 2008. "The Role of Gender Identity in Explaining Sex Differences in Business Owners' Career Satisfier Preferences." *Journal of Business Venturing* 23: 244–56.

Gallo, M. A., and J. Amat. 2003. *Los Secretos de las Empresas Familiares Centenarias.* Barcelona, Spain: Ediciones Deusto.

Global Entrepreneurship Monitor (GEM). 2010. "GEM Annual Report Bogotá 2009–2010." Bogotá, Colombia: Universidad de los Andes and Cámara de Comercio de Bogotá.

Goffee, R., and R. Scase. 1985. *Women in Charge*. London: George Allen & Unwin.

Greenhaus, J. H., and S. Parasuraman. 1999. "Research on Work, Family and Gender: Current Status and Future Directions." In *Handbook of Gender and Work*, edited by G. N. Powell. Thousand Oaks, CA: Sage Publications.

Hup, A., and P. Richardson. 1997. "Business Ownership as an Economic Option for Middle-Income Educated Urban Women in Bangladesh." *Frontiers of Entrepreneurship Research*. Babson Park, Wellesley, MA: Babson College.

Kets de Vries, M. 1977. "The Entrepreneurial Personality: A Person at the Cross-Roads." *Journal of Management Studies* 14 (1): 34–47.

Kourilsky, M., and W. Walstad. 1998. "Entrepreneurship and Female Youth: Knowledge, Attitudes, Gender Differences and Educational Practices." *Journal of Business Venturing* 13: 77–88.

Romero, M. 1993. "El Empresariado Femenino en España. Riesgo Económico e Identidad Femenina." Thesis for the PhD degree in sociology. Universidad Complutense de Madrid.

Sandín, B. 2003. "El Estrés: Un Análisis Basado en el Papel de los Factores Sociales." *International Journal of Clinical and Health Psychology* 3 (1): 141–57.

Stevenson, H. H. 1987. "General Management and Entrepreneurship." Working paper. Harvard University.

Vega, G. 2006. "Familia y Empresa." In *Actualizaciones para el Management y el Desarrollo Organizacional*, edited by L. Marchant. Valparaíso, Chile: Universidad de Viña del Mar.

)

Chapter 10

Work–Life Balance and African American Women Entrepreneurs

Tina Houston-Armstrong
and Krystel Edmonds-Biglow

Interest in the mechanisms for improving balance between one's work responsibilities and home/family commitments has increased. In March 2010, President Barack Obama released an executive report on "Work–Life Balance and the Economics of Workplace Flexibility" (Obama 2010). This report highlighted the dramatic changes that American families have undergone in the past 50 years, with respect to an increase in the number of women participating in the workforce. The report noted that the shift in roles was in large part due to a rise in cost of living, gender role flexibility, and the women's rights movement. Women now comprise roughly 50 percent of the workforce (Obama 2010). In spite of this expansion in opportunity, women still continue to carry the bulk of responsibility for home/family duties in addition to working outside of the home. Child-rearing, elder care, and overall household maintenance continue to be a significant part of the woman's domain. With greater demands on a limited supply of resources and time, working women must devise strategic methods for balancing their work and home obligations.

Due to this increase of women in the workforce, there is an ongoing body of research that seeks to understand the implications of balancing both home and work responsibilities. The literature in this area has predominantly been organized around two dominant constructs: *role theory*, which focuses on the strain resulting from the responsibilities of both roles; and *enrichment models*, which focuses on the beneficial linkage between work–family roles. In late 2012, a third paradigm became available, which offered an additional model for exploring the relationship between work and home obligations. The *work–home resources model* (ten Brummelhuis and Bakker 2012) focuses on the interface of work–home obligations and the ecological influences that determine the individual's experience on both fronts. Using Brofenbrenner's (1992) ecological systems theory, coupled with Hobfoll's (2001) conservation of resource theory, Brummelhuis and Bakker (2012) developed a complex matrix by which positive or negative experience related to the work–home interface could be explained. Brummelhuis and Baker (2012) highlighted the conditional factors that influence work–family roles, where the intersections of culture, marital status, social equality, skills, knowledge, self-efficacy, and self-esteem, to name a few, are taken into consideration when examining this phenomenon. This groundbreaking paradigm of taking into account the influence of ethnicity, culture, and socioeconomic status, as it relates to work–home responsibility, is a novel approach that serves as a guide for this present research study.

The majority of available literature relating to work–life balance and women often focuses on women as a large group, and does take into consideration the unique conditional factors of ethnicity, cultural, and socioeconomic status. As such, the concerns that affect the psychological well-being of ethnic minority women have been grossly underrepresented in psychological research (Wyche and Graves 1992). Furthermore, the literature addressing the unique experiences of African American women entrepreneurs and their work–life balance is slim to none. However, as Brummelhuis and Bakker (2012) suggest, understanding such conditional factors is critical when investigating the impact of work–life balance, and should therefore be taken into consideration. To date, this study is the only one known of, that takes into account the interplay of ethnicity, culture, and socioeconomic status, as it relates to work–life balance strategies and the lived experiences of professional African American women entrepreneurs. Given the dearth of literature in this area, a qualitative phenomenological study was conducted (Giorgi 1997), to serve as a foundation for further investigation and conceptual exploration within this population.

Expanding the Definition of Entrepreneurship

For the purposes of this chapter, the term *entrepreneur* has been expanded from its more traditional meaning to reflect the experiences of the women in this study. Though entrepreneurship is commonly operationalized to include those who launch an independent enterprise (Brockhaus 1987), in today's society, the definition of entrepreneurship has broadened (Baum et al. 2007). Precedence for expanding the definition of entrepreneurship within the African American community has been documented in the work of Cochrane (2010). As such, entrepreneurship has taken on a definition that includes elements of autonomy, professional status, flexibility, and economic freedom. For this group of women, entrepreneurship is connected to both their wage work and traditional forms of enterprise, including running a company and/or thriving private practice. The women in this study were identified as being entrepreneurs by placing emphasis on their ability to provide a professional service that allowed for economic gain.

The Study

This chapter is based on the preliminary findings in a qualitative study of 10 professional African American female entrepreneurs. The purpose of this phenomenological study is to explore the lived experiences of professional African American women as these experiences relate to work–life balance. The women participated in an in-depth, semistructured interview in which they were asked questions pertaining to their work–life balance. The construct of work–life balance was explored on four domains of well-being: general well-being, spiritual well-being, physical well-being, and relational well-being. *General well-being* was defined as common beneficial actions that participants engaged in to improve their work–life balance and decrease their overall stress. *Spiritual well-being* referred to activities that promoted connectedness to a force or being greater than self, which provided a source of meaning and purpose in life. *Physical well-being* focused on an individual's behaviors that promoted physical integrity and health, whereas *relational well-being* addressed the use of intimate relationships to foster feelings of attachment and connection to others.

Prior to being interviewed, all the participants had to meet the criteria of (a) being a professional/entrepreneur and (b) actively engaging in activities to promote balance between their home and work obligations. All of the participants in this study endorsed being a member of a professional association, where nine of them earned doctorate degrees, for which they are currently practicing in their field, and one earned an MBA. They all also endorsed being actively engaged in the process of balancing their home and work duties. The women in this study ranged in age from 34 to 65 years. Collectively they shared a variety of caregiving roles, including caring for adult children, very young children, elderly parents, or grandchildren. From the open-ended interview questions themes emerged. The themes were generated from reflective analysis, coding, and interpretation of the women's stories, as it was part of the phenomenological approach. In these interviews, the women described a variety of challenging situations related to their work–home roles. The analysis of participant responses presented identifiable themes and insights. Two salient themes that emerged from this data were (a) barriers that prevented the achievement of work–life balance (reducers) and (b) strategies that promoted work–life balance (enhancers). In the rest of this chapter, we will focus on the analysis and interpretation of these two themes.

Balance Reducers

Balance reducers are those obstacles that detract from an individual's ability to successfully navigate the responsibilities of work and family life (Matheson and Rosen 2012). Balance reducers decrease the sense of well-being by presenting barriers to achieving work–life balance. The participants identified not scheduling personal time, procrastination, insufficient work–home boundaries, and competing pressure from work and family responsibility as barriers that reduced their overall well-being.

Ignoring "me-time." Ignoring "me-time," or not scheduling personal time was frequently noted as a factor detracting from the well-being of the participants. One of the challenges frequently cited by the women was having "no me-time," the forgoing of engagement in activities that benefited them directly. Finding time to relax, refocus, rest, and connect with others in reciprocal interactions was often limited or nonexistent. The needs of family and work trumped their personal "me-time" activities. As one woman put it, "I don't have enough space for me." Several of the participants indicated that even after a long hard day at work they would come home and care for their family despite their exhaustion. While the participants made it a point to complete the majority of their work-related duties, they underscored their daily challenge of finding time to address their own well-being. Spending time focusing on personal desires or interests at the expense of work or the needs of family members resulted in conflict. One participant reported feeling torn/split. Some of the women alluded to experiencing an underlining guilt if they were to prioritize their needs over the needs of others. "I'm thinking about what I need to be doing to help the children or my parents and it interferes with the personal things that I want to do to detach and take care of my personal needs." One participant noted how she is more likely to take exercise out of her routine than to forgo the needs of work or home. A lack of time spent pursuing interests or experiences that do not benefit others may negatively influence their ability to feel a sense of balance. These women in particular struggled to engage in activities that only benefit themselves. They appeared to be socialized to prioritize the needs of others, and their identity is often associated with the quality of their connections to others. This may be compounded for both African American women and women from other ethnicities who are socialized in collectivist cultures.

Procrastination. Though procrastination has the capacity to be a coping strategy, the women articulated how choosing to delay undesirable duties or tedious projects interfered with their abilities to enhance balance. Over the long run, those who repeatedly avoided high-priority action items reported experiencing more stress and anxiety. The women reported that procrastination in some instances led to sleep deprivation (staying up all night to complete tasks), abandoning exercise, and unhealthy eating (eating high-fat and processed snack foods), which diminished well-being. Some of the women found that they thrived on using procrastination as a short-term solution to getting their action items completed, even though sustained procrastination led to unhealthy behaviors. "I've found for myself that I thrive on procrastination and waiting until the deadline. I'm not sure what that is about . . . I will wait almost to the deadline to do it, so I may be up late at night." While it is common to choose a preferred activity over a nonpreferred task, there are adverse consequences in doing so. "I tend to wait till the last minute to do work things, actual work tasks." Waiting until the last minute may not only ensure that the task is completed but it can also ensure that one's sense of well-being is impacted in the process. Because women are governed by an ethic of care (Gilligan 1982), they may also prioritize time spent with family members or loved ones over professional tasks that do not provide the same type of immediate gratification. Social interaction may be preferred because it reinforces the identity of women compared to achieving goals or completing tasks in nonrelational contexts.

Choosing motherhood. A few of the women discussed how motherhood is wrought with fear, anxiety, and a preoccupation with the needs and well-being of their children. Again, this can be linked to one of the primary mechanisms for the socialization of women. The health and well-being of their children affirm their worth, and thus become a significant focus. Their professional accomplishments are often perceived as secondary virtues and professional achievement may serve to reinforce their dominant source of identity, because their achievement often results in securing resources for children and other family members. A desire to excel in both roles may create another conflict, as it is certain that, at some point, the demands of one obligation will overlap the demands of another. These sentiments were especially salient for one participant who recently had a newborn, and for another who was eight months pregnant and expecting her first child. Both of these women were in their 40s and had delayed motherhood while they were pursuing their careers. Another participant in her mid-30s noted that she would like to become a mother one day, but has chosen to delay motherhood in hopes of becoming more firmly established in her career. These women described the struggle that they endured surrounding the timing, benefits, and consequences associated with choosing motherhood. Conceiving children becomes increasingly difficult as women get older; a struggle to conceive is often met with emotional distress, as many professional women are not solely fulfilled or affirmed by accolades in the workplace. Albeit they all agreed that, the decision and hope of becoming a mother someday outweigh the many challenges as one participant says:

> *This has been a challenge. Just thinking about how much do I want to give away of the time I have with my daughter when she is young, verses how much time do I want to give away professionally without keeping up with my skills and expertise. The fear is that I will lose competence, and the challenge is that my baby will only be small once and I would like to treasure that time with her also.*

Inherent in this statement are the complexities related to professional women choosing to become mothers and the reality-based fear that in choosing motherhood, a woman may be required to temporarily leave the workforce, which may impact her career in a detrimental way. The fear of becoming obsolete or losing ground in one's career development has historically been a threat for women who have chosen to scale back their careers to pursue motherhood. Being an entrepreneur and professional however may offer some protections. One of the participants noted that being a professional and entrepreneur has afforded her flexibility to transition into motherhood while maintaining a part-time work status. Yet she reported feeling the pressure to do more, mainly due to fears of continued relevance in her field. The perceptions associated with the definition of a good mother can weigh heavily on achieving balance.

Insufficient work–home boundaries. As stated earlier, women are often affirmed by relational interactions that secure their identity. As a result, relational interactions may be preferred over task-related activities, which are required for most professions including those that are service oriented. Working as an entrepreneur creates unique challenges, in that there is often less regulation about the use of time. The women of this study chose to work as entrepreneurs to facilitate flexibility and autonomy. Individuals who work for others tend to have greater structures in place to assist in the management of time. Such individuals typically go to work at a prescribed time and leave at a set time. Further, when individuals work for others, they are often required to work away from home. The physical separation from the demands of home, coupled with specified periods for working, helps to facilitate productivity for many. It is much easier to focus on work when there are no physical distractions reminding you of the demands of other responsibilities. Feeling a sense of balance between professional and domestic roles can be especially daunting for entrepreneurial women who work from home, or who are required to take work to home. To reduce the potential for emotional distress resulting from being overwhelmed by various life roles, women who work from home need to take extra care to create an environment that will facilitate the same opportunities for focus and success that exist in traditional work environments (Edwards 2008). Creating a schedule, designating a specific work space, and creating reasonable work-related goals associated with time allotted for specific tasks are essential. Without structure, the opportunities for becoming overwhelmed by various demands can lead to one being less effective in either role. A lack of a structured approach to work-related tasks may also result in an excess focus on work during times when it would be more beneficial to focus on family/ domestic obligations. Women are then vulnerable to feel guilty about not being available to the people who are significant in her life, which can lead to feelings of inadequacy. "The most difficulty I experience is trying to find time where I am not working."

The women interviewed for this study reported being consumed with work. "Professional life takes the majority of my time." "Just to find some time where I am not working is my difficulty." Due to a lack of planning and structure, the women reported finding it challenging to "spend enough time with family and . . . self." The women discussed wanting to establish and keep to more consistent boundaries; however, due to the demands of life, they often fanaticize about "wanting to be in two places at one time" to keep up with the demands of life. For this group of women with demanding careers, there is no sense of separation as they are constantly engaged with managing the aspects of their businesses/careers. "I leave one job, go to another, come home and have another one to do." The stressors and demands of work combined with not setting boundaries can be overwhelming and affect one's well-being. By not setting boundaries, it ensures that an individual will not have enough time to maintain obligations, relationships, and a commitment to personal interests not related to their career or care for others:

> It's the stress of work . . . and people needing your time, and reports being done, and promises you made for your work life needing to be kept . . . And then how will you fit in meeting with friends, going to see your grandma, taking care of your kids.

Placing insufficient limits on roles can present grave consequences that affect one's mental health and physical health. As one participant put it, "The difficulty is trying to find some gratification in the professional life, so it doesn't overtake the personal life." Being able to find a degree of satisfaction and then being able to walk away contented with what you were able to accomplish in a limited span of time is ideal. Women who are high achievers struggle to be present in the current moment, as they are always thinking and planning for their next achievement. They then feel guilty for their absence (physical or otherwise) in the lives of people who are important to them, as reported by the participants in this study.

Balance Enhancers

Balance enhancers are activities or actions that participants engaged in to improve their ability to manage the responsibilities associated with their work and family life (Matheson and Rosen 2012). Balance enhancers support work–life balance while expanding one's sense of well-being. The participants were asked to discuss enhancers that affected their general well-being, spiritual well-being, physical well-being, and relational well-being. The first domain to be discussed is that of general well-being enhancers.

General Well-Being Enhancers

Participants identified general beneficial actions that they used to improve their work–life balance. The women identified six common strategies that supported their balance, including enlisting the help of others, perspective shifting, finding enjoyment at work, setting priorities, time management, and a structured approach toward attending to all responsibilities. The participants noted that attention to these tools proved beneficial, by decreasing stressors and increasing a sense of balance and well-being.

Enlisting help from others. The participants noted how essential it was to their well-being to seek out supportive assistance in getting their needs met and tasks completed. Several of the participants commented on just how vital it was to their own work–life balance to "enlist the support of others." Though most women endorsed the value of this tool, it remained underutilized. With demanding careers and home obligations, it can be challenging to meet all the demands requested. Enlisting the help of others is a critical way of getting the support needed. Being able to ask others for help is an important tool for enhancing work–life balance. This appeared to be particularly challenging for this group of women, of whom all were high achievers and had received a significant amount of recognition in their professional life. Women and people of color may have particular difficulty seeking the assistance of others as they avoid being perceived as weak or inadequate. Internalized racism, sexism, or both cause this compulsion for some; although there is an unconscious narrative of inadequacy or worthlessness that women and people of color may live with, they strive to overcome these through their higher achievements. This could also impact this group of women who struggled to seek assistance in domestic responsibilities, as they did not want others who depend on them to feel abandoned or insufficiently cared for.

Perspective shifting. Women and people of color must have some awareness of how their behavior is influenced by their socialization. Further, they would benefit from learning how their expectations are often unrealistic or unnecessary for feeling a sense of accomplishment and peace. Becoming aware of the influence of how one looks at a given situation influences what they would see, as it was for this group of women. They found that by shifting their perspective and being open to other interpretations of a given situation, their perceptions shifted, enhancing balance. "Trying to put things in perspective . . . helps." For example, when mothering and trying to spend adequate time with your children, but having to cut it short to complete tasks for work, one should not beat themselves up for being overextended, but reframe the situation. "Knowing your kid will be okay, even if they do not get the [full amount of] time you want to give them," is a form of perspective shifting. Being a "good enough" mother as opposed to a perfect mother is a huge perspective shift that allows for freedom from internal pressures and anxiety. Utilizing this strategy in other domains of life is equally beneficial for reducing stress and enhancing balance.

Another approach that leads to shifting perspective is turning to historical figures as sources of empowerment. Consulting with historical figures can be a perspective-enhancing tool that provides insight and solutions to how to deal with a variety of experiences. One participant noted how she looked to the first published African American female poet, Phillis Wheatley, as a source of balance enhancement. "I've began to think about being a Phillis Wheatley, writing myself to freedom . . . I will not give up even though it is difficult." Understanding and recalling the challenges that Phillis Wheatley's journey took her on became a source of strength. Recognizing that Wheatley's journey of being the first is similar to many other professional African American women, who are also the first in their industry, company, field, or department. Drawing from historical figures and uncovering their stories provide an alternative perspective on how to be the first while still moving forward. In instances like this, Phillis Wheatley and other important figures become a source of encouragement to persevere and a model of how to shift perspective to enhance balance.

Enjoying work. Finding ways to enhance enjoyment at work has been one of the tools that the participants viewed as important to creating balance. "I try and make it fun when I am engaged in the work." By making work more pleasurable and enjoyable it increases the likelihood that an individual will be more available and engaged in the process. Another strategy to enjoy work included frequently recalling the benefits of one's work role and recapturing the initial enthusiasm when life at work gets tough. This process often led to recovering the enjoyment of one's chosen profession. One participant increased enjoyment at work by seeking out ways to make her job beneficial for both her and the client. The participant became actively involved and intentional in searching out mutually gratifying options whenever possible. An additional strategy in increasing enjoyment at work is to avoid being too serious on all occasions. Being flexible and lightening up on the job can reduce stress and enhance balance. "Not taking yourself so seriously, as if when you don't get xyz done that the world will fall apart" can increase your well-being. Not taking self so seriously allows one to discover the lighter and funnier side of life and serves as a reminder of that which is and is not of paramount importance.

Priority setting and time management. The participants identified several different prioritization and time management strategies to enhance their overall balance and well-being. Being consciously aware of how one spends her or his time and making effective decisions with time has the capacity to reduce stress and influence her or his sense of balance. All of the women indicated that because balance is important to them, they chose careers that provide flexibility, allowing more opportunities to engage in their multiple roles. "I have tried to pick jobs that had flexible schedules, so if I wanted to do something with family or take time for self I could do that." While reflecting on the various roles and responsibilities that they have chosen, they noted the importance of prioritizing self and scheduling "me-time" on their calendars. They described that to be successful in prioritizing self, it took serious effort, including blocking out time in their appointment book or PDA. The women noted that if they were not taking time to prioritize self-care, then they are at greater risk for being less effective in all their roles.

Establishing boundaries. Setting clearly articulated boundaries can enhance the quality of life and balance. Boundaries are those invisible lines that help to define limits, roles, and responsibilities, which create clear parameters to work in. Boundaries offer clear guidelines, which foster accountability and efficiency. Without setting adequate boundaries there is no consistent and dependable structure to reinforce stability, which may minimize overall functioning. Intentionally setting clear boundaries is essential for effectively managing a demanding lifestyle. As one participant put it, "it requires concentrated efforts" to cope with an intense way of life. Being deliberate with setting limits on the amount of time spent at work and home, and adhering to these limits has proven to be beneficial in enhancing balance. Whether it is sticking to only working a predetermined number of hours a day, or choosing to alternate weekends for work and others for pleasure, or working early in the morning or late at night as to avoid interfering with social events, each person has to find a solution that works for them. The women acknowledged the importance of clearly articulating guidelines and boundaries that serve to enhance their balance.

Spiritual Well-Being Enhancers

Spiritual well-being refers to the sense of meaning and purpose in life that one is granted via their connection to a higher power. The participants were asked if they engage in any spiritual/religious activities and if so, how do their practices provide strategies or support to manage the demands between work and home. All of the women indicated that indeed their spiritual/religious practices contributed positively to how they negotiated their various roles, while discussing the centrality of their spirituality to their overall well-being. The participants identified a variety of strategies and daily practices that they used to enhance their sense of balance and spiritual well-being. The women expressed that their spirituality is a central philosophy of life, where they integrate their spirituality into all aspects of how they live their life. In addition, the women discussed the use of prayer and meditation, church attendance, service to others, and the bible as practices and strategies to increase connectedness, centeredness, and balance.

Prayer and meditation. Prayer and meditation were frequently used as a tool to connect to the divine and enhance well-being and balance. Including prayer and meditation first thing in the morning was a strategy used by some of the women. Connecting with the divine first thing in the morning offered guidance and reduced feelings of isolation throughout the day. For these women, prayer and meditation provided opportunities to express gratitude, thankfulness, and to request guidance from the divine. It also provided a safe space to be silent and listen for a response. "Answers and things are around you all the time, answers that help to guide you; prayer helps you to be in tune to the answers/help and wisdom that is around." Prayer and meditation have the capacity to quiet the mind and allow attention to be open to possible solutions. Knowing that there is a higher power that is ultimately in control provided a sense of hope and trust that all things, no matter how they currently appear, will eventually have a resolution. For one participant, prayer and meditation were key practices:

> *These activities help keep me focused on the priorities of life that mandate that I achieve balance between work and life. They remind me that my work does not define all of who I am. They remind me that though I see my work as part of my spiritual work/vocation, my life is more than that. They give me the standard, blueprint and built-in support system to make balance a priority.*

Being able to put your trust and hope in a power greater then self relieves the worries of having to figure it all out, can decrease stress, and serves as tool to support work–life balance.

Church attendance as social support. Attending church served many functions, however, the women tended to focus on the aspects of social support that corporate worship provided. One participant stated, "My religion gives me the people to talk to; it gives support in doing my work." Another participant noted that attending church helped her to feel "much better and more centered." Church attendance also fulfilled other practical needs including serving as a "reminder to rest," to slow down and enjoy life. One participant noted it was a great place to find child care. Being a part of a larger body helps to reinforce that one is not alone but connected to others. Being joined in community for a cause larger than self can foster feelings of solidarity and strength. Attending church provided a space for reflection, an opportunity to regroup, and a chance to emotionally recharge. One participant stated, "Weekly worship creates a space to cognitively reframe, provide support, and replenish emotionally." For some participants, church attendance also included participating in small groups. These close-knit settings provided opportunities for the participants to have a greater sense of social connectedness, where they were known and had the opportunity to get to know others. Close social connections helped to buffer stress and other adverse experiences, and support positive coping practices that enhance balance and well-being.

Spirituality as a way of life. Participants made it clear that they did not divide their lives into compartments, where spirituality was simply one component, for them spirituality was integrally interwoven in the fabric of who they are. "Throughout the day God is at the center of all that I do so, I do not compartmentalize." Their spirituality was the central philosophy on how to live life; it was the blue print for life. Spirituality had the capacity to make them feel good inside. Spirituality helped the participants "to stay centered and focused on what is important" in life. Spirituality as a way of life helped them to persevere. They reported inviting their higher power into every moment "throughout the day," where they were in "constant contact with God." Being in "constant contact" provided reassurance that their higher power was ultimately in charge and governing the world, allowing them a certain degree of freedom to relax and do just their part.

Bible as guidance. For many of the women who subscribed to spirituality as an integrated life philosophy, they also identified the use of biblical scriptures as a tool for guidance. One participant discussed how for her, the bible had everything needed "to get through life." The bible served as a tool for encouragement, support, wisdom, and knowledge for all things pertaining to life. "If I have a problem or a question I go to the scriptures and I often have scriptures in my work office, home office, and throughout the house that serve to encourage me." The support and guidance offered by the Holy Scriptures provided hope and courage to thrive in the face of difficulty. One participant referenced a commonly known scripture, Philippians 4:19. "I can do all things through Christ . . . He will give me peace that passes all understanding." These types of scriptures provided a supportive foundation in times of difficulty.

Service to others. Stepping outside of self and meeting the needs of others was a very practical and concrete way that participants practiced their spirituality. Service to others provided an opportunity to look beyond self and one's own personal challenges to meet the needs of others. This form of giving to others seemed to engender a sense of appreciativeness and gratitude, an appreciativeness of being connected to something greater than self, and an awareness of each individual's role in giving back. One of the women provided a powerful example of how service enhanced her connectedness to a purpose greater than self:

> *In 7th grade, my teacher asked us to do an assignment where we wrote what we wanted our tombstones to say. I remembered writing that "I am happy that she was here." If there is any way I can be a blessing or assistance to someone I want to help them. When I'm gone, I want them to say I was happy she passed through, not that I was happy she is gone.*

The spirituality of service affects not only the individual who is receiving the gift but also the helper, reminding them that they have a greater purpose in this life.

Physical Well-Being Enhancers

The participants discussed using exercise, nutrition, and personal care as tools to enhance their work–life balance and overall physical well-being. Physical well-being takes into account that by optimizing components of physical health, an individual is also increasing overall health functioning and well-being, based on the assumption that the mind and body are integrally connected.

Exercise. The women described participating in a variety of physical activities to increase health, eliminate stress, and enhance balance. Walking, swimming, hiking, dancing, and yoga tended to top the list of activities that offered a release of stress and rejuvenation of energy. One participant said, "Taking African dance, yoga . . . those things have helped to alleviate the stress that comes with the intensity of the work." However, what was equally as important as the type of activity that was participated in was the frequency in which they engaged in the activity. The women reported exercising between two and five times a week, for at least 30 minutes to an hour. Given their demanding schedules and tendency to eliminate the "me-time" when faced with time challenges on the job or at home, the participants offered creative solutions on how to increase the likelihood of participating in an exercise routine. The women suggested personalizing their physical activity and choosing an enjoyable activity to improve sustainability, thereby ensuring they receive the balance-enhancing benefits of exercise.

Strategies enhancing physical activity and follow through. Identifying and incorporating pleasurable physical activities seemed to be of paramount importance for improving sustainability. Activities that were easily accessible and did not require a lot of setup appeared to have the advantage. For one participant who loved to dance, dance videos were the convenient choice. Not only did she derive pleasure from dancing and listening to music, but also it was time efficient. It took her only a few minutes to get from her bed, dressed, and in front of her TV versus getting into the car and driving to the gym. Convenience was a key factor in supporting her commitment to physical well-being. For those who thrive on interpersonal accountability to spur them on, one participant noted enlisting the assistance of her neighbor. In the mornings, she and her neighbor would walk their dogs together, fulfilling practical needs on many fronts. This camaraderie added pleasure to an ordinary task and increased the odds of her engaging in physical activity. Another strategy used to increase physical activity was exercising early in the morning. This early morning placement eliminated conflicting needs of appointments with clients and competing needs of children or spouses. Executing an early morning exercise routine however required advance planning. In order for the participant to be alert and ready to exercise, she had to make sure to get adequate sleep the previous night. "Going to bed on time helps me to be able to get up in the morning so I can have time to exercise." Though the strategies are varied, the messages are similar; to increase sustainability, an activity must be enjoyable, convenient, and reasonable to do.

Nutrition. Another factor in enhancing balance and physical well-being is incorporating healthy eating behaviors. Over half of the women identified eating nutritious food as a mechanism for enhancing their overall health. Eating a well-balanced meal was described as an integral component of their health care routine. Healthy nutrition behaviors included "eating things that are healthy, less salt, less poor carbs and including more roughage, fruit and vegetables." In addition to "just eating healthy," another participant identified other sources for increasing healthy nutritional habits. "I take vitamins, I drink 8 glasses of water a day, [and] I have a cup of green tea." With a complex work–home schedule, prioritizing healthy eating habits has to be intentional. Making smart food choices required advance preparation. "I make sure I have food with me and that it is healthy food so I can eat even if I am busy." Packing healthy food is a strategy that has proven helpful to defending against grabbing highly processed vending machine snacks or sugary fast-food items. Another participant agreed that by avoiding fast-food and eating on the run she has been able to increase healthy eating behaviors. For this group of women, proper nutrition augmented their sense of balance.

Personal care. Attention to personal care has been another important aspect of maintaining good health practices for these women. The participants discussed how personal care activities, such as personal grooming, are ways in which they engage in self-care. Personal grooming served to improve self-esteem and self-image. It has been said that when you look good, you often feel good. As a participant noted, getting her hair done professionally is a way that she takes care of herself. Another participant described how she regularly incorporated professional massages into her personal care regimen. For her, a massage decreased stress and enhanced relaxation, which supported her work–life balance. In efforts to maximize personal care, another participant discussed how she schedules and routinely attends her doctor's appointments as preventive medicine. Much like how regular attention, protection against humidity and temperature, and proper cleaning help in maintaining the sound and quality of fine instruments, routine visits to the doctor assist in maintaining the health of the human instrument. Establishing healthy practices and personal health norms makes detecting abnormalities or slight changes in health more apparently, for which remediation can be prescribed. Playing was also described as being essential to personal care, where engaging in an activity that brings enjoyment and pleasure, was a form of personal care. Playing provides an opportunity for letting go, being present, and participating in pure delight. As one participant put it, "I work hard and I play hard." Attending to one's personal care comes in many forms and fulfills a vital role in supporting balance and physical well-being.

Relational Well-Being Enhancers

Intimate relationships can foster feelings of attachment and belonging, which have the capacity to influence well-being and mitigate stressors associated with work–life balance. The participants were asked to address how their relationships have influenced their ability to manage their work and home life. The women discussed a number of ways that their relationships supported their balance. For them, relationships have the capacity to be "powerful in terms of

. . . spiritual development." Relationships presented opportunities "to practice being loving, nurturing and caring." Relationships were instructive and provided help when focus was lost. Relationships "act[ed] as a listening/sounding board to help manage issues related to work or family." In addition, trusted relationships offered "wisdom and truth." When intimate "relationships are aligned," they can fuel individuals with needed strength "to face challenges at work and elsewhere." For these women, relationships are valuable resources that provided a host of benefits. There appeared to be three major themes that spoke to how these women used relationships to enhance their overall balance, including maintaining strong support systems, choosing supportive partners, and using close relationships to get perspective and refocus.

Maintaining strong support systems. "People need community, a group of people who are there for them." This was a sentiment shared by all of the participants who reflected on the importance of being connected to others. For a group of women with demanding lifestyles, "relationships are key." Being deliberate about tending to and nurturing these friendships and relationships was critical to enhancing balance. Making "a conscious effort to stay in touch with and rekindle old relationships" was vital. Keeping personal relationships strong and healthy served as a protective factor and promoted well-being. "Having good friends, family support, colleagues at work that can be trust[ed], is the key to success." Good relationships provided a buffer during challenging times and joy during comfortable times. Some relationships helped the women to "get through problems" that arise in their lives. For this group of women, a strong support system or community was not marked by quantity, but quality. You do not have to have "a lot of people . . . but just a core group of individuals that [can be] trust[ed] with my weakness and strengths." Trusting others served as a healing process and created a space to be fully known and appreciated. Maintaining strong support systems offered many powerful experiences.

Choosing supportive partnerships. Various women discussed how having "a very supportive partner" had been a major component in helping them to balance the demands of their personal and professional lives. Utilizing the collaborative nature of relationships and working as a team had been a helpful survival strategy. "I am learning that there is power in two, when [we] work together. It's reinforced that I do not have to find balance alone." Supportive partnerships and romantic relationships offered support and nurturance, where both individuals felt "taken care of." Being intentional about finding a partner with whom they shared a common outlook on life contributed to the supportive nature of the relationship. Having a shared spiritual base was also important when choosing a partner. Maintaining a common "belief system . . . really makes a big difference." Sharing a core belief system enhanced the experience of collaboration. Having trusted individuals to share intimate thoughts and ideas with was invaluable. Choosing intimate relationships, friends, and supportive networks with mindfulness supported their well-being.

Perspective shifting and refocusing. Some of the women alluded to how they look to their personal relationships as a way to get guidance and advice. The guidance and advice that they received helped them to improve their well-being. Getting another person's opinion or insight on a problem or challenge allowed for the possibility of new solutions to emerge. Having a trusted fellow who gave "honest advice" and provided "the real deal and not just what I want to hear" was needed to gain greater self-awareness. This type of frankness was beneficial, especially in elucidating blind spots. "If I try and do things by myself and only look to me, I don't have the perspective needed." Relationships served as a way to enhance one's outlook on life and refocus priorities. "My relationships challenge me to keep faces before me when I feel so driven to only focus on getting ahead at work." With demanding schedules it is all too easy for these women to stay in work mode and not make time for other parts of life, however, their relationships helped them "to keep the big picture in mind" and strive to live a more integrated and balanced lives.

Conclusion

In conclusion, this group of professional African American women offered insight into their lived experiences in balancing both their home obligations and work responsibilities. The exploration of their challenges with work–life balance, as well as their strategies to promote well-being, serves as lens to understand the unique experiences of these women. As the themes unfolded, it became evident that the intersections of ethnicity, culture, and socioeconomic status influenced strategies that these women engaged in. In an ever-increasing diverse marketplace, it of paramount importance to continue to explore how such conditional factors impact the overall well-being of professional women, in this case, that of African American women entrepreneurs.

References

Baum, J. Robert, Michael Frese, Robert A. Baron, and Jerome A. Katz. 2007. "Entrepreneurship as an Area of Psychology Study: An Introduction." In *The Psychology of Entrepreneurship*, 1–18. Mahwah, NJ: Lawrence Erlbaum Associate Publishers. Available at: PsycINFO on EBSCOhost. Accessed March 2, 2013.

Brockhaus, Robert H. 1987. "Entrepreneurial Folklore." *Journal of Small Business Management* 25 (3): 1–6. Available at: PsycINFO on EBSCOhost. Accessed March 2, 2001.

Bronfenbrenner, Urie. 1992. *Ecological Systems Theory.* London: Jessica Kingsley Publishers.

ten Brummelhuis, Lieke L., and Arnold B. Bakker. 2012. "A Resource Perspective on the Work–Home Interface: The Work–Home Resources Model." *American Psychologist* 7 (October): 545–56. Available at: PsycINFO on EBSCOhost. Accessed March 3, 2013.

Cochrane, Philip. 2010. "African American Entrepreneurial Venues and Social Capital." *Journal of Developmental Entrepreneurship* 15 (3): 287–300. Available at: PsycINFO on EBSCOhost. Accessed March 2, 2013.

Edwards, Carolyn Coleman. 2008. "Assessing Entrepreneurship and African American Women: Factors of Success." Northcentral University. ProQuest, 2008.

Gilligan, Carol. 1982. *In a Different Voice: Psychological Theory and Women's Development.* Cambridge: Harvard University Press.

Giorgi, Amedeo. 1997. "The Theory, Practice, and Evaluation of the Phenomenological Method as a Qualitative Research Procedure." *Journal of Phenomenological Psychology* 28: 235–60.

Hobfoll, Stevan E. 2001. "The Influence of Culture, Community, and the Nested-Self in the Stress Process: Advancing Conservation of Resources Theory." *Applied Psychology* 50 (3): 337–421.

Matheson, Jennifer L., and Karen H. Rosen. 2012. "Marriage and Family Therapy Faculty Members' Balance of Work and Personal Life." *Journal of Marital and Family Therapy* 38 (2) (April): 394–416. Available at: PsycINFO on EBSCOhost. Accessed March 3, 2013.

Obama, Barack. 2010. "Work–Life Balance and the Economics of Workplace Flexibility. March 2010." Executive Office of the President Council of Economic Advisers. Available at: http://www.whitehouse.gov/files/documents/100331-cea-economics-workplace-flexibility.pdf.

Wyche, Karen F., and Sherryl B. Graves. 1992. "Minority Women in Academia: Access and Barriers to Professional Participation." *Psychology of Women Quarterly* 16 (4): 429–37. Available at: PsycINFO on EBSCOhost. Accessed March 3, 2013.

Chapter 11

Putting the "E" in Entrepreneurship: Women Entrepreneurs in the Digital Age

Janet Salmons

The Internet, with its broad potential for communication and exchange, has changed the strategy, operations, and sales for businesses of all types and sizes. Due to the ability to reach customers, vendors, allies, or partners anywhere through low-cost websites, blogs, or social networks, barriers to starting a new business have come down. Conducting business with these technologies goes beyond a simple transaction of buying and selling tangible goods and services, because online business importantly includes connecting with and building relationships with key stakeholders. While 20th-century entrepreneurs depended on *financial* capital to build stores and factories, 21st-century entrepreneurs rely on *intellectual* and *social* capital—innovative ideas combined with the ability to build mutually beneficial networks of partners, allies, and customers (Adler and Kwon 2002; Carolis and Saparito 2006; Ottósson and Klyver 2010;, Robb and Coleman 2010; Xiong and Bharadwaj 2011).

Changes regarding the ways new enterprises are started and run have impacted both male and female business owners. However, the study discussed in this chapter focused specifically on women entrepreneurs who are taking advantage of emerging opportunities unique to the globally connected contemporary milieu in order to launch new ventures.

Of course even in the digital age, large-scale, multinational enterprises are still being envisioned by contemporary entrepreneurs. Indeed, the gadgets and devices used to connect with social networks are being invented, manufactured, and distributed much the way as was yesterday's clunky telephone or typewriter. Male entrepreneurs such as Steve Jobs (Apple), Michael Dell (Dell

Computers), and Jeff Bezos (Amazon Kindle) are well-known and wealthy as a result of their success in manufacturing innovative technology products. It is at the other end of the spectrum, where the entrepreneurial effort is hatched, lives, and breathes in a digitally connected milieu, the most profound changes are occurring. And at this end of the spectrum, women entrepreneurs are actively engaged.

To what extent have these new developments affected women entrepreneurs? Sorensen, Folker, and Brigham (2008) describe women's "collaborative network orientation" and suggest that women prefer to organize in networks, create collaborative and cooperative relationships within these networks, and use these networks to build and run businesses. Similarly, Bird and Brush (2002) contend that women view the world "holistically," as a "web of relationships". It seems logical that women are well suited for business on the social-capital-intensive World Wide Web.

The lowering of entrance barriers and greater focus on social capital may be contributing to the increase in women entrepreneurs generally. The 2010 Global Entrepreneurship Monitor (GEM) (Kelly et al. 2010) reports a narrowing in the gap between men and women entrepreneurs in the United States: 47 percent for females compared with a rate of 53 percent for males. GEM found that in 2010, women showed a 5.6 percent rate of start-up activity (5.0% in 2009), while the rate for men was 6.7 percent (dropped from 8.8% in 2009). The National Women's Business Council analyzed the 2007 U.S. Census and small-business data in the 2012 report, "Women-Owned Firms in the U.S." This report shows that women owned 7.8 million businesses, representing 28.8 percent of all companies in the country, with the growth of women-owned firms outpacing the growth of other firm types (Nagle, Mittapalli, and Hannum 2012). Most of these businesses were founded—not acquired or inherited. They were often very small; 88.3 percent of women-owned businesses were *nonemployer firms*, meaning they had no full-time regular employees (Lewis et al. 2011; Nagle, Mittapalli, and Hannum 2012). According to an analysis of data from the Kauffman Firm Survey (Fairlie, 2011), women-owned, technology-based firms were smaller than firms owned by men, fewer were organized as corporations (54.1% vs. 76.1%), and more were likely to be home-based sole proprietorships (Robb and Coleman 2010).

While these reports show diverse types of businesses owned by women, the majority of the businesses (77%) had individuals as customers, with the balance serving other organizations or businesses (Nagle, Mittapalli, and Hannum 2012). It is logical to assume that a business based on sales or services to individuals would find online communications a boon. Indeed, the National Entrepreneurial Assessment for the United States of America 2010 report describes the perception that starting an Internet business is a lower-risk proposition than other business options (Kelly et al. 2010). Kelly et al. (2011, 32) observe that "In 2010, 17.4% of early-stage entrepreneurs (compared with only 4.5% of established business owners) reported starting out as an Internet business. Continued innovation of the Internet (e.g., Web 2.0) seems to have created new opportunities for early-stage entrepreneurs to start businesses."

Of course, not all consumer services are delivered online. Still, the Internet is emerging as a significant factor for small, consumer-oriented businesses that thrive on ongoing relationships.

Interesting as they may be, cited reports from the National Women's Business Council, Kauffman Foundation, GEM, and studies that referenced them are the result of quantitative analyses of large data sets. As valuable as statistics are for tracking broad trends, these analyses do not provide insights into the motivations, aspirations, and day-to-day practices of today's women entrepreneurs. The numbers suggest the need for a qualitative study into the lived experiences and personal perspectives of women who start and run their own businesses.

Using findings from an interview-based qualitative grounded theory study and recent literature, in this chapter, we broadly explore the influence of information and communication technologies (ICTs) on women entrepreneurs' goals, options, and choices. We compare and contrast women entrepreneurs who use technology to build businesses and sell physical or local products and services with those who use technology to build businesses and sell products and services that are electronic. Points of comparison will include the e-business strategy; relationships with allies, partners, and customers; and personal and business goals.

Redefining Entrepreneurship

Emerging forms mean redefinition of the concept of *entrepreneurism*. Dheeriya (2009) defines *online entrepreneurship* or *e-entrepreneurship* as any venture conducted solely on the Internet or the World Wide Web. Online entrepreneurship encompasses the activities of a regular entrepreneur, but the mode of operation is technologically based (Dheeriya 2009). *Home-based internet business (HBIB)* refers to business conducted online, from a home office (Marco van, Sayers, and Keen 2008). When HBIBs are run by mothers, they are called *mompreneurs*—in England *mumpreneurs* (Kelan 2008; Nel, Maritz, and Thongprovati 2010). *Women entrepreneurs* are defined as those who have initiated a business, are actively involved in managing it, own at least 50 percent of the firm, and the business has been in operation for one year or longer (Nixdorff and Rosen 2010).

In this study, a distinction was made between women who are real-world e-entrepreneurs and those who are digital e-entrepreneurs. The term *real-world e-entrepreneurs* refers to those who use online communications with vendors and customers, partners and allies, and for promotions and advertising. However, products and services are physical, and in some cases, inherently face-to-face, delivered, or purchased on location. The term *digital e-entrepreneurs* refers to those who similarly use online communications, but are in the business of selling electronic products and services. Electronic products and services could include online writing, teaching, training, consulting, web design, or programming. Important considerations for both types center on entrepreneurs' motivations for using online technologies and the ways they use them to communicate. Is the strategy successful, and how do they define and measure success?

Either e-entrepreneur type may have a local, regional, national, or even global geographic scope or operations. Online marketing may draw local customers to a retail shop, or international customers to a blog, community, or store on the web. One entrepreneur described the "awesome experience of standing in an Internet café in Hong Kong and watching her website pop up—and realizing that at that very moment, she could order her product halfway round the world from her home-business base in Orlando" (Abarbanel 2008, 31). Geography does not constrain the e-entrepreneurial imagination when communications are global.

Push–Pull Factors and Women Entrepreneurs

Entrepreneurs choose to start a business for a number of personal, professional, or economic reasons to meet their own immediate or long-term goals. Prospective entrepreneurs may be tired of following someone else's vision, and instead see their own avenue for success, an opening that may be impractical and risky but nonetheless irresistible. Barriers—cultural and financial—face women who try to launch new ventures, so there must be some considerable impetus to make the effort (Shinnar, Giacomin, and Janssen 2012).

Entrepreneurs' motivations to transform an idea into a business have been widely categorized as either *push* or *necessity* factors, or *pull* or *opportunity* factors (Kariv 2011; Schjoedt and Shaver 2007). According to this way of thinking, the would-be entrepreneur may feel pushed from the workplace to start a business. Necessity or push factors include economic necessity caused by job loss or absence of job options, discrimination or limited advancement options, and poor fit with the job or organizational culture (Kariv 2011; Schjoedt and Shaver 2007). If a business is started by necessity, there may be a lack of planning or strategy, so ventures that result from a push are sometimes seen as having a higher risk of failure.

Entrepreneurs are *pulled* into starting businesses because they have ideas or opportunities to pursue. Hayton and Cholakova (2012) argue that the idea for a new business is not the same thing as the opportunity, but "without the idea, the opportunity could never be brought into existence" (Hayton and Cholakova 2012, 45). Additional factors related to the desire for independence, self-fulfillment, wealth, social status, and power may pull someone out of a conventional job and place into an entrepreneurial effort.

Gender has an influence on how push or pull factors are perceived and acted upon; clearly, women are pushed or pulled into entrepreneurship in different ways than are men. The National Women's Business Council (2011) reported on two studies, "Are Male and Female Entrepreneurs Really That Different?" and "Business Creation in the United States: PSED II Initial Assessment," which found statistically significant differences in motivations and expectations between men and women when examining reasons for starting a business. Both studies found that men were motivated by wealth creation and women by the desire for more flexibility and independence (Lewis et al. 2011).

Mattis's (2004) earlier study of women who left jobs to start new businesses showed both push and pull factors. She identified three push factors: perception of gender-related barriers to advancement that are not always overtly visible, also known as the glass ceiling; being unhappy with the work environment; and being unchallenged. Unhappiness with the work environment sometimes occurs because women face sexism or sexual harassment in the workplace.

Some women are unhappy at work because they perceive an inability to attain the kind of leadership position or level of authority that enables them to make a difference or to shape the organization (Orhan and Scott 2001; Patterson and Mavin 2009). They may be dissatisfied with rigid corporate structures and managerial approaches, and desire more autonomy and control (Patterson and Mavin 2009). They may be frustrated by enduring disparities in compensation (Kulich et al. 2011). Participants in Patterson and Mavin's (2009, 180) study of women's transitions from corporate to entrepreneurial work reported that "despite what they considered to be their best efforts, it was felt that their ideas and opinions frequently went unheard." Kephart and Schumacher (2005, 2) connected the glass ceiling with a push toward entrepreneurship:

> For years, women have been fighting within all types of organizations for equal roles in the workplace, equal pay for equal work, and equal respect alongside their male counterparts . . . In fact many female workers are calling it quits in terms of the attempt to succeed equally alongside their male counterparts

particularly within the traditional and old boy's network type organization. Instead, many women are starting their own traditions, their own way, within their own organizations.

The glass ceiling, combined with a general reduction in opportunities for meaningful work, may influence women to start their own businesses. In an essay titled "The Rise of the Independent Workforce," Alexandra Levitt, a mother of two who works virtually from her own consulting business, observed the choice to start a business: Independent work is a choice that . . . I have made. Not every worker has, or will have, that choice. But the way the corporate world is going, I think that many workers need to prepare for the possibility of going out on their own someday. (Levitt 2012, 8)

However pervasive the push factors may be, especially in times when the job market was unreliable, the pull factor *flexibility* was noted significantly in Mattis's and later studies (Kariv 2011; Schjoedt and Shaver 2007). Flexibility was named as the number one attraction of an entrepreneurial option in all of the studies reviewed for this chapter, conveying the point that regardless of the type of organization or position, it is preferable to work in one you have created yourself.

Flexibility is not necessarily related to the number of hours worked, but about the ability to choose those hours. While many see *flexibility* as a code word used to describe mothers' needs to balance work and child-rearing, mothers of young children are not the only ones whose visions for a creative and satisfying work life may include nonwork factors that are not possible in the earlier than nine and later than five nature of today's business life. Abarbanel (2008, 31) observed:

Socially, stage-of-life shifts are also stoking the entrepreneurial engine. If fifty is the new forty, then there are vast numbers of women who have many years of productive, high-speed living ahead of them. As they ponder fresh ideas about how to spend that time, many baby boomers who've made their mark in corporate jobs are exploring new work options more attuned to their changing self-images and aspirations.

Women entrepreneurs want to balance work with other priorities to invent a creative and satisfying work life. Sullivan et al. discussed an "entrepreneurial lifestyle" with a set of values and priorities that influence career choices as they relate to the potential for personal authenticity and balance among many priorities for stimulating work, relationships, caregiving roles, and other nonwork aspects of life (Sullivan et al. 2007). Eddleston and Powell (2012) explored ways in which positive work–family interdependencies were possible with entrepreneurial lifestyles. They point to the need for more research on the influences of family in business support and household support—or marital situation on women entrepreneurs' success (Eddleston and Powell 2012).

To appreciate the pull of the entrepreneurial lifestyle, it may be useful to understand the worker–job–workplace relationship. Scholars interested in person–vocation fit look at the congruence between individuals' interests and abilities and the characteristics and requirements of their vocation; those who study person–organization fit, look at the congruence between individuals and their organizations (Edwards and Billsberry 2010). Several recent studies note that job seekers' and employees' priorities have shifted from priorities based on good matches of knowledge, skills, and abilities with specific jobs to a desire for a fit between an individual's personality, beliefs, and values with job characteristics and with the organization's culture, norms, and values (Andrews, Baker, and Hunt 2011; Morley 2007; Wheeler et al. 2007). Clearly, contemporary workers want more than a paycheck; they seek what the Buddhists call "right livelihood," a way to work that allows for what Edwards and Billsberry (2010) call a "multidimensional fit."

Clearly, women face cultural barriers when they try to launch new ventures (Shinnar, Giacomin, and Janssen 2012). Several studies argue that women have less access to venture capital and financial backing, thus the glass ceiling extends into the entrepreneurial realm (Bosse and Taylor 2012; Robb and Coleman 2010; Sullivan and Meek 2012). But at least some prospective women entrepreneurs may look beyond those barriers with a vision of an independent, creative, and satisfying work life that matches their skills, interests, and passions. If they do not fit in an existing workplace, they are pulled toward creating their own.

Research Approach and Methodology

While scholars have explored online entrepreneurs and women entrepreneurs, little research has linked the two. This qualitative study aimed to explore potential connections. The central research question was, "What is the influence of ICT options on women entrepreneurs' choices for their businesses and their goals for the future?" I was curious about how the availability of online communications technologies affects women entrepreneurs' choices for business models or plans, mode of operation, how they experience relationships with partners or collaborators, and how they envision the future potential of the business.

By using this qualitative approach, the study adhered to the recommendations that Stevenson made in 1990, when she suggested that quantitative approaches are not adequate when studying women entrepreneurs. Stevenson (1990, 442) observed:

> Entrepreneurship is a process, a highly personal, subjective process. One becomes an entrepreneur as an evolution—through the process of encountering, assessing, and reacting to a series of experiences, situations, and events. Until we know more about this process, it is inappropriate to try to measure it using structured, survey research methods. To understand the process of entrepreneurship, it is critical to understand how individual entrepreneurs attach meanings to these events and circumstances.

Theoretical Frameworks

Constructivist epistemology and social capital theory were appropriate to this study. Constructivists assume that we interpret experiences, build meaning, and construct reality based on our perceptions of the world (Bruner and Kearsley 2004; Charmaz 2003). From this position, it was understood that participants constructed their own meanings in different ways, even in relation to the same phenomenon (Gray 2009), with each interpretation as valid as the other (Crotty 2001). The constructivist researcher uses inductive reasoning to examine how people interpret observations of the world and integrate fragmented phenomena into meaningful explanations of their experiences (Denzin and Lincoln 2003; Lincoln and Guba 1985).

The digital network that underlies online business relationship is based on the development of social capital. Nahapiet and Ghoshal (1998) labeled the dimensions of social capital as *structural, relational,* and *cognitive.* While Nahapiet and Ghoshal described *structural social capital* as the properties of the system and patterns of connections among social contacts, and *cognitive social capital* as shared representations and understandings among those contacts, it is the *relational dimension of social capital* that best explains the perspectives and practices of women e-entrepreneurs. Relational social capital theory describes the trust, respect, and friendship that develop over time with social contacts (Nahapiet and Ghoshal 1998). As Alfred (2009, 5) describes it, relational social capital theory recognizes that "the goodwill of others toward us is a valuable resource to be harnessed."

This study explored both the structural and relational aspects of the participants' social capital. Constructivist studies of technology use the term *sociotechnical,* coined by Hughes in 1986 and used "to convey that technology is never 'just' technical or 'just' social" (Faulkner 2001, 82) and to argue that both gender and technology are socially constructed. Thus, by using both constructivism and social capital theory, our study aimed to take a holistic view of women e-entrepreneurs (Dautzenberg 2012).

Grounded Theory and Situational Analysis

To apply grounded theory, researchers build on an understanding of individuals' experiences to generate theoretical principles. They look at categories discovered in the data and construct explanatory theoretical frameworks, which provide abstract conceptual understandings of the studied phenomena (Charmaz 2003, 2006). The framework (Spencer, Ritchie, and O'Connor 2003) approach to analyzing content was used to organize these categories.

Situational analysis is a style of grounded theory. Situational analysis looks at the social situation, while grounded theory looks at the social process (Clarke 2005). Situational analysts diagram elements in the research situation to capture the complexities and show relationships in the data by making use of three kinds of maps: situational, social worlds/arenas, and positional maps. These maps situate the aspects of the research phenomena by not only mapping the data but also by calling out for discovery of otherwise unseen relationships. New theoretical constructs are thus grounded in the data from participants who have experienced the phenomenon. Grounded theory can help explain practice or provide a framework for further research and more formal theory development. The researcher uses inductive reasoning to look for and compare patterns and associations in the data and to locate linkages between sets of phenomena.

The study used a situational analysis, called postmodern grounded theory approach (Charmaz 2006; Clarke 2005), to generate an abstract framework, concepts, and themes for further research. Grounded theory methods depend on the kind of flexibility afforded by interview data collection (Charmaz 2003). Charmaz (2003, 314), who advocates a qualitative approach to grounded theory, calls such interviews "unfolding stories" where the interviewer starts with the participant's story and fills it out by attempting to "locate it within a basic social process." In this study, participants' stories were located within the entrepreneurial situation.

By looking at the situation, I could explore participants attached meaning to their stories around conceiving of, developing, and running the business. The situational analysis approach allowed me to look for interrelated experiences with human (entrepreneur, partners, allies, customers, etc.) and nonhuman aspects (technology, events, etc.). Social capital theory enabled a view of the situation through lens that focused on the benefits of electronic networks of trusting relationships with allies, partners, online followers or friends, and customers.

This study was not designed to generate a new theory or model, as is often the goal for grounded theory. Given the minimal extant research on topics related to women entrepreneurs who operate online, this study's purpose was to look for, surface, and explore the dimensions of the phenomena and to identify potential themes for future study. A very open, generative research approach, with few prior assumptions, was appropriate to this purpose.

Sampling

A stratified purposive sampling approach was used to achieve maximum variation. A stratified approach allows the researcher to identify subgroups that facilitate comparisons (Miles and Huberman 1994). For this study, the main subgroups were defined as real-world e-entrepreneurs and digital e-entrepreneurs. This meant I needed to recruit entrepreneurs who use the Internet to market or carry out other business activities for operations that occur in the physical world. And I needed to recruit entrepreneurs who use the Internet to market or carry out other business activities for operations that occur online. Given the exploratory nature of the study, I wanted a maximum variation sample, with each research participant in a different line of business.

Online recruiting included descriptions of the study posted on my website, social media sites, and related professional and academic e-mail lists. I also searched for entrepreneurs online in specific areas and personally invited them to participate.

All participants completed an informed consent agreement. Note that some participants chose to be named and quoted directly, while others chose to remain anonymous in the reports of this study. Limitations were explained at the outset: no proprietary or financial information was requested for the study.

Real-World E-Entrepreneurs

For the purpose of this study, real-world e-entrepreneurs were defined as those who use online communications with vendors and customers, partners and allies, and for promotions and advertising. However, the nature of the products and services were physical, and in some cases, inherently face-to-face, delivered, constructed, or purchased on location. Six participants fitted this definition, including Ms. Agacayak who had multiple businesses that fitted both categories. Essential characteristics of the participants are outlined in Table 11.1.

As Table 11.1 shows, the real-world e-entrepreneurs who participated in this study ran diverse businesses. Some sold physical products, that is, beaded

Table 11.1 Real-world e-entrepreneurs

	Products and Services	Uses ICTs to	Main ICTs
Tara Agacayak	• Selling work by Turkish artisans to Western customers • Organizing shopping tours for people visiting Turkey	• Promote business • Conduct e-commerce: sell products through eBay • Communicate with new and existing customers	• Site: http://www.behindthebazaar.blogspot.com/ and http://www.taraagacayak.com/ • Social media: yes • Primary communication technology: mix of ICTs
Catherine Jaffee	"Honey Tasting Walking Tours," a project that combines tourism in remote Turkish villages with the support of the local women beekeepers	• Promote business • Communicate with supporters and customers • Attract funding through crowdsourcing with Kickstarter.com • Communicate with team	• Site: http://balyolu.com/ • Social media: yes • Primary communication technology: mix of ICTs
Anna Holland	Beaded jewelry using global ethnic artifacts and beads	• Promote business • Find and build relationships and do business with vendors • Communicate with customers • Sell products retail	• Site: http://www.dorjedesigns.com/ • Social media: no • Primary communications technology: e-mail
Jessica Swift	Graphic arts products for the home, stationery, and fashion accessories. Also licenses designs for use on other companies' products, and offers design services	• Promote business • Attract funding through crowdsourcing with Kickstarter.com • Network with other entrepreneurs • Communicate with customers • Sell products wholesale and retail • Offer online courses for graphic artists	• Site: http://www.jessicaswift.com • Social media: yes • Primary communications technology: mix of ICTs

(Continued)

Table 11.1 (Continued)

	Products and Services	Uses ICTs to	Main ICTs
Participant 1	Architecture and interior design	• Promote business • Solicit input on projects • Communicate with and educate potential customers and people interested in the built environment and green building	• Website: yes (withheld) • Social media: no • Primary communications technology: e-mail blast
Participant 2	Clinical psychologist	• Promote therapy practice • Welcome new clients with online intake forms • Manage appointments and scheduling • Work with assistant on billing • Offer background information on website	• Website: yes (withheld) • Social media: no • Primary communication technology: e-mail/text for admin only due to HIPAA regulations

Abbreviations: HIPAA, Health Insurance Portability and Accountability Act; ICTs, information and communication technologies.

necklaces, crafts, or artistic items, and others sold services that must be offered face-to-face, that is, building design or therapy. All of them had websites and most used social media. Not surprisingly, those who used social media used a variety of communication approaches, while others relied on e-mail.

Digital E-Entrepreneurs

For the purpose of this study, digital e-entrepreneurs were defined as those in the business of selling electronic products and services. While a physical, hard copy version may exist, the nature of their work primarily involved electronic products or services.

As Table 11.2 shows, digital e-entrepreneurs who participated in the study were involved in online marketing or advertising, and online communities. These entrepreneurs facilitated, developed, trained, or served other online entrepreneurs, social entrepreneurs, or nonprofit groups. These entrepreneurs made heavy, varied use of different online technologies including websites and social media. However, one participant, whose work was conducted one-to-one, used e-mail almost exclusively.

Data Collection and Analysis

The primary data collection occurred through interviews and related e-mail communications as needed for clarification or follow-up. Additionally, blog posts, media, and documents were reviewed and analyzed to gain more understanding of the motivations, choices, and business practices of women e-entrepreneurs.

Interviews were semistructured, with eight main open-ended questions:

1. Briefly explain what technologies you use and how you use them.
    a. What technologies do you use for business-to-business communication?
    b. What technologies do you use for business-to-customer communication?
2. What is your start-up story?
3. What were the significant transition points?
4. Did the availability of communications technology have a role in enabling you to move from one stage to the next? If so, how?
5. Do you believe your business model is successful?
    a. How do you measure success?
    b. How do you measure the success of technology tools and how do you determine which to continue or discontinue using?
6. What are your goals in terms of business size?

Table 11.2 Digital e-entrepreneurs

	Products and Services	Uses ICTs to	Main ICTs
Tara Agacayak	Online community	• Community building, networking, and training • Marketing advice available for "members"	• Site: http://www.globalniche.net/ • Social media: yes • Primary communication technology: mix of ICTs
Crystal Stemberger	Marketing and advertising for blogs in personal finance and travel	• Promote business • Conduct business • Network with other entrepreneurs in personal finance and travel • Communicate with advertisers • Communicate with bloggers • Respond to inquiries	• Site: http://www.budgetinginthefunstuff.com/ • Website: yes • Social media: no • Primary communication technology: e-mail blast
Nancy White	Community building and facilitation	• Provide services • Provide information and facilitate informal learning experiences for others interested in online facilitation and online communities • Learn about trends in the field and communicate with a broad network of people with similar interests • Communicate with collaborative partners • Communicate with clients	• Site: http://www.fullcirc.com/ • Social media: yes • Primary communication technology: mix of ICTs

Susan Eddington	Marketing and transmedia storytelling	• Promote business • Negotiate contracts • Conduct sales transactions • Communicate with collaborative partners, contractors, or project teams • Communicate with clients	• Site: www.images-images.com • Social media: no • Primary communication technology: mix of ICTs
Participant 3	Editor for academic writers	• Learn about the trends in the field and others in similar line of work • Communicate with potential clients and follow up on referrals • Send documents back and forth	• Site: no • Social media: yes • Primary communication technology: e-mail and phone

Abbreviation: ICTs, information and communication technologies.

7. What other thoughts do you have about technology use for your work?

8. Anything else you want to add?

Follow-up probes were determined based on responses to these very broad questions. Participants were encouraged to construct their own subjective realities and express their own experiences about becoming an entrepreneur and their related choices for using ICTs to achieve their goals. The study aimed to avoid the shortcomings Helene Ahl observed in her 2006 article, "Why Research on Women Entrepreneurs Needs New Directions?" Ahl (2006, 598) pointed out that studies on women entrepreneurs often fail to offer a full picture because assumptions bias the responses:

> Research on women's entrepreneurship holds certain assumptions of business, gender, family, society, the economy, and the individual, all of which influence the research questions asked, the methods chosen, and the answers received. The assumptions also include what is excluded, i.e., factors or circumstances that are not perceived as relevant for entrepreneurship research.

By asking very broad, open-ended questions and allowing for comments unrelated to a stated question, participants could choose what factors to discuss in terms of their values, priorities, and choices.

Online Interviews to Study Online Phenomena

To reach geographically dispersed participants, interviews were conducted in Adobe Connect. The decision to collect data from interviews conducted online went beyond a simple decision to use an ICT that allowed for a synchronous conversation. When the direct interaction between researcher and participant occurs through computer-mediated communications, technology is more than a simple transactional medium (Salmons 2010). Studies of online communication show that the perceptions of presence, immediacy, and warmth—qualities so important to interview communications—are experienced differently than they are in face-to-face communications (Baños et al. 2008; Shin 2002; Suler 2003). In this study, we used both asynchronous e-mail communications and synchronous meetings with participants.

Preinterview e-mail communications allowed for the initial development of trust and rapport with the participant. In the interviews, participants could see me on the webcam. Since most of them revealed a lot about themselves online, through detailed biographies and photographs on their respective business blogs and websites, enabling them to see *me* allowed for some parity, and also helped develop a sense of researcher presence in the interviews. The conversational tone of the synchronous Adobe Connect web conferencing meeting space allowed for the development of rapport and exchange. Main questions were posted on

PowerPoint slides, which gave visual cues and maintained focus on key areas of inquiry. One question included an interactive diagram, which allowed for visual representation of participants' comments. The diagram showed a continuum, with options for a solo business, small business with employees, mid-size company, or corporation. This diagram was used to elicit responses about each participant's views about growth, types of growth, and goals for the future.

Findings: Descriptive Accounts and Situational Maps

The framework approach includes three broad steps: managing the data, making sense of data through descriptive accounts, and seeking implications and applications through explanatory accounts (Spencer, Ritchie, and O'Connor 2003). To create descriptive accounts, the researcher works with a systematic overview of the data to identify key dimensions, to map the range of diversity of each phenomenon and to develop classifications and typologies (Spencer, Ritchie, and O'Connor 2003). The creation of descriptive accounts involves movement from synthesized or original text to descriptive categories and movement into higher levels of abstraction.

Situational and positional maps (Clarke 2005) were used to organize and present descriptive accounts, offering the basis for discussion and conclusions. Classifications were drawn from the data using Clarke's approach for dissecting and depicting the situation with ordered situational and positional maps (Clarke 2005). Clark posits that such maps *situate* the aspects of the research phenomena by not only mapping the data but also by calling out for discovery of otherwise unseen relationships. Human and nonhuman (i.e., technologies) internal and external factors are teased out to offer new views of possible relationships and new understandings of the situation.

Descriptive Accounts

Classifications and Themes

I immersed myself in the data, listening and reviewing each recorded interview several times. I also transcribed the interviews, which allowed me to review the data in written as well as audio forms. Using the questions as broad initial categories, I inductively looked for patterns and themes in the aspects participants explained the ways they used technology, and the ways the availability of technology influenced their business models and decisions.

Thirteen key themes emerged through this analysis of interview data; they are outlined in Table 11.3. Themes 1–4 relate generally to the motivation for starting and managing the business. Themes 5–13 relate to the choices entrepreneurs make about the technologies they use, and how and why they use the ICTs they have chosen.

Table 11.3 Descriptive themes

Themes	Description	Quotes from Participants
1. Pull is stronger than push.	Motivational factors that can be categorized as push and pull were discussed by all participants—not only in the context of venture formation but also persistence in continuing with the business. In this study we found that one participant was laid off, four quit, two started working entrepreneurially right out of college, and two have other jobs.	"I was disgusted working for a large corporation and I just couldn't stomach it any longer…now, I get to do what I want to do and I get to say." "We have different ways of working across our life cycles, we are not compromising to have it all, we are blending in different ways. Technology enables me to move from one stage to the next."
2. Creativity/quality control is more important than business growth.	Creative work life, autonomy, and control over the direction of the business were not only pulls at the start-up stage, but also for determining the way the business would operate on an ongoing basis. Most participants named these factors as the most important to them—even more important than income level or business growth.	"I know several people who do the kind of jewelry that I do, whose name is on the product but they are not really doing it. With this kind of product it needs to be personal and small." "I put every penny into savings so I had the freedom to go where I wanted and needed to go …and I didn't get stuck in a channel that didn't feed me emotionally and intellectually. Often during the course of my work, there have been opportunities to 'build a business,' hire people, and really focus—but my frugalness allowed me to follow my heart. I want to be an explorer, not a dynasty builder, I want to live on the edge."

3. Grow out, not up and down.	When asked about goals and growth, participants largely preferred the idea of partnering/joining efforts with other like-minded entrepreneurs to the idea of growing into a large company. As noted in #2, participants would rather hire support staff than others who would be hands-on, creating the product or service.	"Keep it simple, keep everyone happy!" "I don't want to put my reputation into other people's hands." "I've been in business for a long time, with multiple contracts and offices. [After losses from Katrina] I've had time to reflect and want to 'follow my bliss.' That meant a new business model...that includes social entrepreneurism." "I don't like management. I don't want to have hundreds of employees. I want to have flexible teams that come in and do what needs to be done."
4. Women entrepreneurs make more entrepreneurs.		"By serving other entrepreneurs...[I am] enabling other entrepreneurs to be able to do their own grassroots businesses." "A couple from western China, they scour bazaars for antique Tibetan turquoise. We have a guy in Pakistan who finds ancient Roman stuff for us from the fields of the farmers. We find people and people find us...the Internet [and mobile technology] allows people in remote places to make a living."

(Continued)

Table 11.3 (Continued)

Themes	Description	Quotes from Participants
		"After moving to Turkey…I had an Internet connection, a digital camera and access to the post office, so I started with e-commerce on eBay. As I built my comfort level, I found I could help other people."
		"Mobilizing those tools [cell phone access] and bringing them into the rural areas [in Turkey, where there is no electricity] to help promote [honey] business is a big part of what we are doing [rural business incubation], especially with women."
5. Choice of ICTs is made strategically.	Entrepreneurs choose ICTs based on usability and alignment with business communications need.	"[What technology tools do you use?] is a particularly significant question, not from a technology standpoint, but how we organize our world, how we organize our work and how we organize our identity in the world. When I talk about the technologies I use I think about them across that continuum [of task and relationship]."
		"[We need to know] how many people go to our website every day? Google Analytics [free] helps with that. We do a once a month blast email telling our customers about new jewelry on the website. It's always fun to see the analytics the next day to see the jump."

6. Free or cheap ICTs work.	While the choice of ICTs is important, entrepreneurs made little or no investment in specialized software or platforms.	"We started one year ago with nothing—no money—but we knew how to use technology really well." "Every time we come up against a challenge, we go to the technology to figure it out how can we get in touch with these people? What communication channels do we have?" "We used free demo software to create our video, so it cost $7.00 and it has been very powerful for getting people to sign up for our trips... Through technology we can share with everybody, we can share our stories."
7. Asynchronous or near-synchronous communications work.	While occasional synchronous telephone or Skype conversations are used, the primary forms of communication are asynchronous or near-synchronous.	"Technology is a godsend!" "I can have a chat room open between a group of collaborators that we leave open over a period of time, so it is almost like sitting next to each other. You pick up the voice part when you need it, but it is mostly just leaving notes." "The instantaneousness of email, being able to shoot a 200-page document across the Pacific Ocean in a minute and get through the screening in Hong Kong so the client can get it when they get up the next morning."

(Continued)

Table 11.3 (Continued)

Themes	Description	Quotes from Participants
8. Relationships matter, and they are sustained with regular communication.	Client/customer experience involves relationships beyond a one-time sale or service. Relationships are built or retained by use of e-mail blasts and RSS subscriptions.	You have an 85% rate of return customers … why? "Our [Dorje Designs] customer service, 1 on 1. If someone emails, we respond as soon as possible … in this kind of business, customer service is everything. Your reputation on the Internet is everything." "Technology for women is very powerful. In a lot of ways it's an equal platform … If you have the persistence and commitment and drive you can succeed in building a following." "We build relationships [with potential customers] by asking for input on decisions. In a residential project, we had come up with two different schemes for the outside remodel of a house, one more traditional and one more contemporary. The client liked them both, couldn't decide which one he liked better, so we put together an eblast with images and sent it out to the list. People could respond and give comments, and we shared them with the client."
9. Direct communication leads to positive ROI.	Participants reported that customer relationships and responsiveness, the personal connection, leads to repeat business and referrals. Also, direct customer communication allowed some of the participants to eliminate the middleman.	"With gallery and consignment sales, I made something, it sits in gallery. And with [gallery] markup, it is not affordable. On the website, we sell for more money, but it costs less to the customer."

10. Choice of ICT depends on the nature of the relationship.	Different ICTs are used for private (clients or customers, collaborative partners, or team members) versus public (wider network, field, or discipline) communication.	"My team stretches across six cities and three continents. We connect on a weekly basis for free with Skype." "Entrepreneurs need to pay attention to internal, task focused, get it done stuff and to the outer world to stay fresh. Little things from external network are extremely important to me as are very focused interactions with clients as we get work done together. Distinguishing between these two has been a helpful practice and help as I think about my work a little differently."
11. ICTS can increase efficiency or increase distractions.	Entrepreneurs who spend a lot of time online have to exercise self-control to avoid being distracted from income-generating work.	"I appreciate the ability to keep an eye on what is going on out there." "It is important to find that balance between what I pay attention to in the torrent of info while getting work done. Technology offers opportunities and challenge." "I don't want anyone fishing about what I do and how I do it."
12. Intellectual property and data privacy are considerations.	While issues of intellectual property are a concern to most participants, their actions varied greatly, from complete transparency, including putting earnings online, to changing from copyright to Creative Commons licenses to encourage sharing, to the decision to not to post any resources or materials.	"I am conscious of audience in terms of updates on LinkedIn; I don't mix business and friends and family." "I believe in abundance, and believe in giving out to the world took all the copyright off all my material and put into Creative Commons—it pays off."

(Continued)

Table 11.3 (Continued)

Themes	Description	Quotes from Participants
	In one case, a participant, who is a therapist, was constrained by HIPAA regulations from communicating directly with clients without investing in a secure web environment.	
13. Plans for future technology use include use of media.	When asked what they plan to do differently in the future, almost all of the participants mentioned using more media.	I/we would like to use "informational videos for website and YouTube" "podcasts" "video with group response using Skype" "augmented reality simulations in educational games in virtual worlds"

Abbreviations: HIPAA, Health Insurance Portability and Accountability Act; ICT, information and communication technology; ROI, return on investment.

Future Aspirations

Themes 2 and 3 are intrinsically linked to the participants' aspirations for their businesses. Using an interactive diagram, I was able to elicit participants' thoughts about where they were now and what they hoped to achieve in the future. The continuum used to explore participants' aspirations for growth included four initial options: a solo business, small business with employees, mid-size company, or corporation. While my question was framed to elicit a straightforward progression of growth, the responses were more nuanced and reflected the social capital theory view of strength through networks. At the solo end of the spectrum, I added two new points to the original model, the networked and the family business, as defined in Table 11.4. The participants were evenly dispersed among the five categories.

Information and Communications Technologies

Themes 5–11 relate to ICT choices and usage. The positional map approach, drawn from Clarke's (2005, 128) situational analysis methodology, provides a way to identify positions and array them dimensionally within the "situation of inquiry." A positional map makes it possible to see when participants used selected technologies and for what purpose. One axis shows the progression from private to public. The other axis shows a time-response continuum (Salmons 2012). This axis describes the span of communications from synchronicity, where both parties were fully engaged in real-time interaction to asynchronous communications at any time. In between, synchronous communications involve some degree of real-time conversation in a context where other activities also occur, and near-synchronous communications offer an ongoing, open conversation with near but not immediate response. As the positional map shows, asynchronous communications are by far the most popular choice. Only conversations with current, active customers or clients merited the full attention of synchronicity.

More about the "Situation"

Descriptive themes outlined in Table 11.4 emerged from the data. Another way to understand the "situation" of women e-entrepreneurs is with what Clarke (2005, 86) calls an "ordered situational map." Clarke (2005, 87) suggests that to create such a map, the researcher draws on the data to answer key questions:

- Who and what are in the situation?
- Who and what matters in the situation?
- What elements make a difference in the situation?

Table 11.4 Type of business aspired to by participants

Type of Aspiration	Participants
A. Solo sole proprietor. May contract or hire support for support services like bookkeeping, accounting, or IT.	Two participants "I know we could be bigger and employ people but I don't want that."
B. Networked sole proprietor. Entrepreneur shares marketing or works collaboratively with a network of others—working online. The sole proprietor may bring together a team to accomplish a larger project.	Two participants "It is a business model for open source, model of experimentation not replication." "I want to network with others, without the responsibility of administration."
C. Family business. Woman e-entrepreneur in business with her husband or immediate family.	Two participants "I wanted a solo business, but it is growing into a small [family] business. My husband will be quitting his day job next year. I don't want to manage others."
D. Small business. Woman e-entrepreneur in business with others or with other employees.	Two participants "We [women previously in family business] were tired of being solo entrepreneurs, we wanted to create something larger, employ more people, with the potential to retire from and sell it at some point in the future. We currently have 5 equal partners, no staff, it is an owner-led firm."
E. Mid-size company. Woman e-entrepreneur in business with others or with other employees, with multiple locations, larger contracts, and larger scope.	Two participants

Abbreviation: IT, information technology.

In addition to drawing from the data to look at the situation of inquiry from new angles, the researcher may need to delve into the literature to answer more contextual questions about the economic and sociocultural elements. Once these questions have been answered, the researcher can look for interrelationships between and among the elements.

The situation of women e-entrepreneurs, their choices of ICTs, and implications of those choices are charted in Table 11.5.

Table 11.5 Ordered situational map: women e-entreprenuers

Individual Human Actors	Nonhuman Elements
• Women e-entrepreneurs—women who start and run businesses that make significant use of ICTs • Family members, partners, allies, employees, and vendors	• ICTs

Collective Human Elements	Implicated Actors
• Professional groups or associations • Kickstarter, a crowdsource funding website community in support of entrepreneurs	• Customers/clients who like buying from or working with—and supporting—grassroots entrepreneurs • Broader network of supporters/potential customers who read e-mails or visit websites, and share information or give feedback.

Discursive Constructions of Individual Human Actors	Discursive Constructions of Nonhuman Actors
• Pull is stronger than push—the top pull into entrepreneurial activity is the desire for creative, flexible, and meaningful work. • Relationships matter, and they are sustained by regular communication. • It is important to be a part of a larger network—in the discipline or field, with supporters and followers.	• ICTs allow for synchronous or asynchronous, visual- or text-based styles of communication. • Choice of ICT depends on the nature of the relationship and whether the communication is public (with the broader network) or private (with existing customers or clients).

Economic Elements	Sociocultural Elements
• Pull is stronger than push—participants chose entrepreneurism; most were not pushed out of jobs. • Free or low-cost ICTs work; economic investment in expensive technologies not needed to succeed. • Creativity/quality control is more important than business growth.	• Women entrepreneurs make more entrepreneurs. • While extant literature on women entrepreneurs notes family responsibilites as a principle motivator for women entrepreneurs, the pull of flexibility may or may not relate to work–family balance.

Temporal Elements	Spatial Elements
• Asynchronous or near-synchronous communications are the most frequent choices. • Synchronous communications are used primarily with existing customers.	• E-entrepreneurs are not limited by geographical location. • Being geographically "untethered" is a priority.

Abbreviation: ICT, information and communication technology.

Discussion and Conclusions

Of the 13 interrelated themes, 3 stand out. Taken together, these themes suggest a powerful pull women feel not only to start a business but also to lead an entrepreneurial lifestyle. The participants helped to define a contemporary version of the entrepreneurial life/work style, which involves varied, vibrant relationships and rich communication. Technology enables these important relationships to thrive—but it is not an end unto itself.

"Pull" Motivation to Start and Continue an Entrepreneurial Venture

Without a doubt, the top motivator for participants was the pull toward creative, flexible, and meaningful work experiences for freedom to do the work they imagined and chose. This pull did not stop after the initial start-up; the participants who had been working in their businesses for a number of years spoke about reinvention, redirection, and renewal in the same terms. Susan Eddington observed:

> I've been in [advertising] business for a long time, with multiple contracts and offices. [After losses from Katrina] I've had time to reflect and want to "follow my bliss" with trans-media storytelling [about the environment and about intimate partner violence]. That means a new business model . . . that includes social entrepreneurism.

Nancy White similarly pointed out:

> but my frugalness allowed me to follow my heart [because I didn't have to take just any contract]. I want to be an explorer, not a dynasty builder, I want to live on the edge.

As noted in themes 2 and 3, while all strive for economic return on their work investments, the desire for flexibility and creativity was stronger than the desire for high-growth or higher income. One participant noted in response to a question about measuring achievements: "I am eating and I am paying my student loans, so I guess that is success!"

The wider discourse, what Clarke (2005) would call *sociocultural elements*, generally speaks of the appeal of independent work for women in the context of family responsibilities. Orhan and Scott (2001, 232) observed, "A pull/push model reflects most entrepreneurial motivations, and one female-specific feature is the push factor of a flexible schedule, reflective of the family caring role that is still expected from women. Because of their mothering role, women experience truncated or stopped careers more often than men." In this small study, participants of different ages spoke of different needs throughout the life cycle and work–life balance, but none of the participants discussed motherhood as a primary motivation to move into entrepreneurship. Indeed, the nature of the businesses discussed in this study may or may not allow for more attention to family than would a traditional job for an employer! Since two participants' businesses grew to the point where husbands were "hired," offering other areas for future exploration in terms of broader discourses about gender stereotypes, family relationships, and women's entrepreneurship.

Social Capital: Relationships Matter

Participants discussed what could be described as multiple tiers of relationships. At the center are the immediate relationships with active or returning customers, allies and partners, vendors, or distributors. In the next tier are potential or recent customers. Important for informal learning and exchange is a wider network of people and organizations in the field, interested supporters or those with shared interests, or communities of practice. Finally, in the outer tier, the broader public offers untapped opportunities for new relationships. As the positional map shows, participants used different technologies and modes of communication with each tier.

While participants were independent thinkers, they valued learning from and collaborating with their respective circles and networks. This point echoes the findings of Thomas and Moisey's study of women entrepreneurs that showed perceived value of the Internet for informal learning as access to informational capital and connectivity to social capital (Thomas and Moisey 2006).

Participants' relationships extended to other entrepreneurs. Several participants intentionally developed other women entrepreneurs as part of their business. In other cases, almost by happenstance, the nature of the business and the kinds of vendors and suppliers allowed participants to develop relationships that were mutually beneficial with grassroots and start-up entrepreneurs. This finding supports Abarbanel's 2008 research, which also found an emphasis on service among women entrepreneurs. Abarbanel (2008, 33) observed that women entrepreneurs "harnass the power of giving back to stoke the engines of entrepreneurial growth."

Technology: Tool and Enabler

After reviewing the data collected from real-world and digital entrepreneurs, the primary distinction was, not surprisingly, the range of ICTs used. The digital entrepreneurs used a wider variety of social media tools than did the real-world entrepreneurs. The nature of the specific ICTs used did not, however, reflect more or less reliance on technology—all participants reported communicating extensively with current customers, wider networks, and the public. Common themes emerged about the use of free, trial, or inexpensive ICTs. None of the participants had invested in a paid or premium service such as a meeting platform. Even those who made use of social media or media such as videos or podcasts still relied primarily on the basics, using e-mail for most communications.

ICTs, whether chosen by trial and error or selected strategically, were the essential factors in the businesses described. While the real-world entrepreneurs could otherwise deliver products and services, they might not have the all-important pool of clients and customers necessary to keep the business afloat.

Real-World and Digital Entrepreneurs: Are They Different?

The study began with an assumption that a distinction could be made between real-world and digital entrepreneurs. A maximum variation sample was selected in order to gain an understanding of a wide range of possible motivations for starting online businesses and choices women e-entrepreneurs make to manage and build their ventures. However, these entrepreneurs had more in common than they had as differences. While participants shared very different kinds of business experiences in the interviews, the responses around the identified themes were fairly consistent. There were no real outliers, or divergent viewpoints. One can imagine that, were they all in the same room, their heads would be nodding as they listened to each other talk about their motivations, experiences, and aspirations.

Limitations of the Study

All participants, even those operating internationally, were from the United States. Literature suggests that the trends in women's e-entrepreneurship are different in other developed and developing countries. For one thing, in places where Internet access is limited and connections may be made over smartphones, rather than desktop or laptop computers, and where delivery may be difficult or unreliable, sales of physical goods online may be more difficult. The research was not designed to study the financial or economic dimensions of the participants' businesses. These topics were beyond the scope of this study.

Given the small sample size, it was not possible to generalize the findings to a larger population of e-entreprenerial women. For example, other women may be more concerned about work that allows them to work from home and care for children, or may be interested in building a large-scale, high-growth potential businesses than did the participants in this study.

Future Research

The central research question for this study was, "What is the influence of ICTs options on women entrepreneurs' choices for their businesses and their goals for the future?" Thirteen themes emerged from the data, in addition to descriptions of positions taken vis–à–vis specific technology tasks and ICT. These findings offer a springboard for future study. Using theoretical sampling, I planned to interview participants whose experiences aligned with the themes and positions to gain a more in-depth understanding of the women entrepreneurs' choices and options. Numerous outstanding questions remain about the motivations, leadership styles, and management approaches used in successful real-world or digital online businesses.

References

Abarbanel, Karin. 2008. "Women Entrepreneurs: Reshaping the Workplace." *Interbeing* 2 (2): 31–34.

Adler, P. S., and S. W. Kwon. 2002. "Social Capital: Prospects for a New Concept." *Academy of Management Review* 27: 17–40.

Ahl, Helene. 2006. "Why Research on Women Entrepreneurs Needs New Directions." *Entrepreneurship Theory and Practice* 30 (5): 595–621.

Alfred, Mary V. 2009. "Social Capital Theory: Implications for Women's Networking and Learning." *New Directions for Adult and Continuing Education* (122): 3–12. doi:10.1002/ace.329.

Ali, Abdul, Candida Brush, Julio De Castro, Julian Lange, Thomas Lyons, Moriah Meyskens, Joseph Onochie, Ivory Phinisee, Edward Rogoff, Al Suhu, and John Whitman. 2011. "Global Entrepreneurship Monitor National Entrepreneurial Assessment for the United States of America: 2011 United States Report." Babson College and Baruch College. Available at: http://blsciblogs.baruch.cuny.edu/field-center/files/2012/03/GEM2010Report.pdf.

Andrews, Martha C., Thomas Baker, and Tammy G. Hunt. 2011. "Values and Person–Organization Fit." *Leadership & Organization Development Journal* 32 (1): 5–19. doi:10.1037/0033–2909.103.3.411.

Baños, Rosa M., Cristina Botella, Isabel Rubió, Soledad Quero, Azucena García-Palacios, and Mariano Alcañiz. 2008. "Presence and Emotions in Virtual Environments: The Influence of Stereoscopy." *CyberPsychology & Behavior* 11 (1): 1–8.

Bird, B., and Candida Brush. 2002. "A Gendered Perspective on Organizational Creation." *Entrepreneurship: Theory and Practice* 26 (3): 41–65.

Bosse, Douglas A., and Porcher L. Taylor, III. 2012. "The Second Glass Ceiling Impedes Women Entrepreneurs." *Journal of Applied Management and Entrepreneurship* 17 (1): 52–68.

Bruner, Jerome, and Greg Kearsley. 2004. *Constructivist Theory.* Explorations in Learning & Instruction: The Theory into Practice Database 2004. Available at: http://tip.psychology.org/bruner.html.

Carolis, Donna Marie De, and Patrick Saparito. 2006. "Social Capital, Cognition, and Entrepreneurial Opportunities: A Theoretical Framework." *Entrepreneurship: Theory and Practice* 30 (1): 41–56. doi:10.1111/j.1540–6520.2006.00109.x.

Charmaz, Kathy. 2003. "Qualitative Interviewing and Grounded Theory Analysis." In *Inside Interviewing: New Lenses, New Concerns,* edited by James A. Holstein and Jaber F. Gubrium. Thousand Oaks: Sage Publications.

Charmaz, Kathy. 2006. *Constructed Grounded Theory: A Practical Guide through Qualitative Analysis.* Thousand Oaks: Sage Publications.

Clarke, Adele. 2005. *Situational Analysis: Grounded Theory after the Postmodern Turn.* Thousand Oaks: Sage Publications.

Crotty, M. 2001. *The Foundations of Social Research: The Meaning and Perspective in the Research Process.* London: Sage Publications.

Dautzenberg, Kirsti. 2012. "Gender Differences of Business Owners in Technology-Based Firms." *International Journal of Gender and Entrepreneurship* 4 (1): 65–78. doi:10.1080/13691060600572557.

Denzin, Norman K., and Yvonna S. Lincoln, eds. 2003. *Collecting and Interpreting Qualitative Materials.* 2nd ed. Thousand Oaks: Sage Publications.

Dheeriya, Prakash. 2009. "A Conceptual Framework for Describing Online Entrepreneurship." *Journal of Small Business and Entrepreneurship* 22 (3): 275–83.

Eddleston, Kimberly A., and Gary N. Powell. 2012. "Nurturing Entrepreneurs' Work–Family Balance: A Gendered Perspective." *Entrepreneurship: Theory and Practice* 36 (3): 513–41. doi:10.1111/j.1540–6520.2012.00506.x.

Edwards, Julian A., and Jon Billsberry. 2010. "Testing a Multidimensional Theory of Person–Environment Fit." *Journal of Managerial Issues* 22 (4): 476–93.

Fairlie, Robert. 2011. "Kauffman Index of Entrepreneurial Activity 1996–2010."[1]

Faulkner, Wendy. 2001. "The Technology Question in Feminism: A View from Feminist Technology Studies." *Women's Studies International Forum* 24 (1): 79–95. doi:http://dx.doi.org/10.1016/S0277-5395(00)00166-7.

Gray, David. 2009. *Doing Research in the Real World.* 2nd ed. London: Sage Publications.

Hayton, James C., and Magdalena Cholakova. 2012. "The Role of Affect in the Creation and Intentional Pursuit of Entrepreneurial Ideas." *Entrepreneurship: Theory and Practice* 36 (1): 41–68. doi:10.1111/j.1540–6520.2011.00458.x.

Kariv, Dafna. 2011. "Entrepreneurial Orientations of Women Business Founders from a Push/Pull Perspective: Canadians versus Non-Canadians—A Multinational Assessment." *Journal of Small Business and Entrepreneurship* 24 (3): 397–425.

Kelan, Elisabeth K. 2008. "The Discursive Construction of Gender in Contemporary Management Literature." *Journal of Business Ethics* 81 (2): 427–45. doi:10.1007/s10551-007-9505-2.

Kelly, L. et al. 2010. "Global Entrepreneurship Monitor National Entrepreneurial Assessment for the United States of America: 2010 United States Report." Babson College and Baruch College. Available at: http://www.babson.edu/Academics/centers/blank-center/global-research/gem/Documents/GEM%20US%202011%20Report%202.pdf.

Kephart, Pamela, and Lillian Schumacher. 2005. "Has the 'Glass Ceiling' cracked? An Exploration of Women Entrepreneurship." *Journal of Leadership & Organizational Studies* 12 (1): 2–15.

Kulich, Clara, Grzegorz Trojanowski, Michelle K. Ryan, S. Alexander Haslam, and Luc D. R. Renneboog. 2011. "Who Gets the Carrot and Who Gets the Stick? Evidence of Gender Disparities in Executive Remuneration." *Strategic Management Journal* 32 (3): 301–21. doi:10.1002/smj.878.

Levitt, Alexandra. 2012. "The Rise of the Independent Workforce." *New York Times* (April 15): 8.

Lewis, Dana, Eun Kim, Julia Kurnik, and Emily Petty. 2011. "2011 Annual Report." National Women's Business Council. Available at: http://www.nwbc.gov/sites/default/files/508%20Compliant%20Revised%20NWBC%202011%20Annual%20report.pdf.

Lincoln, Yvonna S., and Egon G. Guba. 1985. *Naturalistic Inquiry.* Thousand Oaks: Sage Publications.

Marco van, Gelderen, Janet Sayers, and Caroline Keen. 2008. "Home-Based Internet Businesses as Drivers of Variety." *Journal of Small Business and Enterprise Development* 15 (1): 162–77. doi:10.1108/14626000810850900.

Mattis, Mary. 2004. "Women Entrepreneurs: Out from Under the Glass Ceiling." *Gender in Management* 19 (3): 154–63.

Miles, Matthew, and A. Michael Huberman. 1994. *Qualitative Data Analysis: An Expanded Sourcebook.* 2nd ed. Thousand Oaks: Sage.

Morley, Michael J. 2007. "Person–Organization Fit." *Journal of Managerial Psychology* 22 (2): 109–17. doi:10.1108/02683940710726375.

Nagle, Barry, Kavita Mittapalli, and Kelly Hannum. 2012. "Women-Owned Firms in the U.S." National Women's Business Council. Available at: http://www.nwbc.gov/sites/default/files/NWBC%20Final%20Narrative%20Report.pdf.

Nahapiet, Janine, and Sumantra Ghoshal. 1998. "Social Capital, Intellectual Capital, and the Organizational Advantage." *Academy of Management Review* 23 (2): 242–66.

National Women's Business Council's 2011 Annual Report 2011. Annual Report. Available at: http://www.nwbc.gov/research/nwbcs-2011-annual-report.

Nel, P., A. Maritz, and O. Thongprovati. 2010. "Motherhood and Entrepreneurship: The Mumpreneur Phenomenon." *International Journal of Organizational Innovation* 3 (1): 6–34.

Nixdorff, Janet, and Theodore Rosen. 2010. "The Glass Ceiling Women Face: An Examination and Proposals for Development of Future Women Entrepreneurs." *New England Journal of Entrepreneurship* 13 (2): 71–87.

Orhan, Muriel, and Don Scott. 2001. "Why Women Enter into Entrepreneurship: An Explanatory Model." *Gender in Management* 16 (5): 232–43.

Ottósson, Hannes, and K. I. M. Klyver. 2010. "The Effect of Human Capital on Social Capital among Entrepreneurs." *Journal of Enterprising Culture* 18 (4): 399–417.

Patterson, Nicola, and Sharon Mavin. 2009. "Women Entrepreneurs: Jumping the Corporateship and Gaining New Wings." *International Small Business Journal* 27 (2): 173–92. doi:10.1177/0266242608100489.

Robb, Alicia M., and Susan Coleman. 2010. "Financing Strategies of New Technology-Based Firms: A Comparison of Women- and Men-Owned Firms." *Journal of Technology Management & Innovation* 5 (1): 30–50.

Salmons, Janet E. 2010. *Online Interviews in Real Time.* Thousand Oaks: Sage Publications.

Salmons, Janet E., ed. 2012. *Cases in Online Interview Research.* Thousand Oaks: Sage Publications.

Schjoedt, Leon, and Kelly G. Shaver. 2007. "Deciding on an Entrepreneurial Career: A Test of the Pull and Push Hypotheses Using the Panel Study of Entrepreneurial Dynamics." *Entrepreneurship: Theory and Practice* 31 (5): 733–52. doi:10.111 1/j.1540–6520.2007.00197.

Shin, Namin. 2002. "Beyond Interaction: The Relational Construct of 'Transactional Presence.'" *Open Learning* 17 (2): 121–37.

Shinnar, Rachel S., Olivier Giacomin, and Frank Janssen. 2012. "Entrepreneurial Perceptions and Intentions: The Role of Gender and Culture." *Entrepreneurship: Theory and Practice* 36 (3): 465–93. doi:10.1111/j.1540–6520.2012.00506.x.

Sorenson, Ritch L., Cathleen A. Folker, and Keith H. Brigham. 2008. "The Collaborative Network Orientation: Achieving Business Success through Collaborative Relationships." *Entrepreneurship: Theory and Practice* 32 (4): 615–34. doi:10.1111/j.1540–6520.2008.00245.x.

Spencer, Liz, Jane Ritchie, and William O'Connor. 2003. "Analysis: Practices, Principles and Processes." In *Qualitative Research Practice: A Guide for Social Science Students and Researchers,* edited by Jane Ritchie and Jane Lewis. London: Sage Publications.

Stevenson, Lois. 1990. "Some Methodological Problems Associated with Researching Women Entrepreneurs." *Journal of Business Ethics* 9 (4/5): 439–46.

Suler, John. 2003. "Presence in Cyberspace." *Psychology of Cyberspace* [e-book]. Available at: http://www-usr.rider.edu/˜suler/psycyber/psycyber.html.

Sullivan, Diane M., and William R. Meek. 2012. "Gender and Entrepreneurship: A Review and Process Model." *Journal of Managerial Psychology* 27 (5): 428–58. doi:10.2307/259271.

Sullivan, Sherry, Monica Forret, Lisa Mainiero, and Siria Terjesen. 2007. "What Motivates Entrepreneurs? An Exploratory Study of the Kaleidoscope Career Model and Entrepreneurship." *Journal of Applied Management and Entrepreneurship* 12 (4): 4–19.

Thomas, Patricia, and Susan Moisey. 2006. "Women Entrepreneurs' Perceptions of the Value of the Internet in Informal Learning." *Journal of Small Business and Entrepreneurship* 19 (2): 183–202.

Wheeler, Anthony R., Gallagher Vickie Coleman, Robyn L. Brouer, and Chris J. Sablynski. 2007. "When Person–Organization (Mis)fit and (Dis)satisfaction Lead to Turnover." *Journal of Managerial Psychology* 22 (2): 203–19. doi:10.1108/02683940710726447.

Xiong, Guiyang, and Sundar Bharadwaj. 2011. "Social Capital of Young Technology Firms and Iheir IPO Values: The Complementary Role of Relevant Absorptive Capacity." *Journal of Marketing* 75 (6): 87–104. doi:10.1509/jmkg.75.6.87.

Chapter 12

You Are What You Brand: Women Share Their Branding Stories

Leah R. Singer

For 25 years, television talk show host Oprah Winfrey would step out on her studio stage, look the audience in the eye (in studio and on camera), and talk about a variety of subjects that ranged from self-improvement to doing good to controlling one's own destiny. No matter what the topic of the day was, the viewer always knew what to expect from Oprah. Whatever the show's subject was, Oprah's motto of "Live your best life" could be found within the subtext.

Every brand begins with a story and ends with a promise (Haig 2011). Whether you are an entrepreneur or a big-company marketer, it is important to remember to tell the story and honor that promise (Vinjamuri 2008). The "Live your best life" and self-improvement concepts are the essence of Oprah's brand. That brand is so strong that it carries across all of Oprah's platforms— from television to her magazine, network, and even the books and movies she endorses. A brand is a story and core purpose, which essentially becomes a promise to the customer. Oprah is a master of personal branding.

Yet one of the basic rules in branding is not to be the face of your company. How have icons like Oprah Winfrey, Martha Stewart, and Rachael Ray successfully branded their businesses as themselves?

In order to understand the concept of individual branding, it is important to look at how one-woman branding began in the 1950s and how it has changed—and not so much—since then. From there, the concept of the brand as an extension of the individual will be examined in order to understand brands based on personalities have the added challenge of maintaining an image that needs to be virtually flawless.

Then, the unintentional brand individual will be discussed. Specifically, how so many individuals (including Oprah) did not see themselves as a brand, nor did they embrace the concept. The importance of authenticity and branding will be examined along with ways to manage branding through processes such as franchise management. Finally, this chapter will look at the key ways to maintain successful branding and why female entrepreneurs like Oprah, Martha Stewart, and Rachael Ray have successfully become their brand.

The First One-Woman Brand

Before there were Oprah Winfrey and Martha Stewart, there was a female entrepreneur who built a business using little more than a business concept, a few dollars, and her name. That woman was Lillian Vernon.

In 1951, Vernon launched a company from her yellow Formica kitchen table in the Mount Vernon suburb of New York City. As a young bride, Vernon's goal was to supplement her husband's income by selling handbags and belts for teenage girls. After placing an advertisement in *Seventeen* magazine, Vernon received 50 orders. Those orders eventually led to the birth of Lillian Vernon Corporation, which later became a specialty catalog retailer with annual revenues of $240 million (Coughlin and Thomas 2002).

Vernon did not set out to build a business brand based on her personality. Yet that is exactly what she ended up doing. The struggles the company faced were the same that many women at the time faced as well: the inability to secure credit loans from banks and mocking and ridicule from male business associates (Coughlin and Thomas 2002). In addition, Vernon started the company more out of necessity than out of a desire. At the time, there were very few jobs for females who needed to earn income. The company and Vernon herself epitomized the struggle of women—and women in the workforce—in the 1950s. She eventually paved the way for future female entrepreneurs and began to illustrate the lesson that while the woman herself may not be the company, she is definitely an extension of the business brand.

The Brand as an Extension of You

One of the challenges with having a business based on an actual person is a simple truism: humans are flawed. If the brand is going to succeed among consumers, it must be seen as credible and trustworthy. As such, brands based on personalities have the added challenge of maintaining an image that needs to be virtually flawless. This is why personality brands are not encouraged, because one false move makes it very difficult to recover.

The brand name must be protected at all costs, which is why these individuals are often upset when photos are used without permission or quotes taken out of context. Oprah's brand, for example, is considered to be the Midas touch for books, people, and products she endorses. She carefully guards her media properties to protect her personal brand. This is one reason only Oprah herself appears on the cover of O Magazine. Her brand communicates exactly what she intends it to communicate (Ross 2010).

Some criticize Oprah for her fierce protection of her name and image. But we have all seen what can happen when a personal brand is tarnished. Tiger Woods and John Edwards are two examples of how a personal brand can go terribly wrong. Once a brand goes bad, it is difficult to recover from the damage (Ross 2010).

One way to remedy this paradox is to make the brand less about the person himself or herself and more about the *personality traits* of the said person. Those traits become the brand attributes of the individual.

Leslie May is the owner of Pawsible Marketing, a consulting and marketing business she founded in 2002. In 22 years of work, May learned to build a strong brand by engaging honestly with current and prospective customers. She is also well known for her deep love of animals and her growing family of dogs and cats. This love of pets inspired May to take her marketing firm into a branded niche service exclusively to help owners of pet-related businesses (Dishman 2010).

May's is an example of a company that is branded based on the attributes or personality traits of the person behind the company. But the company itself is not named after May. This key distinction will help May should she ever decide to sell her business. Once the company is sold, she has relinquished Pawsible Marketing, but she has retained the more valuable right to her own name.

The Unintentional Brand

Oprah Winfrey admits she had a difficult time admitting she was a brand. "I had no intention of being a brand. My intention was to do the work and represent the truth in the work every day. But I guess that's what a brand is.....Being true to yourself is what creates a brand, and as long as you are true to yourself you don't have to worry what the brand is or how the brand is doing or how the brand is fairing in the world" (Bercovici 2010).

Gina Alagata is the founder and CEO of San Diego–based Women Inkorporated (WINK), a women-only networking company launched in April 2010, which offers meeting venues for women in business to connect, grow, and learn. Alagata is the face and brand of WINK. But like Winfrey, that was not her goal when she started the organization. She notes that in the beginning, she did not think her personality had much to do with WINK. But as time went on, she had realized that it was intertwined with the company.

People told me that WINK was warm and friendly. I wanted it to be the most friendly and welcoming organization in town. Those are core messages of my brand and who I am. I am personally friendly, warm and encouraging. (Alagata 2012)

Alagata admits wanting separation between herself and the company brand when she began her business. But as time went on and as she has helped fellow female entrepreneurs and business owners, she realizes that it is not just the business that has done this, it is Alagata herself. Now she says that it is less about her company and more about her role.

Like many female entrepreneurs, Alagata has found that she has had no trouble being the brand associated with WINK so long as she has stayed authentic and true to her personal and professional mission. It is maintaining that authenticity that keeps so many personality-driven brands successful.

The Importance of Authenticity

The concept of authenticity is one that is stressed heavily in brand management. That is, being authentic, honest, and true to the core value of the brand. This idea has not always been a guiding principle in brand management. In the past, companies preferred to have more of a "faceless" quality. But in today's economy, being faceless does not work. Personality is the key element behind what a brand stands for and the story that products tell customers (Bhargava 2008).

The biggest challenge most organizations face today is discovering how to go from a brand that people consume to one that they are passionate about. Every element of business—from the interactions with customers to the packaging of product to the company spokesperson (who may be the brand himself or herself)—is an element of the brand personality (Bhargava 2008). Every one of these interactions must be created in an authentic way in order to maintain trust and consistency among consumers.

This concept of authenticity relates especially to the individual as the brand. In today's culture, this includes Facebook posts, e-mail messages, tweets, and tabloid photos. Martha Stewart came close to losing her brand image and reputation in 2001 when she was accused of insider trading and later was sent to jail. The woman who built her brand around impeccable style, home décor, and decorating was now facing a new reputation as a criminal who may not be trusted by common people. This shift in image was due to a newly discovered sense of inauthenticity among her fans.

Rebecca Tall Brown is the owner of Tri-Line Marketing, a boutique marketing agency based in San Diego, California. As a marketing professional—and the daughter of a small-business owner (who happens to be the brand of his company)—Brown echoes the importance of authenticity as it relates to branding.

Brown says, "Every interaction people have with you is a chance for you to brand. Your image will become stronger the more it's consistent. Every interaction can reinforce the image, either in a positive or negative way." She also notes that a brand is transparent, meaning it cannot hide anything. If insecurities exist within the company or the personality, they will show through in branding.

Brown believes her personal brand is a direct reflection of her values: integrity, travelling light, and ease. While these can sometimes be a challenge to convey, those elements differentiate her from other marketing firms. She is transparent and does not pretend to be something she is not. Brown travels light and has a light sense of humor. (In fact, she rode her bike from her home to give her interview for this chapter.) Her brand is a direct reflection of who she is as a person.

Whether you are Martha Stewart or Rebecca Tall Brown, being authentic is a key element of successful branding. As long as a person is honest and true to himself or herself and values, the brand will remain intact. Another way to keep a brand intact is by the actual management of the brand itself, mainly through a franchise option. The next section will examine franchising as a brand management strategy.

Franchising and Brand Management

One strategy women entrepreneurs have used to keep their brand consistent throughout business is the process of franchising. One of the advantages of franchising is that the franchisor is able to dictate the brand identity and apply the branding guidelines consistently to all of the branches. This includes the look and feel of the outlets, posters, banners, flyers, and all marketing and branding campaigns (Black 2011).

All of these items help the individual maintain a consistent brand image. Consistency is the cornerstone of franchising and brand development. As such, franchisors often create and refine the franchise brand before bringing franchisees on board (Black 2011).

Felena Hanson is the founder of Hera Hub, a spa-inspired, collaborative workspace for female entrepreneurs based in San Diego, California. While Hera Hub includes more than 200 members, it is Hanson who is the face of the business and she takes her role as the brand ambassador seriously. When

Hanson decided to expand Hera Hub beyond one location, she opted for the franchise route. One of the driving decisions behind the decision to franchise was control of the brand.

Hanson said, "My biggest goal and challenge is to find myself and replicate myself in other cities. I'm gregarious, a people pleaser, connector, drop everything and listen . . . I'm excited, and want to serve. My hope is to find franchisees in other cities like that" (Hanson 2012). Hanson continues to explain that franchising will help keep her brand intact and differentiate Hera Hub from other women's networking organizations.

Hanson also feels the items that differentiate Hera Hub from other coworking spaces are the things she wants to keep intact and mandate within future franchises. She explains how she has a list of approximately 10 items that must be attended to at Hera Hub on a daily basis. For example, the thermostat must be set at a specific temperature and candles must be lit in the lobby area. Those are also the things she believes make Hera Hub unique. Hanson explains that with franchising, she can mandate color palates, music choices, and candles. Those are the items that help build Hanson and Hera Hub's brand. Hanson notes that this is a big advantage of franchising with respect to branding.

While franchising is certainly one way to manage a brand, it can be successful only if the right elements exist at the brand's core. The next section will examine the key to what makes a brand successful and if you do not have those elements, the brand will likely not stand out among its competitors.

The Key to Successful Branding

A successful brand should differentiate a product from all the others. Successful branding programs are based on the concept of singularity. The objective is to create in the mind of the customer the perception that there is no other product on the market quite like one's product (Ries and Ries 2002). This concept is especially true for individuals who are seen as the brand, or containing the brand attributes.

Liz Goodgold is a branding expert with more than 20 years of experience in marketing and branding. She has worked for such major clients as the World Trade Centers, Sharp HealthCare, Quaker Oats, Pfizer, and Univision. Goodgold tells companies and individuals that they can stand for only one thing, and every person must remember and achieve the concept of "flawless recall." Goodgold continues, "People need to remember you in order to do business with you. To have exceptional flawless recall, you need to keep it simple and stand for one thing." She advises all her entrepreneurial clients to get flawless recall, and focus on the one thing they do.

With Rachael Ray, the one thing that set her apart from the crowd was the 30-minute meal. For Martha Stewart, it was impeccable lifestyle taste. The Oprah brand tends to focus on living your best life. These three women focus on one concept that people can recall easily, and that is the key to successful branding.

It has been more than 50 years since Lillian Vernon started a successful mail-order catalog business and soon became the face of female entrepreneurs of the 1950s. Yet the lessons of personal branding have not much changed from then to now when Oprah Winfrey graces the cover of O *Magazine*. Both Vernon and Winfrey—and Stewart and Ray—realized having learned that being a personal brand requires authenticity, control, a clear vision and direction, and a strong sense of self. While none of these women set out to become the brands they are today, they are all clear about what they stand for and how they differ from others.

References

Alagata, Gina. 2012. Interview by Leah R. Singer. Personal Interview November 27, 2012.

Bercovici, J. 2010. "Oprah Winfrey: It Was Hard to Accept Being a Brand." *Daily Finance*. Available at: http://www.dailyfinance.com/2010/10/05/oprah-winfrey-being-a-brand/. Accessed December 11, 2012.

Bhargava, R. 2008. *Personality Not Included: Why Companies Lose Their Authenticity and How Great Brands Get It Back*. New York: McGraw Hill.

Black, L. 2011. "Franchise Branding." *Your Business*. Available at: http://bizmag.co.za/franchise-branding/. Accessed December 12, 2012.

Coughlin, J. H., and A. R. Thomas. 2002. *The Rise of Women Entrepreneurs: People, Processes, and Global Trends*. Westport, CT: Quorum Books.

Dishman, L. 2010. "10 Ways to Build Your Personal Brand." *Business Insider*. Available at: http://www.businessinsider.com/10-ways-to-build-your-personal-brand-2010-4?op=1. Accessed December 11, 2012.

Haig, M. 2011. *Brand Failures: The Truth about the 100 Biggest Branding Mistakes of All Time*. Philadelphia: KoganPage.

Hanson, Felena. 2012. Interview by Leah R. Singer. Personal Interview December 7, 2012.

Ries, A., and L. Ries. 2002. *The 22 Immutable Laws of Branding*. New York: Harper-Collins Publishers, Inc.

Ross, M. 2010. *Branding Basics for Small Business*. Bedford, IN: NorLights Press.

Vinjamuri, D. 2008. *Accidental Branding: How Ordinary People Build Extraordinary Brands*. Hoboken, NJ: John Wiley & Sons, Inc.

About the Editor and Contributors

Editor

Louise Kelly is a professor of strategy at the School of Management at Alliant International University in San Diego, California. She has a PhD in strategic management from Concordia University, Montreal. She specializes in international strategic leadership research—looking at top management team leadership from a social network perspective. She has published widely in the area of top management team leadership in such journals as *Entrepreneurship: Theory and Practice, Journal of Developmental Entrepreneurship, International Journal of Management Decision Making, Academy of Administrative Sciences,* and *Journal of World Business.* She is the coauthor of *An Existential Systems Approach to Managing Organizations* (Quorum Press, 1998). Dr. Kelly has consulted for firms in Canada, the United States, Mexico, Kenya, and Vietnam. She is a cofounder of GlobalMind Center for Strategic Consulting, and has been designated as an outstanding scholar by the U.S. federal government based on her international scholarship and publications. She also cowrote *A Dictionary of Strategy: Strategic Management A-Z* (Sage, 2004), and her latest book is *The Psychologist Manager: Success Models for Psychologists in Executive Positions* (Hogrefe, 2012). In 2013, she was voted as the outstanding professor at the Alliant School of Management and was invited to the National Executive Board of the Academy of Management's Sigma Iota Epsilon, which is dedicated to excellence and ethics in business as a professional practice.

Contributors

Clare Brindley is professor of marketing and entrepreneurship at Nottingham Trent University. She is an elected fellow of the Royal Society of Arts and has served as a trustee/director of the Institute of Small Business and Entrepreneurship and Nottingham Women's Centre. Her research is multidisciplinary and has two central themes—the small business sector and supply chain risk. Her work has been funded by the Economic and Social Research Council, the British Academy, the Department of Trade and Industry, the Academy of Marketing, and the European Social Fund. She has published widely in journals such as the *International Journal of Operations & Production Management, International Journal of Agile Supply Management, European Journal of Innovation Management, International Journal of Entrepreneurial Behaviour & Research, Journal of Small Business Management*, and the *International Journal of Retail & Distribution Management*. Clare's papers have been chosen by Emerald for its reading lists of top 50 publications in both the logistics and supply chain and the intellectual underpinnings of entrepreneurial small business categories. She is also an editorial board member of several leading publications. Her work has been presented at international conferences including the British Academy of Management and the Academy of Marketing.

Candida G. Brush is a professor of entrepreneurship, chair of the Entrepreneurship Division, holds the Franklin W. Olin chair in entrepreneurship, and serves as the research director of the Arthur M. Blank Center at Babson College. She holds an honorary doctorate from Jönköping University, Jönköping, Sweden, and she has visiting adjunct appointment to Nordlands University, Bodo Graduate School of Business. Professor Brush is a founding member of the Diana Project International and winner of the 2007 Global Award for Entrepreneurship Research. Her research investigates women's growth businesses, angel investing, and strategies of emerging ventures. She has authored 9 books, 120 journal articles, and other publications. She serves as an editor for the journal *Entrepreneurship: Theory and Practice*, and is an angel investor and board member for several companies and organizations.

Professor Eileen Drew (BA, MSc, Dip. MIS, PhD) has taught in the School of Computer Science and Statistics and Centre for Gender and Women's Studies at Trinity College, Dublin. She has undertaken extensive research in the statistical analysis of national and European Union (EU) data sets, including an international Comparative Leadership Survey of women and men in 27 industrialized countries. Her current fields of interest are gender in entrepreneurship and leadership, gender gaps in science, technology, engineering, and mathematics, work–life balance, the gender pay gap, family leaves, and protection of part-time workers. Professor Drew is the national senior expert for European Fundamental Rights Agency and European Gender Equality Institute, and has worked as the gender mainstreaming expert for the Social Security Reform Co-operation Project in China, supported by the European Commission. She was appointed as a gender equality expert to the EU Network of Women in Decision-Making in Politics and the Economy. She is currently a principal investigator for an EU-supported Framework Programme 7 project called Institutional Transformation for Effecting Gender Equality in Research (INTEGER). The objective of this project is to create sustainable change in education and research institutions to improve the career progression of women scientific researchers.

Dr. Linda F. Edelman (MBA, DBA from Boston University) is an associate professor of strategic management at Bentley University. Before coming to Bentley, she studied at London Business School and was a research fellow at the Warwick Business School, Warwick University, for two years. Professor Edelman is the author of over 15 book chapters and 30 peer-reviewed journal articles. In addition, she has made over 50 scholarly and professional international presentations. Her work has appeared in many of the top management and entrepreneurship journals such as *Journal of Business Venturing, Entrepreneurship: Theory and Practice, Industrial and Corporate Change,* and *Organization Studies.* She serves on three editorial boards, is an ad hoc reviewer for the National Science Foundation and other scholarly organizations. Currently, Dr. Edelman teaches strategic management to undergraduates, graduates, doctoral students and executives. Her recent research examines strategic industry dynamics, women and nascent entrepreneurs, internationalization of small and medium enterprises, and entrepreneurial finance.

Krystel Edmonds-Biglow (PsyD) is an associate professor at the California School of Professional Psychology at Alliant International University. In her role as a core faculty member, she teaches a variety of intervention courses related to traditional clinical practice as well as community clinical psychology. Dr. Edmonds-Biglow also serves as the course coordinator for the intercultural processes/human diversity course, required for all first year students. Additionally, she is a licensed clinical psychologist who provides consultation to community-based organizations and direct services to individuals, families, and couples. These services include psychotherapy and psychodiagnostic testing. In addition to her role as a faculty member and service provider,

Dr. Edmonds-Biglow is on the editorial board for the *Journal of Child and Adolescent Trauma.*

Jay M. Finkelman (MBA, PhD, ABPP) is a professor and chair of industrial/organizational business psychology at The Chicago School of Professional Psychology (CSPP), Los Angeles. Dr. Finkelman is a licensed psychologist in California and New York and board certified in forensic psychology and board certified in organizational and business consulting psychology. Previously, he was the vice president of academic affairs and chief academic officer of the CSPP. Before that, he was a professor and system-wide director of the Organizational Psychology Division at Alliant International University's California School of Professional Psychology. He served as a senior manager, consultant, and expert witness in employment, staffing, and human resources management for over two decades. He has had hundreds of retentions and depositions, and had testified at trials, as an expert in employment practices, 51 times, equally for plaintiffs and defendants. He authored over 100 publications, including coauthoring three books: *The Psychologist Manager: Success Models for Psychologists in Executive Positions* (Hogrefe Publishing, 2012), *The 7 Attributes of Highly Competitive Staffing Firms* (Crain Communications, Inc., 2010), and *The Role of Human Factors in Computers* (Human Factors Society, 1977). Dr. Finkelman is an industrial and forensic psychologist as well as a certified professional ergonomist. He holds a PhD in industrial/organizational psychology from New York University and an MBA in industrial psychology from the Bernard M. Baruch School of Business of The City College of The City University of New York (CUNY). He was a tenured full professor of industrial psychology at The City University of New York as well as the dean of students at Baruch College. He also served on the Doctoral Faculty in Business, specializing in organizational behavior, at the Graduate Center of CUNY.

Dr. Carley Foster is a reader in retail management at Nottingham Trent University. Her research explores diversity issues, such as age and gender, associated with retail and marketing careers and retail service encounters. She has published widely in these areas, and her work has been funded by a number of research and professional bodies.

Tina Houston-Armstrong (PhD) is an assistant professor of clinical psychology at the CSPP. Dr. Houston-Armstrong's research and clinical interests focus on wellness and resilience among underrepresented populations. Currently she is investigating work–life balance and well-being of professional African American women. In addition, Dr. Houston-Armstrong consults with the Institute on Violence, Abuse and Trauma, where she has been instrumental in the development and initiation of the Child Advocacy Studies Training Program (CAST). CAST is a training program designed to provide trainees with a multidisciplinary approach to responding and treating families impacted by child maltreatment. Prior to joining the CSPP-Los Angles faculty, she served as a full-time staff psychologist and supervisor at a local community mental health agency, where she specialized in working with young children and their families impacted by violence.

Anne Laure Humbert is a gender expert (research, statistics, indices) at the European Institute for Gender Equality, an European Union (EU) agency. She has done extensive work in the area of women and/or gender within the economy and society, with particular attention to work and organizations, entrepreneurship, and the integration of work and life. Her work includes the development of the Gender Equality Index, a measurement tool at EU level to monitor the effectiveness of gender equality policies.

Jan Inge Jenssen is the head of the department and an accomplished professor of economics and business administration at Agder University in Norway. He is widely published in the areas of entrepreneurship and strategy and the start-ups of new organizations.

Christine Janssen-Selvadurai is currently a full-time lecturer and the director of the entrepreneurship program in the Gabelli School of Business at Fordham University in New York City. She recently developed and launched a new entrepreneurship program (Fall 2011), is the adviser of the student-run entrepreneurship society, and is the cofounder and codirector of the Fordham Foundry, Fordham's premier business incubator. For her efforts in inspiring and engaging students in entrepreneurship, she received the Adviser of the Year Award in April 2011 and the Dean's Award for Excellence in Teaching in May 2012. She holds a BS in marketing from the University of South Florida (Tampa, FL, 1993), a global MBA in communication and information systems and finance from Fordham University (New York, NY, 2000), and a PhD from New York University (New York, NY, 2010). Her dissertation was a qualitative study (phenomenology) entitled "On Becoming: The Lived Learning Experiences of Female Entrepreneurs."

Tatiana S. Manolova (DBA, Boston University) is an associate professor of management at Bentley University, Waltham, MA. Research interests include strategic management (competitive strategies for new and small companies), international entrepreneurship, and management in emerging economies. During 2010–2011, she was a visiting professor at Kind Saud University, Riyadh, Saudi Arabia, and conducted research on entrepreneurship in Saudi Arabia in affiliation with the Prince Salman Institute for Entrepreneurship. Tatiana is the author of over 40 scholarly articles and book chapters. She serves on the editorial boards of *Entrepreneurship: Theory and Practice*, *Journal of Business Venturing*, and *Journal of Global Entrepreneurship Research*.

Dr. Virginia McKendry is an assistant professor at the School of Communication and Culture at Royal Roads University in Victoria, BC, Canada. Earning an MA in women's studies (Simon Fraser University) and a PhD in history (York University), she is an interdisciplinary scholar whose work focuses on understanding the ways that cultures change and resist change, with a specific interest in discovering the foundational metaphors that inform the dynamics of culture and communication in organizations of all kinds. After completing her doctorate, she worked for a national public relations firm and an Internet development company. As an academic, she has taught cultural studies, communication studies, and gender studies courses at Wilfrid Laurier University and Royal Roads University. Since 2005, she has participated in applied research initiatives with Canadian communities, nonprofits, governments, and educational institutions seeking guidance on how best to effect values-based, sustainable cultural change.

Bett Mickels is the founder and president of WorldWideTeams Consulting in San Diego, CA. Bett has 20+ years' experience in franchising, improving business operations, and developing teams for Fortune 300 multinational organizations. Bett is comfortable leading large-scale international project teams and working alongside small business entrepreneurs. From her experience, research, and interviews with business leaders around the world, Bett advises clients on (1) business expansion, (2) business profit solutions, and (3) best practices for high-performing teams. Bett has a doctorate in business administration and MBA. She can be reached at bettmickels@worldwideteams.com.

Yenni Viviana Duque Orozco is a researcher and assistant professor at the Faculty of Economic Sciences at Universidad Militar Nueva Granada in Bogota, Colombia. She completed her undergraduate studies in business administration at Universidad Militar Nueva Granada (2005). She received a master's degree in business management (2011). As a researcher, she has worked on studies concerning corporate social responsibility (CSR) and entrepreneurship. She is a coauthor of *Las Mujeres Empresarias en Colombia*. Her main interests are in research in CSR and sustainable development. She plans to start a doctoral program in sustainable development.

Maria Carolina Ortiz Riaga is a researcher and assistant professor at the Faculty of Economic Sciences at Universidad Militar Nueva Granada in Bogota, Colombia. She is a psychologist and studied at Pontificia Universidad Javeriana, Colombia (1988). She received a master's degree in education (2009). She is a professor of entrepreneurship and research methodology. As a researcher, she has worked on studies concerning women-owned businesses and entrepreneurship. She is the author of several books including *The Entrepreneurial Personality Development* and *Women Entrepreneurs in Colombia*. She plans to start a doctoral program in education.

Janet Salmons (PhD) has been serving on the Graduate Faculty of the Capella University School of Business since 1999 as a dissertation supervisor for doctoral learners. She was honored with the Harold Abel Distinguished Faculty Award for 2011–2012 and the Steven Shank Recognition for Teaching in 2012 and 2013. She is an independent researcher, writer, and consultant through her company, Vision2Lead, Inc. Publications include editing the *Cases in Online Interview Research* (2012) and writing *Online Qualitative Interviews* (2014) and *Online Interviews in Real Time* (2010) for Sage Publications.

Dr. Rotem Shneor is an associate professor at the Centre for Entrepreneurship at the University of Agder, Norway. He is the academic coordinator for entrepreneurship education programs at the university for bachelor, master and PhD students. His research interests span various aspects of entrepreneurship and international management, including—cognitive aspects of entrepreneurship, gender issues in entrepreneurship, cross-cultural and cross-country comparative studies of entrepreneurship, and international marketing and strategy of new ventures.

Leah R. Singer is a writer and marketing strategist who helps businesses, nonprofits, and educational institutions to explain their story through words. She writes regularly for *The Huffington Post* and numerous other national websites and blogs. Before starting her business, Leah was a speechwriter for two presidents at San Diego State University (SDSU), served as the director of communications for the SDSU Enrollment Services Department, and did marketing and public relations for KPBS public broadcasting station. She has a master's degree in communication and a bachelor's degree in journalism and political science, both from San Diego State University.

Jennifer Walinga (PhD) is the director of the School of Communication and Culture, Royal Roads University, Victoria, BC, Canada. After teaching English for 20 years, Jennifer combined her passion for communication and athletics in pursuing an MA in Leadership where her research focused on the impact of experiential training programs on organizational performance. Jennifer went on to earn my PhD in organizational studies from the University of Victoria, where she developed a problem solving and coaching strategy called Integrated Focus, which she continued to apply with individuals and organizations from a variety of realms. In designing communication, change, and performance interventions, she blends theories from organizational, educational, and sport psychology and draws heavily upon her experience as a member of Canada's Commonwealth, World, and Olympic gold medalist rowing teams (1983–1992). Her research interests include team dynamics, creative insight, innovation, and high performance. She teaches courses in research methods; organizational, interpersonal, and small-group communication; and leadership. She is currently conducting several studies: training creative insight, problem framing within the research process, stress thriving, learning and technology, energy management, and the personal and social value of sport participation. She is a mother of three and an active member of the athletic and educational communities in Victoria, BC.

Dr. Dan Wheatley (FRSA) is a senior lecturer in economics at Nottingham Trent University. He completed his PhD dissertation entitled "Working 9 to 5? Complex Patterns of Time Allocation among Managers and Professionals in Dual-Career Households," in December 2009. His particular areas of interest are work time, work–life balance, travel to work, subjective well-being, and dual-career households. His work has appeared in journals such as *American Journal of Economics and Sociology; Gender, Work & Organization; New Technology, Work and Employment, Personnel Review; Review of Political Economy;* and *Review of Social Economy.* He can be contacted at: daniel.wheatley@ntu.ac.uk.

Index

Note: Italicized page numbers indicate a figure. Page numbers followed by *t* indicate a table.